The

Dear a

Good luck on

your "journey".

May you have

health, joy and

happiness.

Your friend from

X Sport Gym.

Rich Crosby

The Journey

Memoirs of a South Side Chicago kind of guy

Richard J. Cronborg

2008

The Journey

"Nothing in the world can take the place of persistence. Talent will not; nothing is more common than unsuccessful men with talent. Genius will not; un-rewarded genius is almost a proverb. Education will not; the world is full of educated derelicts. Persistence and Determination alone are omnipotent. The slogan, "Press On", has solved, and always will solve, the problems of the human race."

-Calvin Coolidge

*I want to thank my author friends who guided me in this process:
My dear friends, C. P. Kaestner and his sweet girlfriend, Nikki, who
encouraged and helped me through my illness and the journaling process.
I want to thank Sarah Biggs-Wudel who always had time to answer
my questions and believed in me. Eric Heinz, who proofread and edited
my final copy. Eric refused payment from me for all the time he invested
in this project. I want to thank my artist friend Chuck Moesch for his
beautiful oil paintings. They grace the front and rear covers of this
Memoir. Chuck worked from photos he took of my mug back in 2005. I
also want to thank Paulette Stobinske, my dear friend, who has shown
my artwork in her gallery for many years, and Larry McAllister who
does all my website construction and updates. Finally, I thank my dear
family for their support and love! They didn't give up on me when the
going got tough!*
*This book is dedicated to my wife Debbie, my daughter Catherine, and
especially to my brother Jim—the "Iron Man"—who passed away in
2007. He was a paragon of persistence!*

MORNING 1954

I woke up to the smell of bacon grease. I was a five-year-old boy in a coldwater flat on the South Side of Chicago. The cacophony of family chatter entered my ears. Like a fog, I now perceive these shrouded memories in my old age. They are a wasteland of what was, mythologized by my minds' eye. I lived on 65th Street and Francisco Avenue, on the South Side of Chicago, in a small coldwater flat. Mom had to heat up water on the little stove, to give me a bath. I slept in a dresser drawer made into a makeshift crib, when I was an infant. I remember coats of paint, flaking off a skeleton of ramshackle stairs, in the back of the shoddy building. Everything was painted industrial gray. I remember a dusty backyard with patches of weeds, interspersed with the grass.

Mike the junkman, makes his rounds. I hear his bell and see his horse-drawn trailer filled with detritus from the alleyways. He kindly gives me a complete set of lead soldiers. I put one of them in my mouth as I watch him travel on to other adventures. I smile and create wartime scenarios in my young mind. I play in the dirt in the backyard of the coldwater flat.

GRANDPA NELS

He didn't say much
He wore fine suits and shoes.
He owned a grand square-faced Hamilton watch.
18-Carat gold.

The inscription read: "From Associates, Armour and Company"
to:

N.C. Cronborg
1923—1952
It was Chicago. City of "Big Shoulders"
The Stockyards.

Grandpa was an Executive. He drove a fancy car.
He had a mistress named Rose.
Now, I sat in his lap.
I watched as he dribbled peach juice down his chin.
He sat in his pajamas, senile at the young age of 54.
He loved me in his silent way.

63rd STREET

The mile or two from Kedzie to Western Avenue on 63rd Street was always full of activity. For me it was a veritable cornucopia of sights and sounds.

The Marquette Theatre had 25 color cartoons for 25 cents.

Taverns flourished on every block.

My father worked or drank in them all.

Butcher shops had sawdust on the floors. Mom watched with "furtive bird's eyes," because sometimes the butcher put his thumb on the scale.

Every penny counted for our poor family.

I loved looking at my amazing skeleton feet through the lens of the x-ray machine at the Florshiem shoe store. Pints of Highlander ice cream cost Mom a dime at Walgreen's. Mom and I quickly ate our bounty before it melted. We both sweat in the oppressive heat of the 3rd-floor flat. Dad was tending bar as usual. Soon the sun would set; we would feel the cool. Mom sang happy songs to deny the sadness in her heart.

THE HAIRCUT—1954

As a kid I loved getting a "Russian Brush" hair cut and a jar of pomade. I was so small I had to sit in a booster chair. Dad was drunk. He hadn't slept all night. Cards, and whores, and drinks in Cicero, Illinois diverted him from his duty to his family. I remember him wearing a homburg hat and white shirts with cufflinks. The shirt, once nicely starched and clean, was a wreck with sweat, wrinkles, and lipstick stains. I smelled the sweet whiskey and cigarette smoke on his breath. We took Grandpa's new Pontiac to the barbershop on California Avenue. Dad let me steer while I sat in his lap. I faintly smelled the Old Spice cologne he splashed on his face generously a few days before. The barbershop brings back childhood memories of racing forms, laughing "red-faced" men waving and whistling at smart young ladies walking by briskly in their high heels. I remember the barber pole. It had hypnotic swirling red-and-white stripes. Leaving the place with a sucker in my mouth, I knew all was good! I was glad, that my father was finally home.

THE CHINESE LAUNDRY

Dad brought his white shirts to be laundered, starched and pressed by a hard-working Chinese family. They owned a "hot house" of a little laundry shop on 63rd and California Avenue. The "California Tap," was around the corner and down the street. Sometimes Dad and I stopped in there for cool drinks if it was a hot day. Each shirt Dad picked up from the laundry was individually packaged in brown paper. Blue, pink, or white paper bands made the packages look like Christmas presents. I hated the heat and the exotic smells of this place. I breathed through my mouth—not my nose—to avoid the sickening sweat, chemicals, and other foreign odors coming from this "hellhole". I observed these poor Chinese, running around like frantic mice. The man kept yelling at the women. The women looked very sad, and sometimes the screaming of the Chinese man frightened them. The youngest girl looked at me, wondering what my world was like. I think she knew what her fate was going to be. I felt sorry for her. I felt sorry for all of them. I even felt sorry for the man who was mean. My dad told me they were better off here in America than in their own land. We left after hearing "rapid fire" broken English, and seeing the forced, false smiles. I thought in my five-year-old brain that maybe Dad would buy me an ice cream cone. I think we went to the California Tap instead.

ROLLING ON THE KITCHEN FLOOR—1956

A little boy can really enjoy rolling on the kitchen floor on Sundays and Holidays!
I always did!
I got to look up all my Auntie's skirts.
My photographic mind was snapping images.
I stored vast multitudes of soft porn images in my prepubescent mind for an: Evening of masturbatory delight!
I liked being alone with my evil little thoughts.
The room was dark and the covers welcomed me to unspeakable joys!
I was always properly remorseful after pleasuring myself.

Afterwards, I always said an Act of Contrition, three Our Father's, three Hail
Mary's and three Glory Be's.

Mortal sin is now expunged from my soul. I am forgiven for my immoral malfeasance. Off to dreamland I go—all-safe—covered and protected. I am happy in my dark, dark, bedroom.

THE PLAYGROUND — 1957

Morning recess was like Las Vegas for little people! I had a lust for marbles. I loved them all! I desired the "Steelies", "Puries", and "Cat's-eye's"! I had skill in trading baseball cards. Making good barters, I always got away with the neat ones!

Playing "Red Rover," I came smashing through the lines! I bought cheap ten-cent balsa wood airplanes with lead weights. The weight slipped onto the nose to make the structure fly straight and true.

Yo-Yos, in their abundance were all over the schoolyard too! I yearned for the tasty chocolate milk at recess. My mom forced me to buy the white milk instead. I thought this was unfair!

Punishments were inflicted and punishments were received. Pecking orders were established by mini-adults. Psyches were developed and psyches were destroyed. The winners and the losers all came to play the game!

Isn't this what American values are all about? We were all involved in the perverse melodrama! The bell sounds! Line up for re-indoctrination! "See spot run"!

THE PARENT-TEACHER CONFERENCE

It was a fearful time! I feared the black-hooded nun who looked like the grim reaper. I felt as if my balls were in a wine press. My nun's sadistic smile broadens with each painful turn of the hideous crank. I endure shame and tears. It's just Mom and me and the evil nun. Dad was gone, tending bar. In my future, he loomed dangerously!

My religion book had sideline notes I had written, blaspheming Jesus and all His Saints. "Sinful" artwork depicted holy men and women as beatniks and prostitutes. Cigarettes were dangling from their mouths and their hands gripped whiskey bottles. "Didn't Jesus love the sinners?" In my defense, my heart silently screamed this logic. The sweet nun presented a showcase of confiscated items from inside my humble desk. We all looked at the pornography, rubber band guns, matches, condoms—all the things that little boys love, but cannot share with the "big people". My mom coldly stared at me as she whisked me out of the office, roughly dragging me by my arm into the streets. I cried a stream of "alligator" tears to save my ass! All Mom said to me for the rest of that evening was, "Wait till your father gets home!" The verdict was in! The minutes were hours now! My execution was only hours away.

POVERTY ISN'T FUN! — 1959

I used to garbage pick for "stuff". In the alley on hot summer mornings, I looked in the garbage cans, being careful to avoid maggots and dog shit. I found pop bottles, discarded bicycles, old tools, records, and all kinds of hardware like washers, and nuts and bolts, and lumber and nails.

One of the greatest treasures I ever found was a discarded vial of mercury. I unknowingly poisoned myself by spilling it in the palm of my hand. I watched its magical properties endlessly...till my mom shrieked with terror one day and took it away from me. For a long time, she observed me closely for brain damage. Kids can be mean to a poor kid. I learned anger and hatred for my peers at a very young age. They always laughed at the patches on the knees of my jeans and one day a few of them jammed dog shit in my cheap baseball mitt. I cried as I cleaned it out. I used a lot of soap and water in the washtubs in the basement. I baked the glove in the sun for a few days. Then I oiled it up. It was as good as new, but when I used it again, the kids laughed at me more than they had before. I stayed in the house a lot that summer. I took solace in Jack London, Edgar Rice Burroughs, Mad Magazine, cheap candy, and masturbation.

WHEN GRANDPA DIED — 1955

Grandpa Nels died in '55. Dad went on a bender for a long time. He blew most of his inheritance. Mom waited for one of Dad's sober moments and confiscated the rest of the money. We bought a nice brick bungalow next to the Nabisco Factory at 7259 S. Homan Avenue, on the South Side of Chicago.

I remember the wonderful aromas coming from the cookie factory, but sometimes the winds changed and came from the Northeast. I was affronted by the dank, dead smells of animal carcasses from the stockyards. The odors forced their way into my nostrils and throat. The stink burned me on these hot summer months of July and August. I played 16" softball in the city streets. When the sun went down and the streetlights came on, I knew it was time to come back home. I heard the bells of the "Good Humor" truck and begged my mom for a quarter to get us a couple of popsicles.

MY BIG BROTHER

When my brother Jim was the age of 13, he was already very responsible and full of pride. He had to be the "man of the house". I was his newborn baby brother, so he excitedly raced home from school to play with me every day before he went to work at the flower shop. After work, he hunted for my father, going into all the smoky bars up and down 63rd Street. Jim usually found Dad slumped over his drink, or with his bald head down, sleeping on the bar. Jim carried him home—heavy like a corpse—to a sparse dinner table, usually consisting of Spam, potatoes, and onions. Mom made due with what was available to her. My brother gave all his money to Mom. Jim had paper routes, odd jobs, and learned from the smart Irish owners of the flower shop about business and finance. My brother, Jim, made work his "God" because he was fueled by anger, resentment, and disgust with our family situation. It was a tough life for my brother in those days. I loved my brother. He was my surrogate father. He always demanded more from me. Now in my old age, I love him because he is "broken". His wealth never healed him from the mental anguish of poverty. Jim always persevered, and continues to persevere. He is the "Iron Man" in my life. He saw the real bad times with Dad.

MY BIG SISTER

Judy, my big sis, was ten years older than me. She taught me how to do the "Stroll" in 1956. We watched American Bandstand in the pre-Dick Clark days when we came home from school. Jim Lounsberry hosted the show in Chicago. Full of the devil, my sister Judy was just like my father. Judy was damaged like the rest of us. She wore heavy eye makeup, tight jeans, and white lipstick. A black leather jacket sometimes adorned her. She looked like a tough girl but inside of her ticked a heart of gold. When she walked into a room with her bright smile, she owned "it". She walked erect like a queen with a regal presence. She ran hot-and-wild, one hundred miles per hour! She ended up with a working-class husband and three beautiful children. They lived in a very modest home. Judy died at the age of 38. She died much too young—and much too drunk—in her garage. Her husband found her body in the morning. Her body was wedged between the red Buick Electra convertible and the garage door. The engine was running, but the lights were out.

MOM

Her name was Irene. She was a simple woman, but displayed great intelligence, humility, and compassion. I never heard my mom utter a negative word about anyone. She was a "rock". She came from Polish-Austrian-German stock. Her father was a Judge. Her mother was a kind woman who took care of the home and eight other children besides my mom. In a "saintly" non-complaining way, my mother suffered all her life with my father. She never spoke ill of him. Mom worked like a slave for us, all of her life. She taught all of us in the family, good values and took us to church every Sunday. Mom died in my arms at the old age of 94. I'm glad I was there for her.

She was the best of us.

Amen

DAD

Dad was not a mean drunk most of the time. Sometimes, he fell asleep with his head in the plate of bacon and eggs that my mom served him in the morning. As a child, I clinically observed him. I noticed he was oblivious to the Chesterfield Regular cigarette burning his brown, nicotine stained index finger. He continued to snore, with his head resting on the table. I often wondered if he realized all the pain he was causing himself and others. He seemed oblivious to the realities of his situation. He turned down an executive position that my grandpa had procured for him at the Armour Company. My father opted for a lifetime of bartending. He bragged to all who would listen, that he was a "professional" mixologist. One time, I saw him mindlessly shit in his pants. It was a terrible thing for a little boy to see. He burned holes in both mattresses and hearts. Sometimes, when he was lucky at the racetrack or at poker games played in the back rooms of nefarious bar rooms, I could persuade Dad to take me to Comiskey Park. This is the home of the Chicago White Sox. I took his big hand in mine and looked up to him. He rubbed my head the way dads do with their little boys. We took a cab to the ballpark. He was always too drunk to drive. He bought me hot dogs, pop, and peanuts. We took the bus back home. I endured the embarrassment of people looking at us. My father snored loudly, with his head hanging. He woke up with "a start" as the bus hit each stop. Diabetes and alcoholism finally had its say. He died with his head on the kitchen table, while the smoke from his "cig" traveled up like a "little soul".

DAD'S FAMILY AND HIS TEN COMMANDMENTS FOR ME

Dad's family was cold and perverse. They had a stubborn German mindset. Grandma Barb was a clean freak. She scrubbed her kitchen floor on her hands and knees at two-in-the-morning. Grandma knew about Grandpa's mistress, and made him suffer for it. Grandma died young of a heart attack while she sat on a clean toilet in her home. My dad had only one other sibling—my Aunt Doris. Aunt Doris liked the "night life" also, but not as much as Dad. I wonder, "Do anal-retentive parents produce anal-expulsive children?" Dad was exempt from rule number ten.

1. "There is no going out on school nights."
2. "The television set is always controlled by me."
3. "Do your homework every day."
4. "If your mother tells me you did anything wrong, you are grounded for a week."
5. "It is your job to shovel snow, take out the garbage, mow the lawn, do the dishes, paint the windows, the gutters, and the walls in the house."
6. "Only speak when spoken to, and always eat what Mom feeds you, without whining or complaining."
7. "I will impose all curfews; you will abide by all the rules, or be grounded for a week."
8. "Do what I say, not what I do!"
9. "When I say 'no', I mean 'no!' Don't ask me again, or you'll get a licking!"
10. "You must attend Mass and Confession with your mother every Saturday and Sunday."

As you well might imagine, these were tough rules for any young man to follow! I endured these rules until I left the house for college. I think my dad probably didn't want me to turn into some kind of "hooligan"! What I felt was rage and anger toward my father. I didn't express it. I just kept it locked up deep inside of me all my life. I learned to keep out of his way. There is no reasoning with a selfish alcoholic. I lived in my room. I constructed an isolated fantasy world for myself. I did the best I could. Many children of alcoholics learn psychological defenses to protect themselves from their parents. Much of what I did in my future life, I don't blame on my father. He was trying to do what was right for me. I made the choices that either helped or hindered me in my life!

THE CAR WASH

Dad drove the new Pontiac into the dark tunnel. There were explosions of suds, flashing lights, and Hula Skirts—those leather-cleaning "thingies" that caress the shiny car body. I was safe inside. I perceived the car wash as a "carnival" of sensory stimulation. The carwash was like a "Fellini" movie to me! Huge fans were blowing beads of water, hither and yon. My ears were popping from the atmospheric changes! The flashing lights at the end of the tunnel signaled the end of my joyous ride. Outside realities began to take shape. Shabby men wiped "her" dry with dirty wet towels. Dad tipped 'em too much, as was his custom. I enjoyed his grandiosity.... I learned from it! We ate liver, or Spam, or canned corned beef hash that night...YUCK!

THE CAMEO LOUNGE

The Cameo Lounge was a couple of blocks down the street from the car wash. I remember riding with Dad past the Continental Can Company, on South Western Avenue. Two blocks to the North, on the West corner of 59th Street, the Cameo Lounge beckoned to us in all of its glory. This restaurant had a fabulous soda fountain and a huge magazine rack with…DIRTY MAGAZINES! In the back was a cocktail lounge with a television set chained way up on the wall, a bowling machine, a gaudy bandstand, a dance floor, and last but not least…some of the most glorious-looking barmaids my young eyes had ever seen! Dad ditched me at the soda fountain and gave me a couple of bucks. He headed back to the bar. I wolfed down a sundae with all the trimmings, or a triple-thick malted milk. These milkshakes were the old-fashioned kind that were served to you in quart-sized metal containers. They were so thick, I couldn't suck them through the straw. I slugged down the ice cream delights quickly, so I could go to the magazine racks. There, I thumbed through "Adam" and "True Detective" magazines. Leering at the scantily clad women, I was in prepubescent heaven! The restaurant also had a great collection of science fiction paperbacks printed by Balantine Press for only thirty-five cents apiece. This is where I discovered great writers like Ray Bradbury and Isaac Asimov. I made my literary purchases and meandered to the back lounge where Dad was drinking a V.O. and seltzer, and smoking his favorite Chesterfield cigarettes. The name of the bartender there was "Uncle Gus", who was a jolly, old, ebullient Greek Immigrant, with a white apron, bow tie, white shirt, and gold cuff links.

Dad always invited Uncle Gus home to our house for Thanksgiving and Christmas, because Gus had no family here. Uncle Gus was really a part of our family! Gus had a shiny bald head and a big old cigar hanging out of his mouth. He "owned" a big smile and was always happy to see me. He joyfully greeted me in broken English and hugged me saying, "Whadda'ya have, young man?" I usually chose a kiddie cocktail with maraschino cherries, or a ginger ale. Then Uncle Gus would "fix me up" with a bag of Chicago's famous Vintner potato chips, or a bag of pretzels. Dad smiled, tousled my hair and threw some change my way for the bowling machine. I remember sounds of baseball games, Perry Como, Doris Day, Frank Sinatra, and laughter from the ebullient afternoon customers. I immediately knew I liked the bar, and vowed I would be a customer some day, just like my dad.

What I loved most were the good-looking bar maids in the skin-tight black-and-white uniforms. They smelled like heaven and had lascivious-looking red lips, which always smiled at me seductively! I loved their black nylons, short skirts and high heels. The young women had beautiful round derrieres with little apron strings dangling on them. The skirt fabric strained, as the girls bent over the tables to serve drinks. On break, the girls sat on the bar stools, legs crossed, skirts hiked way up high. They drew heavily on those filtered cigarettes with their "pouting" red lips. Their bras pushed their tits up out of their outfits. Wow! My little penis got rock hard, watching all of this! I looked at the lipstick-stained cigarettes in the ashtray and was tempted to steal them away to my home. I wanted to taste the lipstick on the discarded filters! The goddesses "sashayed" away from the bar with a rehearsed jiggle.

I was totally awestruck by the beauty and seductiveness of it all. I felt like Lucifer was sitting right on my shoulder. I knew I would burn in hell for my thoughts, but I didn't care. I gave up my senses to every single moment with those women!

Sometimes one of the girls would come over and embrace me, telling my father, "He is just the cutest little boy!" She pulled my face to those exposed globes of flesh and I breathed in as deeply as I could, enjoying this "heavenly" moment; I wanted to last for an eternity! The perfume entered my nostrils, and made me "light-headed". It all was such a wonderful aphrodisiac for a young man!

This whole experience allowed me to have a secret bank of memories, where withdrawals could be made at any time. Tight asses and full breasts—swinging to-and-fro—was my Nirvana! I was a student of voyeurism! I envisioned a lifetime of joys to come! I wondered if these vixens knew they were planting seeds of lust in my dark, little heart? "Yes," I thought, "they knew!"

PLAYGROUND INSANITY

I knew there was something wrong with me...
When I experienced, "anomie".

Whirling children were all around me...
Yet I was alone.

Something dark came over me...
It took away reality.

Like a vapor, I disappeared...
I was no more!
This was the score!

No one heard the scream from me!
It blackened my individuality. I was "rubbed out."

These frightful moments began early for me...
In my playground lurked insanity. The children laughed for what
seemed...
An eternity.
They never knew the horror of my dysfunctionality!

THE JOYS OF CYSTIC ACNE

I couldn't just get zits like normal kids. I would have welcomed blackheads. No, I had giant weeping pockets of pus, which left pockmarks all over my face and body. I looked like a "lunar landscape". All the remedies were tried, applied, and finally denied by me as useless. Prayer, meditation, masturbation, exacerbation, strained relations, no copulation and sweet isolation were a part of my life. All was caused by my pizza face.

I wish I had read the great Charles Bukowski, at the time. He might have given me some relief, with the knowledge that some other human being having a creative soul also had experienced this cruel torture. "Alas," I thought, "I was alone." Bukowski, the skid row poet laureate, who was the owner of the condition known as "Acne Vulgaris," and a more severe drinking problem than I would ever aspire to have, might have comforted me in my teen years. We had much in common. We both made out. We got laid, we got paid, and as I learned from his writings, we all got "way layed" in life.

So ye of not-so-fair-complexions, raise your glasses high, and drink to your imperfections! There are greater joys and woes, coming for you around the corner, pizza face!

HIGH SCHOOL

Ah, high school! These were the days of glory and pride, of sock hops, and hooligans from the neighborhood running wild through the streets. I attended a staunch, Irish-Catholic High School, proudly run by the Augustinian Fathers. The campus was composed of Gothic-style buildings. You could actually sense the "ghosts" of past glories and traditions, emanating from the austere classrooms.

It was the grandest of Catholic academic penal institutions. The Fathers and lay-teachers were totally dedicated to developing boys into "good" Catholic young men—mentally, spiritually, and physically. The school had solid alumni who believed in a grand mythology of "manliness" and "morality" in an ungodly world.

The great responsibility of tutelage and personal example was placed in the hands of these austere Augustinian Fathers and some good Catholic laymen. These men shared the duty of enforcing our enlightenment through mental manipulation, and varied administrations of corporal punishments.

I was in awe. We were issued instructional manuals, class schedules, and dress codes. We were swiftly and surely propagandized into the combine of high school Catholicism. Bells, P.A. systems, and heavy wooden paddles ensured that the reaper-like figures in the black robes would deal with any frivolity or disorderly behavior by us, immediately. We young men were required to wear ties and white shirts, dress slacks and polished shoes.

❧

Tie color was to designate class standing, from freshman to senior year. I felt as if I were in the military. For me, 1963 was a grand year to be a freshman. Our football team didn't lose a game and was ranked #1 in the National Polls. It was a hell of a way to start freshman year. One thing that stands out in my mind is the ingenuity and craftsmanship that went into the design of the "ass whooping paddles" made by the cretin woodshop students who weren't college bound. These paddles were works of art. Some were long and some were short. All of them were aesthetically beautiful. Some had holes drilled through them for less wind resistance! This allowed for "supersonic speed" in the swinging of the varnished monstrosity to the buttocks of a victim student. I dreaded the command from the priest to, "Bend over and hold your jewels!" I held my scrotum with one hand, and my ankle with the other. Usually I took 6 swats.

The pain felt like an electric bolt. It moved swiftly from the ass cheeks, up the spinal cord, to the pain centers in my demented teenaged brain! By the time I took 3 swats, I was praying to God and all the Saints for the strength to endure the pain from the rest of the swats to my sore derriere. Oaths regarding the improvement of my personal conduct quickly rambled through my muddled brain. The priest sadistically smiled with glee through the entire hazing process!

A lot of the priests and laymen teachers were alcoholics and cigarette smokers. Some were real "head cases".

I learned quickly which ones I had to steer away from. My experience was very much like adapting to "yard life" in state penal institutions!

In spite of it all, I received a pretty damned good education at this school. They prepared me for what I was going to encounter academically in college. In Catholic high school, I always took home two to three hours of homework every night. Every college I applied for accepted me. After all is said and done, I have a place in my heart for this school. I learned loyalty, discipline, and responsibility. I also learned to have a healthy fear of what might be coming after me! Maybe we need more schools like this today...AMEN!

HOT SUMMER NIGHTS IN CHICAGO

Way back in 1967, it was a ritual between fathers and sons in Chicago, to sit on the front porch on hot summer nights. At age 17, I put a pack of "cigs" on the dinner table in front of my dad, and asked him for permission to smoke. I feared his response, but to my surprise he respected my bravery, and from that day on, allowed me to smoke in front of him. Dad and I sometimes sat on the front porch. In the dark, the city streetlights hummed their electrical song. We listened to the Chicago White Sox on my old Motorola transistor radio while we smoked cigarettes.

I learned how to flick the butts over the bushes into the street, just like my dad. My dad loved these times. There was a cup of coffee for him and a coke for me. There was no air conditioning in our house. Mom was singing and sweating in the kitchen, joyfully hand-washing dishes. We listened to her through the wooden screen door. Dad sat in his lawn chair. I opted for the coolness of the concrete stairs. I must have looked like some type of "minion" sitting at my fathers' feet. Mom brought Dad more coffee, warning me that I would get "piles" from sitting the way I did.

SUMMER BEFORE COLLEGE

My Dad got me a job, as a crane operator's helper in order to save money for college. He knew the business agents and the President of Local #150, the Heavy Equipment Operator's Union. These fellows were "rough and tumble" construction men. They wore fancy suits, which denied this fact. They drank hard booze and flirted with the waitresses at the fancy bar where my dad worked day shift. The union hall was in a small office across the street, near Midway Airport.

The "fix" was in, because they liked my dad. I was off and running with a Union Permit, making $4.05 and hour. This was some "big time" money back in 1967. I loved this work. My acne subsided because of my exposure to the hot sun. I started to develop some musculature due to the hard physical work. I loved the men who taught me how to run the machines. The best things they taught me, I thought, were drinking shots and beers, and chasing women. I didn't appreciate them turning me on to chewing tobacco. They forgot to tell me not to swallow. I must have turned a million shades of green, as they rolled around in the dirt, laughing like hyenas at my predicament.

I learned a lot about a man's world the summer before college.

I gained quite a bit of respect from my teenaged peer group and started dating a few pretty-darned-good-looking girls before I ventured down to Southern Illinois University. I couldn't wait to start college!

In the evenings, my best friend Bill and I played 16" softball with the neighborhood guys or threw a football around in Marquette Park. Afterwards, we bought a couple of quarts of "Schlitz" beer and a couple of Chicago hot dogs from the street vendor. You never put ketchup on a Chicago hot dog. We always garnished the "holy dog" with mustard, relish, tomato, onions, and a pickle. Now that's Chicago-style cuisine. Bill and I sat on the park bridge and peered into the waters of the lagoon. Slugging down the beer and eating the hot dogs was pure joy. It was a bonding experience between best friends. We looked at the stars and talked all about our dreams for the future. We were going to set the world on fire! Bill was headed for DePaul University in the city. We spoke of girls and sports, and how we would meet up again at Thanksgiving time. We were "drunk" with the joys of adolescence.

SOUTHERN ILLINOIS UNIVERSITY, PRE FRESHMAN VISIT—1967

Imagine taking a Greyhound Bus from downtown Chicago. It's a dingy station with panhandlers and nefarious characters all around. I experienced the smells of urine, popcorn, and sanitary sewers. This was the Chicago I knew as a boy. My beat up suitcase was stored in the "belly of the beast". My soul longed for adventure. This was going to be the first time I would see what was to be my home for the next four years.

We rolled through the cornfields of Central Illinois, and in Springfield picked up a myopic fat guy a few years older than me. He plopped his rumpled body in a seat next to mine. I didn't know it at the time, but this was a stroke of luck. Gradually, he initiated a conversation. He was starting his junior year at S.I.U. and was living off campus in a seedy efficiency apartment. He started drawing me into his interesting ramblings.

He spoke of the "Fugs", a band from the Lower-East Side of New York, whose claim to fame was a song titled, "Up Against the Wall, Motherfucker". "This dude is hip," I thought. He was abysmally fat and shoddy, but hip. He possessed a "middle aged" kind of demeanor for a 20-year-old. He smelled of patchouli oil and wore some type of icon on a woven leather strap, which lay boldly on his Buddha-like belly.

He clutched the Wall Street Journal in his fat sweaty hand and spoke of Alan Ginsberg, Jack Kerouac, Ken Keysee, Alan Watts, and lord-only-knows whom else. The "dude" had a good mind!

I hadn't a clue about what the hell he was talking about, but really enjoyed it all. I wanted to hear more. He invited me to "crash" at his sloppy apartment, called the "Pyramids". I figured I was strong enough to over power him if he was a pervert, so I threw all caution to the wind. I also figured that staying on campus would mean no beer, and that keeping company with the other "neophytes" in town during pre-registration would be a drag. They didn't know what the hell was going on, and neither did I. With the fat guy, at least I was off campus.

I looked like Lou Reed with acne. It was 100 degrees and I had a greasy ducktail with a pompadour. I wore a black ban Lon shirt and sharkskin pants. I had those pointy-style "Beatle boots," which zip up on the sides. There I was, bopping down these hippie-oriented Carbondale streets. People must have thought I was a sideman for some obscure outdated "soul band" or a freakin' hillbilly. Anyhow, I felt I looked like a space alien.

My fat benefactor was kind and gave me a tutorial on what was cool...He showed me his blues and psychedelic album collection. He turned me on to the bars that served younger-looking guys with fake IDs (which I had purchased in Chicago for twenty bucks).

I smoked my first joint with this guy, while listening to the "Fire Sign Theatre" and "Frank Zappa and the Mothers of Invention". I loved this humid "armpit" known as Carbondale, Illinois. Walking through the campus at night, all I heard was the mournful, tribalistic sounds of The Door's first album. It pulsated with social change.

It eerily invited me to put oil paint on my cheeks and to rip my clothes off. I was invited to join this infant nation of alternative youth, and change the world! I knew my life was going to change significantly in Carbondale.

The sweet smell of marijuana was burning everywhere. All around me were head shops. Hippy-looking girls, with ripe young tits in halter-tops, no bras, hip huggers, and "soulful" knowing smiles, invited me to the "dance". I wanted to taste their luscious fruit and be initiated into the subculture!

I pre-registered at the academic war machine. I lined myself up, for my classes. All tasks were completed now. I felt the campus was awesome! I didn't want to leave. I made the journey back to Chicago on the Greyhound bus, now a changed young man. Now I "holed up" in Mom and Dad's bungalow, counting the days until I could leave the South Side of Chicago.

I listened to alternative music on WSDM radio. Psychedelic "mamas" were the disc jockeys here. I started changing the way I looked and the way I talked. I started to read more incendiary literature. The Revolution was going to change my life. Most people my age were listening to the new music. It was the music of a disenfranchised youth. The music spoke of drugs, sex, revolution, and the Viet Nam war. It spoke of social change and righting the wrongs of our parents. Middle America was incensed by our behavior. They called themselves "the moral majority". We knew how immoral they were! These were the people voting for the destruction of an innocent culture on the other side of the world. They sacrificed 58,000 of their children before the war was over.

THE ARRIVAL AT S.I.U. — 1967

Dad and Mom rented a brand new "boat" of a car. It was a big old red Ford LTD, from the local Hertz "rent-a-car". I think, maybe O.J. Simpson was jumping over turnstiles in their T.V. commercials at this time.

We began the magical journey from Chicago via Route 66 and then down old Highway 51. Interstate 57 was non-existent way back in '67, so the trip to Carbondale was about an eight-hour drive. We stopped for a country lunch in some "po-dunk" town along the way. The food was glorious! We enjoyed fried chicken, mashed potatoes and gravy, grits, and homemade biscuits! I was amazed that only 200 miles south of Chicago, a deep-south "flavor" proliferated in culture, thought, and food! This was my beautiful state of Illinois! The cultural diversity amazes me to this day!

We arrived at Warren Hall, frazzled, sweaty, and anticipant. Students checked in their dorm rooms with stereos, hot plates, clothes, trunks, suitcases, guitars, and all kinds of junk. It was total chaos—like when you disturb an anthill with the toe of your shoe. We set my possessions up in my designated dorm room. I then proceeded with the cursory drama of hugs and kisses and the tears streaming down my mother's cheeks. The final goodbyes were said and I waved to Mom and Pop as they went on their way back to Chicago, where they would continue their elderly way of life.

The next stage of the weird psychodrama was the meeting of new roommates, dorm-mates, and so forth.

❧

They were all there: farm kids, urban blacks, isolationists, revolutionaries, foreigners, hippies, clowns, and the physically-and mentally-challenged.

I was going to love this! A veritable melting pot of the world...I was feeling the ebb and flow...it was sooooo sensory overload!!!!! I was totally alone, but surrounded by a multiplicity of weird people. It was strange, man!

We sized each other up. The blacks went with the blacks, the nerds went with the nerds, the foreigners went with the foreigners, the disabled went with the disabled, the hippies went with the hippies, the farmers went with the farmers, and those who were left behind found some type of identifying symbols, or "warm fuzzies" from a few students they could rally around. Here was all this diversity and we all were prejudiced because of fear. No new ideas would come into our heads, by God!!!! There always is safety in numbers. American Democracy at work once again!

DENNIS THE QUADRIPLEGIC — 1967

Dennis hailed from Park Forest, Illinois. He had been a number-one-ranked Illinois State champion gymnast! He specialized on the rings. He bragged that he could do the "iron cross" better than anyone in the U.S.A. before the accident. The rings "did him in".

This fateful accident severed his spinal column. He was damned to spend the rest of his life in an electric wheel chair. He had a catheter inserted in his penis and a urine bag strapped to his leg. Dennis had limited use of his hands, but learned how to write with a pencil. He lived in the dorm room next to mine, in our first year at Warren Hall.

In spite of life's cruel joke, he was philosophical about his condition. He reasoned that if he had never had the accident, his mind wouldn't have developed to its full intellectual capacity. The man was on his way to getting his Ph.D. in Psychology. While he was an athlete, he claimed that he was "mindlessly walking through life". At least now, he was "rolling" through life with a modicum of cognitive power! I liked this guy a lot! He was a fine example of bravery and determination.

Dennis required an attendant to get him dressed, bathe him, and help him go to the toilet. His younger brother was appointed by Dennis' parents to be his "prime caregiver" at the university. This was a bad idea. Soon, I heard arguments in the room next to mine. The younger brother was cracking under the pressure, and full of resentment toward Dennis.

Ultimately, the younger brother moved on to an apartment off campus, to smoke dope with his laconic girlfriend.

The new attendant was perfect for Dennis. Scott came from the New York area and was also a star gymnast in high school. He was bright, and possessed a good nature. He was happy for the opportunity to make a few extra bucks looking after Dennis. He and Dennis had a lot in common! They became fast friends. I enjoyed their friendship as well. Together, these two guys were full of the devil! They told a lot of jokes and pulled a lot of pranks!

The three of us used to call a cab and load Dennis and his wheel chair inside the vehicle. We ventured into town to a popular "watering hole" called the Club. The bar was on Main Street right next to the Varsity

Theater. We drank countless pitchers of beer there, our freshman year. The policy of the tavern was never to "card" students, who brought the disabled into the bar. The students who frequented her establishment fondly called the owner of the bar "Fat Judy". She was a huge gal, over six feet tall, weighing in at about 300 lbs. She had a beautiful face and big blue eyes. Her hair was blonde and coiffed up in a beehive hairdo. She had a threatening voice and if she yelled at you, "out on the street" you would go! Lord only knows where she came from, or how she came about owning this bar. I only know that she was something to behold! She was menacing, fat, and beautiful—all at the same time!

I loved this bar! It was a grimy, crowded place. Beer-chugging contests were in vogue and the most popular song on the jukebox was "Take your Love and Shove It, I've Had My Fill of It".

Dennis, Scott, and I got drunk as Lords, smoked a million cigarettes, and laughed like hell every Friday night. Of course, Dennis' pee bag filled up, and the one of us who was the "most sober" would have to close the valve on his catheter and empty the "pee-bag" into the toilet. You can imagine how much fun we had with the entire group of bar patrons who watched this exercise.

The beer cans were made out of steel back then and a "church key" was required to open them. I'd punch a couple of holes in the top of the beer can and one in the bottom. I put my thumb over the bottom hole, really quickly so I wouldn't lose any of the amber liquid. A 3rd party with a stopwatch yelled, "Go!"

The two "chugging" competitors sucked their beers down as fast as their gullets would accept the frothy treat! I think my record for inhaling beer with this method was around three seconds. There is nothing like supercharging cold beer down your gullet. College students were proving that there were practical applications for Newtonian Physics! These were the true joys of higher education. College was a lot of fun for me in 1967.

VIET NAM, PSYCHEDELIA, AND OTHER THINGS

"Hell No, We Won't Go!" I was safe for four years. I received a nice 2-S deferment from my "dear friends" at the Selective Service System. As long as I maintained a gentleman's "C" average at the educational combine, they couldn't ship me half way around the world to shoot at innocent little yellow men. All these little guys wanted to do was squat in the fields and grow rice! In essence, they just want to be freakin' left alone! That was OK with me!

After a few months at Southern, I threw away the "Lou Reed" look for long hair and "John Lennon" glasses. I started inculcating new values and developed a new-world view. S.I.U. was very much a Republican, "good old boy" University. It fostered all the ideals of the military-industrial complex, and wasn't at all ready for the "radicalization" of its student body.

I found the atmosphere of the university was "charged with an electric excitement" in the good old 60's. It was a great time to be alive. Everything was moving really fast, and social change and counter culture were becoming more and more mainstream every day. The "old guard" was paranoid beyond belief! They overreacted to everything radical. We knew we had 'em by the short hairs! My generation played a lot of "mind games" with authority figures!

Since I had a working-class mindset, I really didn't want to change the freakin' world; I just wanted to learn. I was paying for this education!

❦

I didn't have the luxury of having a rich mommy and daddy! This dichotomy proved to be problematic for me sometimes.

To some extent, I thought "mass insanity" was taking over our society and mainstream rationality was being left by the wayside. Sides were being drawn. I encountered two diametrically opposed ideologies. Both sides of the culture war had those "glazed eyes" and a "true believer" mentality to match.

My answer was to get into my books during the week and smoke dope or drink on the weekends. I got more and more into social isolation. I stayed by myself a lot now. I studied way too much. I felt I was falling through the cracks of society and nobody cared. I was an eccentric and I relished my eccentricity. I came home that summer, but it didn't feel like home to me anymore. My identity was changing.

I felt as if I was living in some sort of strange dream. What I thought were solid roots and stable values, evaporated in my mind. A cosmic practical joke was being played on me! I cognized, that all my adolescent realities were really just "smoke and mirrors". Huxley was right: this was a "Brave New World!"

BAD ACID AND NIGHTMARES — 1968

Studying and isolation became the norm for me. Heavy partying on the weekends and looking for female companionship was a "dead alley". I had a yearning in my guts to just hold a soft hand. I wanted to hear a sweet feminine voice telling me that I was "someone special". The "Barbie and Ken" sorority and fraternity types paraded around me, arm-in-arm. Their public displays of affection were driving me insane. I was dying inside! I was becoming a hebephrenic, neurotic, acne-laden, intellectual monster!

I drove myself harder in the classroom. I was studying around the clock. I only stopped when I had to eat, or urinate. I slept a meager three or four hours a night. I talked to people sparingly. Depression snuck up slowly and surely, then it blindsided me—the victim—with an effective right cross! What finally drove me into "crazyland" was a hippie dude who wanted to "do the nasty" with my date at a Friday-night house party. He dropped a big dose of LSD in my beer and I was off on my first trip. I wandered home, running sometimes. My heart was beating so fast, I thought I was going to have a heart attack! I felt like I was losing my mind. I was lost, ending up in familiar places, that didn't look too familiar anymore. I was "freaking out!" I saw solid walls melt, auras of light, and heard strange sounds.

I finally made it home to my bed and curled up in a fetal position. I stayed in my room for two days, but it seemed like an eternity. I was afraid to get out of my bunk.

I snapped out of the nightmare, but I realized I was transformed into a different person. I was experiencing a deep and dark depression. I knew I had lost something important. This "thing" I lost was never to be regained. I mourned the loss of it. It felt like my soul—the essence of what constituted my being—was gone for good! I was in a pit. I was raped, and left for dead. I walked through the rest of the school year "zombiefied!" My concentration had left me and my soul was screaming: "I am broken!"

I came home to Chicago at the end of May. I gutted out spring quarter and somehow managed to pass all my classes. I remember living for two weeks in my dark bedroom, surviving on Thorazine and beer.

I finally told my Freudian shrink, to shove the Thorazine "up his ass". I began running on the Marquette Park quarter-mile cinder running track. I made myself do chin-ups, pull-ups, and push-ups. I pushed my body to extremes and started coming out of my funk. In three or four weeks, I was ready for construction work.

I learned, the best cure for the "hole in your heart" and the "devils in your head" is sunshine, exercise, hard work, and good food. A quart of beer everyday didn't hurt me either...at the time...AMEN

RISING LIKE A PHOENIX—1969

The media, I fondly remember, called 1969 the "Summer of Love". It was a year that was especially significant for me. I finally lost my virginity at the elderly age of twenty! I moved into an efficiency apartment off campus and was glad to be out of the dormitory complex. My first love was twenty-four years old, blonde, Swedish, and beautiful. She was urbane, older, and sexily Rubinesque! She fell in love with my intellect in Sociology class! It's funny what gets a guy laid! Go figure!

We drank cheap wine, made love, and burned candles and incense. We listened to psychedelic music. We got "high". The "grim reaper" had finally left my soul! My new confidence led me to Barbara. She taught me erotic joy! This was the special joy of "the first time". A young man or woman never forgets these first tender kisses. They have a special purity to them. We gave ourselves to each other freely. She taught me companionship and affection in our relationship. I was totally smitten. I was in a mature love for the first time in my life. After three or four months, it was over. She left me for a graduate student. He was older and had more to offer her. Now, I guess, he was the "Cadillac" and I was the "Chevy". God! "I was back in the pit again", I thought! Somehow I survived my broken heart, and went on the next girl in my life, as all young men do! Eventually the anxiety went away. I smile whenever I think of her now! She knew I would be all right! She was tender in the way she let me go. I never will forget the sweetness of my first love!

MORE ON THE SUMMER OF LOVE — 1969

At Southern Illinois University, one beautiful fall afternoon in 1968, my 1962 Ford Galaxy was turned into a psychedelic work of art! My freaky friends and I had a painting party. Now, every color in the rainbow was on the body of my old Ford. The car looked like a poster from one of Bill Graham's rock concerts at Fillmore Auditorium, in San Francisco. It boasted wild bursts of color and swirls of beautiful paint. It was a very "Peter Max"-looking ride!

At the end of the school year in the summer of 1969, I met Sandy. I hadn't seen her since Catholic grammar school! She never looked like this! She had grown some very nice breasts, by God! Back in grammar school, she was a quiet, mousy kind of girl. She wore that boring Catholic schoolgirl uniform. Yuck! Now, she was thin and shapely. She had lovely dark hair, parted down the middle—hippie-chick style. She had nice, pert breasts, and a lovely bottom in her hip-hugger jeans. YUM!!!!... This babe was looking good!

We swam in one of those "sorry" four-foot plastic pools in back of her house. Her parents were home and she freaked me out, by rubbing up against me in the pool and telling me she wanted "it" right out there! She was like a "cat in heat", man! She was one of those liberated females! Wow! I didn't want to do "it" right there in the pool. My survival instincts were "red-flagging" that idea. I thought that her parents catching us was not a good scenario at all! She said, "We can go do it in my bedroom. My parents don't care." Double-WOW!

I remember entering her sweet vagina and listening to the Rock Opera "Tommy" by the "Who". She put me in heaven! In my old age, I still play this CD, and am instantly transported to that "Summer of Love".

On our next date, we went dancing to live bands in various "gin mills" on the South Side of Chicago. We were bombed, buzzed, and horny. It was four-in-the-morning and she inadvertently dropped a burning cigarette or joint in the back seat of my car. I think she became too relaxed from me jamming my tongue down her throat! As I was feeling up her breasts, she made the sexiest moans I ever heard, so I quickly escorted her to my mom and dad's back yard in order to "bang her brains out".

I had to work fast, 'cause the sun was coming up and I didn't want the neighbors walking to the bus stop to catch us. As we finished, I was gloriously proud of myself! I pulled my jeans on and half-carried my new love interest back to the car in front of the house.

The first thing to meet my eyes, were billowing clouds of smoke just pouring out of my Ford! My heart was pounding like crazy! I was in terror! I ran to the side of my mom's house and grabbed the garden hose to extinguish the fire. I was praying to God, this old hose could reach my smoldering car! The rear bench seat was smoking. While I was freaking out, my mom woke up.

She stuck her head outside the window. She yelled, "Holy Mother of God, what are you doing!" All I remember saying was, "Geez, Mom, not right now. Can't you see I have a problem here?!" Thinking of all my options and moving really fast, I decided to drive to the Chicago Fire Department!

The fire station was down the street on 81st and Kedzie Avenue. Sandy is drunk in the front seat, just roaring hysterically with laughter. She lights up another joint, and says, "This is just the best date I've ever had!" She is laughing and saying, "Rich, if we don't die first, my old man is going to kill us!" This statement didn't do the least to fortify my courage or my resolve to solve the problem at hand! The drive was about 5 minutes from my house, but it seemed like an eternity. When we pulled into the fire station driveway, the fire chief said, "Are you kids insane?! You could have blown yourselves and the gas tank, sky high!"

I drove Sandy to her Mom and Dad's house about 6:30 a.m., both of us stinking of smoke. We also smelled like booze and refer. Geez, we had red eyes and sunken hearts, fearing the consequences of our actions.

Walking through her front door, I viewed the angry scowls of her mother. We sauntered to the "cheery" breakfast table. Her huge, Irish-Catholic, police-sergeant-of-a-father was eating his eggs and drinking his coffee. He stared holes through me with his crystal clear blue eyes. I was scared to death and felt that at any second he was going to spring from the table and take his nightstick to me or put his big hands around my neck!

He said, "Son, you will never, ever, see or call my daughter ever again. Do you fully understand what I am telling you?"

I said, "Yes Sir! Oh, thank you Sir!" Without so much as a glance at Sandy, I bounded out her front door. As I got into my burnt out car, I glanced at the springs in the back seat. I smiled as I thought, "Some rags for stuffing, some Lysol, and some blankets stapled to the main frame will fix this problem!"

I got back home and Mom fixed me a "killer" breakfast. I had bacon and eggs and toast. She brought me lots of pancakes with Karo syrup, while she ranted and raved about waking her up. She wanted to know if I "had a hole in my head". With a full belly, I went to bed happy. I fell asleep, thinking about where I was going to go that night. It was Saturday night and the "hunt for chicks" must go on!

SENIOR YEAR: THE TRAILER, JERRY AND GOOD TIMES — 1971

Ah, it was senior year and the best of college times were to come! A guy I knew from Chicago's South Side and I hooked up and rented a trailer just outside of the city limits of Carbondale, on old Route 51. My new roommate's name was Jerry. He was a big, happy Polack! I loved the guy from day one! The trailer had two bedrooms with locks on the doors. The bedrooms were on opposite ends of the trailer for privacy. This was cool, because we planned on entertaining a young lady or two while we were there. In the middle of the trailer was a toilet and shower. We also had a small kitchenette with a tiny electric range and standard size refrigerator. Added to the place was a small living room with a cheap sofa. There was enough room in the living room for a TV and a stereo system, plus our weights and barbells.

Jerry was 6'5" tall and weighed in at around 285 lbs. He lifted weights, and had a thick body on him, like a lineman on a pro-football team. His kind face, thick glasses, and beaming smile denied his ominous-looking body. This "ginormous" guy was as gentle as a lamb! We got along famously, both as roommates and as friends. We looked for good times and we had plenty of them together! Surprisingly, Jerry got me interested in pumping iron. Usually, on Thursday nights, we purchased a couple of six packs, a few bags of chips, rolled a couple of joints, and settled down to watch "Gunsmoke", "All in the Family", and "Hawaii Five-O". Life was great with Jerry!

❧

We owned a raggedy-looking black cat called "Stokely", who was named after the Black Panther, Stokely Carmichael. This cat loved marijuana. He jumped up on our laps when we lit up. He begged us to blow the smoke into his nostrils. When the cat was stoned, he chased "non-existent entities" and rubbed himself all along the walls of the trailer. When we watched our crazy cat, Jerry and I laughed so hard, we almost wet our drawers!

Our diet for the week consisted of hot dogs, frozen hamburger patties, and chicken cooked with Shake-and-Bake. We bought Van Camps pork-and-beans, Hormel Chili, frozen pizzas, potato chips, pretzels and ice cream. We washed all this junk down with a lot of beer. Jerry and I were really into healthy eating. College students today worry too much about their diets. We knew we were never going to die! We were too young for that stuff.

Jerry and I smoked some "primo" pot. This stuff was the best dank, odiferous shit you could buy at the time. There were no stems or seeds in these bags—just a lot of buds in our dope! In those days, this stuff probably came from Southeast Asia. We figured the war was good for something, at least! Anyway, a guy could score a "lid", (5 shot glasses of grass) for $20. My roommate and I could stay stoned for the whole week if we liked. I liked saving it for the girls. God only knows how much a big bag of reefer like this would cost me today. I could probably buy an "Ipod" for what I would have to pay for a lid of this today. If you blew a half joint of the shit we had, you would be totally wrecked. "Wrecked," meant "f***ed up" in our lingo, back in the 60's.

One time, I remember looking at the "Endless Summer" poster of a couple of surfers, hanging on our wall. I was high on grass. I actually saw the waves moving, and the surfers catching the pipeline! WOW! (We said "Wow" a lot back then.) The way to look at a poster is under black ultraviolet lights, with Hendrix playing riffs in the background. I listened to the Beach Boys' Endless Summer album now, to bring me back to those days. At the age of 58, I'm still insane; I admit it. The only difference is that I haven't had drugs or alcohol for years!

Jerry called me the "Paranoid Pigeon". He said I worried too much about things. Someone had to worry. My God, we had some narrow escapes. Jerry was finally in graduate school. It took him 6 years to get his undergraduate degree in Geology. He was a "lifer". I suppose it took him at least another 6 years to get his Masters Degree! I was long-gone by then. He was a professional student and enjoyed every minute of it! On Fridays, real early in the morning, we went bass fishing. We went to a great spot on "Little Grassy Lake" called the spillway. We each brought a six-pack of beer, to take the "edge" off. Sometimes we picked up a keg of beer and a tapper on Thursday nights and threw it on ice in a huge washtub, for Friday night parties. It sat in the shade by the side of the trailer, wrapped up in blankets, to keep it good-and-cold. We cleaned fish when we came home, and froze 'em for a fish fry during the week.

Friday-night parties were awesome. We charged three bucks at the door for the party and the beer. The grass was for Jerry and me. We only turned on the very best, good-looking babes. This was a good investment!

❧

By the time party people started coming to our trailer, Jerry and I would be half-in-the-bag from hitting on the keg all afternoon. We lifted weights outside and listened to rock-and-roll. We sweat in the sun and worked on our tans, while quenching our thirst with the "golden brew". About 6 p.m. we showered up, brushed the old teeth, and slipped on our fresh tank tops and cut off jeans. We liked to show off our tans and pumped-up muscles. We were both ready for "action". Action always came to us; we didn't have to go looking for it!

Jerry and I listened to rock music while we waited for the crowd to come. We laughed and sipped on our beers, vowing that we would never leave this place because it truly was "heaven on earth". We packed in anywhere from 25 to 40 people for our trailer parties. People actually lined up outside, because we were known to throw one "helluva" party. We made some pretty good money from the parties, which financed our marijuana purchases and dates with girls.

Good-looking girls could crash our parties anytime, for nothing. Letting them in for free was good business and usually worth our while!

It all was so awesome. The stereo blasted the great songs of Santana, Sly and the Family Stone, Hendrix, Joplin, The Doors, Country Joe and the Fish, and The Moody Blues — ad infinitum. This was bacchanalia at its best! It all was so tribal. It was erotic. It was surreal and psychedelic!

❧

Bodies swayed to the pulsating beat of the music. People were sweating, hugging, kissing, humping, fighting, crying, stinking, and puking. It was a great psychodrama! This was being fully alive! It was a feast for all the senses, and Jerry and I were the ringleaders. Ours was a strange, 1960's kind-of-world.

It was like an "Andy Warhol" production. Jerry and I were lucky. I guess we had good Karma because we never got busted. We did this party at least twenty or thirty times. As I said before, we never wanted it to end!

❧

MORE ON JERRY AND WEIGHT TRAINING

Jerry amazed me. He pumped those barbells with those huge arms he had on him and I watched his muscles GROW, right before my very eyes! His veins popped out everywhere. The guy looked like the "Incredible Hulk" on steroids. I wanted to look like that, damn it! Jerry taught me how to do curls, upright rows, the military press, bench press, squats, tricep extensions, "super sets" and more! He taught me how to eat massive amounts of protein to get bigger!

He screamed at me like a Marine Drill Instructor—"One more rep, you weak, paranoid pigeon you! You're a damn pussy! Push! That's it, that's it! Now one more! You can do it! Yeah, don't stop now! Yes! Attaboy, Richie baby!"

Gawd, I felt like I was going to puke every day! Sometimes he worked me so damn hard, I did "lose my cookies". We worked out every day for at least 2 hours. After about 6 weeks, people were noticing the change in me. I was looking good. I just loved the feeling of getting my muscles all pumped up—the blood filling up my arms and legs and chest. It's the best rush in the world! It's better than any drug! Only those who are in this weird subculture of muscle-heads and runners know about the "high".

Jerry had a simple sensitivity to his nature. By no means was he a mental giant, but sometimes he surprised me with the depth of his understanding. He was truly, a good and gentle man. He displayed a wonderful humility and joy for life. I never expected to see this in a man of his size and stature.

I guess I loved this man because he was genuine. He also had an uncanny ability to make me go insane with laughter. I enjoyed watching all of the crazy things he said and did. There was always a new adventure to be experienced with this guy. I learned a lot about friendship living with Jerry during my senior year in the trailer.

HOT CHILI IN YOUR "FRUIT OF THE LOOMS"

Jerry had a "buzz on". He was drinking some rock-gut whiskey and "Old Milwaukee Beer" chasers all afternoon that fateful Friday. Why the hell anyone drank "Old Milwaukee" was beyond my comprehension. The stuff always gave me the "screamin'mimi's". In common layman's terms: "THE SHITS".

He got the munchies, so I opened two 16-ounce cans of super hot chili, with meat and kidney beans for the "big ol' boy". I knew this "feast" had to sober him up. At the very least, it would clear his sinuses. Ten minutes after he inhaled this huge dinner, (along with a box of stale saltine crackers), he was off to the "porcelain throne" to take a dump.

I thought I fixed him up, but after a half-an-hour, I decided to check on him and nudged the bathroom door open. He was passed out, with his "whiteys" around his knees. It looked like his head was gazing into the "cotton abyss" of his under shorts. He was snoring like a wounded bear. "Hey! Wake up asshole!" I said. He mumbled something unintelligible and started snoring again. This surely was not a pretty picture. I didn't appreciate him sleeping on the damn "head". I had to take a "whiz" myself. Next thing I know, I made a huge mistake by shaking him. He "ralphed" up some of the nastiest puke I had ever seen in my life, smack dab in the middle of his under shorts.

I ran outta' there, laughing my ass off, down the street to Hippie Mike's trailer. I needed to borrow his Nikon camera. This was going to be a Kodak moment! I relieved myself at Mike's place, and told him what he was going to see. We both ran back to my trailer, camera-in-hand, chortling like a couple of schoolgirls.

First off, we got some great camera shots of poor Jerry. We knew we would have all kinds of fun with these snapshots later on, when the "big guy" was sober! All of a sudden, Jerry pulled up his "pukey"undies and jeans. He burped and exclaimed, "I feel great now! When's the party going to start?" Oh, no! Mike and I got a five-gallon plastic bucket, and filled it with warm, soapy water. I found the big sponge we used to wash the cars. We stood Jerry up in the shower stall, stripped him, and went to cleaning him up. You can imagine what strength this took on our part. Jerry was a mountain of drunken, dead weight.

Mike held him up as the shower water hit his big Polack head. I had to do the dirty work. I put the wretched undies and jeans into a garbage bag and buried them out in the woods. Burying a fresh corpse would have been easier! God it was yucky! Once we got Jerry squeaky clean, we put some fresh "whiteys" on him and tucked him in his bed, all safe and sound. I told him we wanted him to go "night-night" for a while. The whole situation was totally hilarious. He was actually smiling, all cleaned and scrubbed up. He looked like a "big pink baby". He drunkenly mumbled what great friends we were and was thankful for all our ministrations. I thought, "Thank God our buddy Jerry isn't a mean drunk. Whew!" I bid adieu to Mike, thanking him for all his help. I'd see him at our trailer party in a couple of hours.

I proceeded to wash down and disinfect the bathroom. Then I showered, and disinfected myself! Sometimes it's hard work being a drunk. It comes with the territory. I wouldn't have done this stuff for just anyone, but for Jerry's sake—God bless his heart—it was all right with me.

LATER ON THAT EVENING

The party was going on as usual. People were asking, "Where the hell is Jerry?" I cracked his door open to give them peeks. "Shhhh! Don't wake him," I said. Everyone was laughing like hell. Jerry's story was a saga now!

In the middle of the party, somewhere around 11 p.m., who the hell do you figure comes stumbling out of his bedroom? He's got nothing on but the fresh underwear that Mike and I tugged up around his big ass. Jerry is all bleary-eyed with a big old smile on his face. He says, "Roll me a joint, Pigeon! Why'd yah let me get so drunk?!"

Every one in the trailer was laughing and giving him a round of applause. Jerry was with us once again! He rose from the dead. He had his favorite beer stein in his big "paw". His eyeglasses were all crooked, and he had a silly smile on his face. His hair was messed up and he looked like hell. His body got him over the top, however. Jerry was in great shape!

In no time at all, he had his big arm around a hot-looking babe. Jerry was one-in-a-million! He made me smile all the time. Our friendship came straight from the heart.

THE SAGA OF THE LONE BEER MUG

It was Friday night and another bacchanalian event was planned at our trailer. This party had been awesome. The trailer was trashed beyond belief! I opened my eyes slowly, and looked at the clock. I saw that it was one in the afternoon. "Oh Christ!" I exclaimed.

The oppressive sun was somewhat filtered by the disheveled, nicotine-stained blinds in my room. My mouth was rancid from the acid in my stomach. I had the worst damned cottonmouth I had ever experienced in my short life. I squinted at the nightstand, and breathed a sigh of relief. It was there. I knew I was going to need it when I passed out the night before, for this morning. Little did I know I'd need it this afternoon!

I lit the joint and inhaled deeply. Immediately, I coughed and hacked just like some elderly emphysema patient. I threw my legs over the side of the bed. I sat there, inert, feeling the calming rush of the dope hitting the nerve receptors in my head. I took another "hit" and peered down at my tan feet. I was soaked with sweat. "It was going to be another hot one today", I thought.

Suddenly, I'm tapped on the shoulder by Lord only knows who! I hear a girlie voice begging, "Can I have a hit?" I turn and look, wondering what I am going to see. "Hmmm, not bad", I thought. "Sure baby, let's wake up Jerry and go to the 'Golden Bear' for some breakfast." She is ecstatic. I never met a woman who doesn't like to be taken to a restaurant. I observed her young body as she put on her clothes. She is smiling at me. I think she knows what we are going to do after breakfast! I know I'm too hung over to study today, and I'm thinking she feels the same way. YUM! I love afternoon delights!

We stumble out of the bedroom, into the narrow hallway and are greeted by a miasma of beer cans, records, cigarette butts, ashtrays, discarded clothing items, and sleeping bodies lying in the filth. "Alright", I say, "the party is over. Let's all get the hell outta' here!" I go to shaking and kicking these poor souls, as they scramble for their belongings. They head out to face the enemy sun and a day of remorse after pounding beers all night. Later, they will smile and relish the good time they had at my trailer. Their pain was to be but a distant memory. They would all come back next week and do it all over again!

Then I saw "IT"...the Monolith! It had to represent something important. I felt as if I was seeing Kubrick's "2001 Space Odyssey" once again! Alone, in all of its majesty, it sat. A perfect 5-foot diameter circle had been cleaned for its presence. The icon sat dead center within its circumference. It was a single crystalline beer mug, filled to the brim with "upchuck". At this very "cosmic" moment, I had a spiritual awakening. I realized something very important: "Human ingenuity has no bounds." Ah, the beauty of it all!

THURSDAY NIGHT AT LEO' S

Leo's was a scummy liquor store on Route 51, South of Route 13, in Carbondale. It stood in all its glory next to the Illinois Central Train Station. The upper floor of Leo's had all the packaged goods. A student could purchase whiskey, beer, cigarettes, Slim Jims, and kegs of beer. The liquor store was always mobbed when S.I.U. students made the train ride back to Union Station in Downtown Chicago after final exams. We were always drunk by the time we hit Champaign, Illinois. Champaign was the home of the University of Illinois. We welcomed the invading "Illini" students with whoops of joy! Their entry onto the train meant more party people carrying booze and contraband. The party was definitely going to get raucous now! We knew that within the hour, we would be injected with more ribald enthusiasm and make more contacts with Chicago females for vacation-time fun!

I'm getting off the subject at hand!

Leo's had a huge basement. We went down the concrete stairs into the "labyrinth." The place was like a cave. On Thursday nights, for only a dollar cover charge, we could "drink our brains out". An unlimited amount of Busch beer in-the-can was available for us all night, for the mere price of fifteen cents! Not only that, we got to listen to a live rock-and-roll bands. We also had the unknown benefit of losing 20% of our hearing capacity, if we were regulars for over a year!

Sometimes, Jerry and I bought our keg for the Friday night party and loaded it in the trunk of his big Buick. Then, we sauntered downstairs for cheap beers and cheap thrills. We were multi-tasking '60s-style and didn't even realize it! Leo's didn't have air conditioning. Plus, it had a lousy ventilation system. Everything down there was dirty and brown with nicotine. Years of partying, and cigarette and marijuana smoke, created a special ambiance. The floor was soaking wet from condensation. Sweat, urine, and beer added to the dampness. We sure didn't want to fall down in Leo's! Blue smoke from fog machines gave the bandstand an eerie elegance. Strobe lights flashed continuously to the driving beat from drums and bass guitar.

My senses were "jack-hammered" by rock and roll. Bodies swayed and sometimes stumbled and fell in this melodrama. Tarantino would love this joint! For three bucks, a guy could get totally hammered and meet the girl of his dreams—or maybe, his nightmares.

The night unfolded like some kind of cheap plastic flower. The fever pitch built and the heat melted the petals, as the drunken patrons made the treacherous march back up the concrete stairs. The drunks moved like wooden soldiers. They weaved and fell. The point was to fall forward! We strived for our goal, which was fresh air, and the dark night outside. It was a weird carnival. It was a tribal ritual of inebriation!

GRADUATION SOUTHERN ILLINOIS UNIVERSITY—1971

Graduation was funereal. No one I ever met, wanted to leave sweet Carbondale, Illinois. We faced Chicago row houses now—the dingy city. Gone were the fishing lakes and wide-open spaces at Giant City State Park. Many keg parties were enjoyed in this great wilderness of the Shawnee National Forest. Gone was our aberrant Disneyland. We were all to going to face the longest unemployment line in American history. Some of us would be heading to the rice paddies and jungles of Southeast Asia. Some of us were going to die out there.

It wasn't a pretty sight, seeing our funky moms and dads smiling "idiotically" with joy. They were so happy for us all, but we were bummed! Didn't they know how horrible this graduation day was for their sons and daughters? They grinned at their little boys and girls. Our parents were oh, so proud! We had to endure countless snapshots. We sweat in our archaic caps and gowns. Some of the girls were flashing the bikinis they were wearing underneath. This was the wonderful "mindset" of my fellow students at Dear Southern Illinois University!

The city of Chicago lurked, waiting to swallow me whole. It was an ominous animal ready to suck me in and spit me out. This evil entity of Chicago had to be confronted and conquered. It was my "Dharma" to take my place as a productive citizen. This conservatism was a far cry from my idyllic trailer life. I graduated as a Dean's List Scholar. My parents were really proud of me. I was the first one in our family to actually graduate from college. Mine was a "lunchbox" family with their first college graduate! All the neighbors were beaming! One of "their kind" had made good! I had to conquer the world now! Everyone expected it of me!

Thankfully, I flunked my draft physical. Central Michigan University accepted me into their Master's Degree Psychology Program. I didn't have a dime in my pocket to attend my school of choice. My game plan was to save for a year or two, then proceed to Michigan and my Masters degree. I then would go on for my Doctorate. I pictured myself in a herringbone sport coat with the suede elbow patches. I'd be smoking a pipe and have a neatly groomed full beard and long hair. I would have that professional professorial look, which comely female graduate students adored! This was my "Walter Mitty" type dream!

❧

Returning home was all right for a while. It gave me a chance to hook up with old friends. I played softball in the park and hung out with the old neighborhood guys at Bruno's tap, on 71st Street. I got all the news concerning the welfare of high school buddies who were serving in Viet Nam. Learning news about our friends who weren't coming back was devastating for all of us in the neighborhood.

❧

Another bar I hung out at was the "Mansart House". This cocktail lounge was located on 69th and Pulaski Avenue. On Thursday nights, they packed 'em in. The ladies drank for free on Thursdays and the dolls that came in this place were absolutely beautiful! They really fixed themselves up. Mini-skirts and Hot Pants were the fashion at the time. For all the young men in my peer group, this was a bonus resulting from the sexual revolution. A guy had to dress up in nice dress slacks and a nice shirt or sweater, to pick up one of these hot babes. On Thursday evenings at the Mansart House, I always tried to score a date for the weekend. The bar was dark and the jukebox played a lot of slow, romantic soul-type music. The chances for future intimacies were fairly obvious to a fellow, after a slow dance.

From Friday through Sunday night, we had choices of hundreds of nightclubs and bars. This was the beauty of Chicago at the time. The scene was faster and slicker than any college campus. Chicago was, and still is, a "party town".

❧

My job now, was to send out over 100 resumes to corporate concerns that might have interest in my skills. I was dejected when I received only three responses from the firms I was interested in working for! They were all nice rejection letters. I was staring at economic reality for the first time, and didn't relish what I was seeing! I had to lower my standards, or Dad was going to throw me out of his house! I took a white-collar job, which I found while I perused the Chicago Tribune want ads. This job was all the way downtown. I was going to be employed as a "headhunter" for an employment agency, putting "pressmen" to work. I had to learn all about printing machines, and how they worked. I dealt with the printing houses and the workers who needed printing jobs. I was going to be paid to be the middleman. I didn't have a clue about any of this stuff! I was speaking a new language that I didn't totally comprehend. The phone was hung up in my ear, more often than not. Nobody in the office took the time to tell me what the hell I was supposed to do!

Some old guy drinking Maalox straight from the bottle tried to break me in. His face was in agony all day long, as he held his guts, and answered the phone. Jesus, this was a major bummer! I wondered sometimes if he was going to make it through the day. After watching him suffer for a week, I realized I was making no commission money! I knew this job wasn't going anywhere, except in the toilet. I saw myself 30 years from now, holding my guts and swilling Maalox, a broken man at 50. I was in the hole about five bucks as a result of paying for the Archer Avenue bus downtown. I parked the old psychedelic Ford on one of the side streets somewhere near California Avenue, around the area of Kelly High School. I hoped the high school kids wouldn't add to the paint job on my car! I took the bus from there. I sure couldn't afford downtown parking. I hated the bus, the traffic and the fumes from the traffic in the city. I longed for the fresh air of Carbondale!

I hated sitting on the bus in my cheap suit, with my brown-bag lunch, lovingly made for me by my mom. Every day I went to work, I faced 8 hours of agonizing boredom and anxiety. My first week of pay was a negative five dollars.

I figured this wasn't a good start for a Dean's List Scholar. Was this my payback for all the fun I had? When you graduate from college, you're supposed to be successful. God was punishing me, I was sure! I had to come home and face the music. I had to borrow $20 bucks from Mom for the weekend, while my father yelled at me. I told him I would start anew, in my search for a job on Monday morning. He said, "You know the paper comes to the house every day. If you know what's good for you, you'll check the want ads tomorrow morning!" What a bummer.

MIDNIGHT SHIFT AT CONTINENTAL LIQUOR— SUMMER 1971

After my horrible failure as an employment agency specialist, things got worse. My dad came home from work all excited about a new position he found for me. My stomach started doing "flip-flops" in anticipation of what I was going to hear. My dad was going to rescue me from economic ruin with a "great" job at a liquor warehouse on Chicago Avenue and Halsted Street. YUUUUCK!!!!!!

This was just what I wanted to hear. No way! Dad knew all the liquor salesmen who came into his cocktail lounge. They told him a smart boy like me, should have no problem moving up in the firm. I didn't want anything to do with it and felt an impending sense of doom. I knew this was going to be a disaster from the "git-go". What made it even worse was that they were putting me on midnight shift. This isn't what a twenty-one-year-old guy wants to do! This meant that I couldn't drink, or chase girls for at least five-nights-a-week. No more beer in the park. No more hot dogs. No more sitting on the bridge with my neighborhood buddies! No picking up girls in Bruno's tap. This "major league" sucked, big time!

I took the job just to keep peace in the family. I remember driving to the liquor house on hot, steamy nights down Halsted Street. The job was a mere eighty-one blocks from my house. The people of Chicago were amused as I drove all the way to work, feeling mortified in my psychedelic Ford. The blanket still covered the burnt out back seat. The Good Lord was punishing me for my carnal sin. I re-painted the car, approximating the original color with a big paintbrush found in Mom's basement. I bought a cheap gallon of red paint from Saxon's Hardware Store on 63rd and Kedzie Avenue.

I knew it wasn't such a good idea to be driving in Chicago with a flower-power car. Mayor Richard J. Daley's "Boys in Blue" still had their Nazi mentality. The Chicago cops maintained stiff "hard-ons" for the "Yippies" and the anarchistic behavior they displayed at the Democratic National Convention in 1969. I didn't want to risk being pulled over every day by a three-hundred-pound donut-eater, with a nightstick and red face, ready to beat the "Be-Jesus" out of me. Cops have good memories and they hated radical kids.

The drive to work was interesting. I loved the smell of the hot dogs and the aromas of other foods on Maxwell Street. I dug the funky clothing store called "Smoky Joes". That's where all the hip black "blues men" bought their rags. I loved Greek Town and the slums. I got to banter with hookers at stoplights and always tossed a quarter to the homeless guys begging up and down the route. This was the Chicago I loved: bums, whores, flop houses, liquor stores, and blacks with radios the size of television sets perched up on their shoulders! There were storefront Baptist churches, stinking sanitary sewers, and Chicago Transit Authority buses cutting me off at almost every light. It might have been a bad dream for anyone else, but I was a Chicagoan at heart and knew how the city worked. A guy had to be tough in this town, or he got his ass kicked!

I worked the midnight shift with guys called "ready men". These guys reported to some beat-up storefront, which posed as an "employment center". The dilapidated men, who were sober enough to stand up and still had a little muscle on their frames, were selected for work. A cigar-chomping manager stuffed them in a van and the drunks were transported to the liquor warehouse. These guys were the real deal! They were bonafide flophouse drunks! They all lived up and down Madison Street. They were going to be my co-workers, all night long! I was living the American Dream! Eh?

I stacked boxes of liquor with these men. The stench coming out of their pores was stifling. Aromas of shit, sweat, wine, whiskey, and God-only-knows what else, attacked my olfactory senses every night! I worked in the oppressive, humid, Chicago summer heat. What's worse is that I worked in a confined area inside a truck trailer, with no ventilation. The trailer offered unique smells of its own and inside of each one of them, it was well over one hundred degrees!

The boxes of liquor kept coming all night long. It was a lunatic, hell-like procession, which went on for an eternity. My wet-brained comrades kept asking me, "What the hell are you doing here kid?" I really didn't know how to answer them. I just stayed "mum" and questioned my sanity. I did this to please my father. My agony soon overcame familial devotion. The job took two months of my life, before I mustered the courage to walk off.

I felt reborn. I resurrected myself and was a free man once again. I knew how a convict felt when his sentence was finally served and the penitentiary gates swung open for him. I saw sunlight again and filled my lungs with the fresh air of freedom. After this experience, I always hated a midnight shift. Your body never knows when to piss, shit, eat, or sleep when you work the graveyard shift. AMEN.

THE MEN'S WEAR SHOP—1971-1972

My dad thought I blew the opportunity of a lifetime! Liquor salesmen make a lot of money! They also become big-time alcoholics. This was not my dream, Dad! I couldn't begin to explain to him, the many horrors I had endured. I had to find a better job to redeem myself in his eyes. Thank God, it was right around the corner for me.

I interviewed with the owner of a menswear shop, at the Ford City Shopping Center on 76th and Cicero Avenue. The owner was a tall, good-looking man in his mid 60's. He was an Irish-Catholic and had a large family. The man looked elegant and his conversational skills were top-shelf. As I shook his hand, I felt a vibe that he liked me. There was an immediate connection. I knew right away, I was going to get this job! I presented my resume to him. As he read it, he arched his eyebrows and said, "You're overqualified for this position Richard. Why do you want this job?" I described to him the horrors I had just experienced with the liquor house. I then expressed my desire to work for a year or two, in order to save money for graduate school. He respected my honesty and integrity and I was hired on the spot. I pumped his hand happily.

He smiled and told me that he would start me at one-hundred-and-forty dollars a week. A 6% commission would grace sales exceeding $2,350 per week over my base salary. I was in heaven! That was a lot more than I was making at the liquor house. He said, "You can start tomorrow, Richard. Welcome aboard!" I thanked him enthusiastically, and told him he wouldn't regret his decision!

The drive home was a short distance—only ten minutes away. I wouldn't have to drive an hour each way to and from work every day. I was happy as a lark and couldn't wait to tell my folks! If I worked hard and learned how to be a top- notch salesman, I had the opportunity to make some big money. Mr. "O" had opened my eyes to a new reality. He wouldn't regret that he had hired me. Looking back now, with pen-in-hand, I have to say that what I learned from this great man was as valuable as the four years of learning at the university. I found something good for me. I did it on my own. This is a bridge that winners have to cross. Sometimes, adversity makes a man focus with a little more intensity.

LEARNING THE ROPES

I learned how to work the floor. I learned the stock. I knew where every shirt and tie was in the place. I cleaned up and stacked every item of clothing neatly. It was all placed back in the bins, after customers left them looking like nuclear bomb devastation.

I began to understand the complexities of the retail clothing business.

The tailor taught me how to "fit" men in suits. I learned how to use the tape measure and the soapstone to mark for alterations. I loved "working" a customer. Being naturally friendly and outgoing is a necessary quality to possess in this type of work. I was a "natural". I could assess a situation and know if I had a "live" one or a "dud".

I used my employee discount to buy some beautiful clothes. To be successful in this business, a man had to look the part. I looked sharp all the time and developed an air of confidence. People relate to success. If you look good, smile, and relate to your customers, they are always willing to spend more money. I used my spiel like an expert! I could make a person believe that their clothing purchase was going to change their lives! I felt more like Elmer Gantry than a clothing salesman. I moved the impressionable buyers all over the store and always rang up some big sales. After all, "clothes make the man". I took to my new job like a duck takes to water!

Mr. "O" just loved me. He had two sons, two daughters, and a son-in-law working in his shop. Amazingly, they all loved me, too! I was having the time of my life. I always got along well with the Irish. Maybe it was due to my four years at an Irish-Catholic high school. The family had some great parties at their Elmhurst home. It was a family filled with laughter and good will. I was invited to all the parties, and was treated like another son. I felt like another member of their family. I was learning more and more every day at the shop. I hired on in August of 1971. By the time Thanksgiving had come, I was the number-one salesman in the store. Retail sales demands long hours and hard work.

As I mentioned previously, a salesman has to restock merchandise and keep everything on the racks and shelves looking presentable to the public. He is running on his feet all day long.

Paper work has to be done and transactions have to be made. The salesman has to look as sharp as a tack all day long and be available to assist a customer at any time. Availability is of the essence. A high level of exuberance and confidence is always necessary for a modicum of success. I was selling three-to-four-thousand dollars worth of merchandise every week. I worked six-days-a-week. I only had to work from noon-to-five on Sundays, but I took Mondays off, so it really felt like a five-day week. Two evenings a week, I stayed until ten o'clock and closed up the shop.

I was earning anywhere from, $180- to $240-a-week gross pay, which was pretty good money back in 1971. I was happy with the $140 back in August, when I first started my employment! I had come a long way. With Christmas coming, I had a whole month to really make some big money. The day after Thanksgiving (which is the biggest shopping day of the year), I single-handedly rang up over six thousand dollars! That, my friends, adds up to over $360 in wages, for one day's work! That evening, Mr. "O" took me to a nice restaurant and treated me to a prime rib dinner with all the trimmings. We also enjoyed a few well-deserved manhattans. As he picked up the tab, he said, "You have a special gift, son. You like people, and they like you. You have what it takes. Knowledge and drive is what makes a man a success in any endeavor." Mentoring from men like Mr. "O" helped me to become a success in life.

My father couldn't provide mentoring because he wasn't wired to succeed at anything. I loved my dad, but as I grew in maturity, his flaws became more evident to me. I had two father figures in my life now. I had my brother, Jim, and Mr. "O". Listening to their advice and doing the work required of me, I guaranteed myself a successful life. They were guiding me in the direction where I needed to go. The most important thing I learned from my two mentors, was that a man needs to show up with his hands out in front of him, ready to work. It was my responsibility to keep my ears up and my eyes open. I needed to listen, in order to be a sponge and soak up the knowledge they so freely were offering to me. This is the greatest gift one man can offer another: Knowledge. A man learns in his heart that knowledge is power!

CHRISTMAS SEASON — 1971

I was really on a roll. Having the confidence of my employer, really stoked my fires. I produced sales like a runaway train! Without a day off, I worked from Thanksgiving Day until Christmas Eve. People were coming to the shop in droves. Wave after wave of customers came through our doors. Their only mission was to empty their pockets. For me, the cash register bell rang "tidings of joy"! I was building a nice little nest egg. Living with Mom and Dad was a great asset.

Mom cooked great meals, and did my laundry for me every week. Room-and-board was only $25 a week. My mom and dad were happy with this arrangement. By the time I sat down to Christmas dinner with my family, I had proudly socked away a couple-of-grand in the bank.

Exhausted but happy, I returned to the shop the day after Christmas. We handled the expected influx of returned items, but I usually persuaded the customer into an exchange. Now this is good salesmanship! Sometimes I managed to sell the customer more merchandise. Mr. "O" really loved this skill I had developed! He was overjoyed with my sales for the holiday season, and gave me a twenty-dollar raise. I really had learned my craft.

I now thought less and less about graduate school. I was thinking more about classy-looking women and fast cars. I wore the latest look in men's fashion and ate and drank in the finest establishments. Maybe my future didn't lie in the realm of academia after all. This is a common error many young men make early on in their careers.

THE NEW CAR—1972

January came to Chicago, and with it the blustery wind known to all Chicagoans as the "hawk". Sales at the shop significantly slowed down to snail's pace and I welcomed the break. I worked long-and-hard the whole Christmas season and felt I earned a rest after the holiday crunch.

The old psychedelic Ford finally died, but my brother and his mechanic-friend Eddie found a gem-of-a-car for me. This car was a beautiful jet-black 1965 Chrysler Newport Sedan. It was in tip-top shape and had low miles. This big old "boat" was as large as a limousine and its interior was flawless. The car had big bench seats that looked brand new! They looked like they just recently had come off the factory line. The windshield was so huge in this car, it looked like the picture window in my mom and dad's living room!

The best thing about the deal was the elderly gentleman who owned the car wanted only $400 bucks for it! Jim, Eddie, and I crawled around the ground underneath this beast, looking for telltale signs of mechanical problems. We couldn't find any oil leaks, so we popped the hood and saw a huge, clean V-8 engine. We all looked at each other and smiled! This baby was super clean! When I got in and turned the ignition key, she fired up like a lion. She idled down quickly and purred like a kitten. Jim and Eddie smiled at me as I slapped down four crisp "Ben Franklins" on the old man's kitchen table.

Later at my brother's house, we drank a few beers, and raised a glass to my good fortune. I drove home in my new car, feeling like a million bucks!

I couldn't wait to dress up in a nice coat and tie the next morning, and drive to work in my shiny new car. The love beads and long hair were abandoned now. That life style seemed a million miles away. I put my college days to rest, in a neat little corner in my mind.

NIGHTCLUBBING AND THE NEW GIRLFREIND

Since I more-or-less raised the level of my standard of living, the drinking establishments I frequented were more upscale. I was meeting professional women now. It was a step up for me. They were classy and beautiful.

In the seedy, Chicago-style taverns I lolled in after college graduation, I encountered a clientele of assorted factory workers, malcontents, drug addicts, alcoholics, crazies, whores, panhandlers, and bullshit artists. These barroom characters were easily found most any day of the week, sitting on the same raggedy bar stools.

These were the bars where, "Everybody NEVER knew your name." Alcoholic dementia and dysfunctional family behavior had rendered most of the old gang either brain dead, or damaged in one way or another. They were the broken people who had given up on their dreams. When I walked in, I didn't get the same greetings from them anymore. Entering Bruno's tavern, I knew the thrill was finally gone. The place was as depressing as the customers. After work sometimes, I showed up well groomed and smelling like a retail dandy. I wore expensive clothes and shoes. I knew I was out of my element and so did my old pals. I wanted to stay, but there was price to pay! I wasn't up to listening to the catcalls, jeers, and insults from some of the drunks.

My old pals said, "Who are you trying to kid? Why don't you put on a pair of jeans and a flannel shirt, and smoke a joint with us anymore?"

Of course, there still were some great people in the bar. These men were happy for my success. I gravitated towards them because they believed in themselves. Rich or poor, if a man has self-respect and dreams, he is worthy of my time and I beg to be worthy of his time as well. I gleaned some astounding wisdom and listened to marvelous stories, told by the elderly retirees, factory workers, policemen, salesmen, and the like. I understood that the "angry others" were venting, because they were fearful of what I represented to them. I was a constant reminder to them of their wasted years. Their personal failures couldn't be blamed on anyone. They knew they weren't going anywhere. I felt sorry for them. To live in a skin like this has to be frightening. A wasted youth is a bitter enough pill to swallow, but a wasted life is hell.

I didn't frequent these haunts so much anymore. I didn't think it was cool to hold a broken cue stick in my hand. I didn't enjoy a Slim Jim in my mouth for dinner anymore! I started searching for nice nightclubs with restaurants and show bands. I loved the large dance floors, with the nice tables and subdued lighting. I enjoyed real tablecloths and paintings on the walls.

All these creature comforts lent to the special ambiance of the establishments I sought out. Scattered around were comfortable chairs and sofas for me to recline on, cocktail in hand. The men's rooms always were immaculate and had porters offering towels and after shave lotion. The "golden handled" sinks were always clean and beautiful. The marble counters offered all types of toiletries, including breath mints or mouthwash. A man could also have his shoes shined, if he so desired. This was the life of people who had money, and I wanted it!

The women and men who spent time in these establishments were impeccably attired. Most were well educated or financially sound. Some had both money and brains—a great combination! Most of these people worked and played hard. All of this elegance was a far cry from the standard Chicago tavern. I loved this new life. Some of the clubs I frequented in my younger days were The Taste of Honey, The Willow Tree, and the Che Si Bon.

They are now long gone, but not forgotten. At the "Che", as we fondly called the place, I was destined to meet my next girlfriend!

DIANA, MY NEW GIRLFRIEND

One Thursday evening, at the Che Si Bon, I saw the prettiest little blonde. She demurely smiled at me. She stood about 5'2" and was wearing a pair of sexy Hot Pants, which were in vogue at the time. I was intrigued!

She had dark nylons on her shapely legs, and high heels. To finish this angel's attire, was a tight knit top, which looked frilly and feminine. I was instantly in love. She wore her hair short, in a fashionable cut. She had lovely eyes and lips. Her figure was slender and sensual—it was to die for.

Immediately, I asked her to dance. I was in luck. She said, "Yes" just as a sultry Smokey Robinson tune came on the jukebox. The lights in the place dimmed and she pushed that sweet body of hers into mine. She looked lovingly into my eyes and with that great smile she had, put her cheek to mine. I felt the heat coming from her neck, ear, and breasts. I held her hand firmly after the dance. I wasn't going to let this girl get away from me. I offered to buy her a drink and she said, "By all means!" We conversed for over a half-an-hour. She was utterly charming and intelligent. She taught elementary school and was a year older than I. Jokingly, I asked her if she liked younger men. She said, "Only if they look like you!" We ended up in my new car, steaming up the windows for an hour or so, on some side street. I went home, with the youthful glow, which comes with infatuation! I was smitten. Cupid did the job on me. I had her phone number, and a date with her the next evening!

Every date with Diana was wonderful. For me, I honestly can say she and I were a perfect match. Everyone who met Diana just loved her! She was honest, and beautiful, a giving and caring young woman. Diana was surely the perfect soul mate for me. We dined at some of the best restaurants in Chicago. We looked lovely together. I treated her like a queen, and she carried herself like one.

Diana was young, fresh, and full of life. She always dressed well. We went dancing all the time. We both loved to dance. We were falling deeply in love. Our relationship was fast and furious. We both were hot for each other, which truly helps in any relationship! Besides, we had all the personality traits that matched us up just perfectly. All was beautiful in our world. I was going to marry this lovely girl. My family loved her so much; they expected me to "pop the question". They thought it was only a matter of time before I did! Little did they know fate would have its way once again. It wasn't in the cards.

THE END OF DIANA AND ME

Diana and I were having the time of our lives. We enjoyed the zoo, the lakefront, nightclubs, and just catching the latest movies at the cinema.

We ended our evenings in my big Chrysler, making love, hot and heavy. I never wanted to rent a motel room. We hadn't consummated our love affair, because I was getting cold feet. I wanted to finish graduate school, or become established in some endeavor that paid better money, before I was ready for the big commitment of marriage. I was afraid I was going to get her pregnant. I didn't want to "have" to marry her and raise a family. This freaked me out.

One evening, we foolishly parked in front of a nightclub, on a busy street. We both had too much to drink. We were going at it pretty good and clothes were coming off. It was around three in the morning. The bar had been closed for two hours. No other cars were in the parking lot. We were sitting ducks. The door swung open, the flashlights were in our faces. We both felt embarrassed and compromised. I felt as if the cops were raping me, just for doing something that is so natural. The only problem with this convoluted logic is that they have every right to stop you from what you are doing. Public indecency is against the law. We went into two separate squad cars and endured two separate interrogations. I begged and groveled like a little girl. I was ashamed of myself. I wondered what they were putting my poor Diana through. She was young and beautiful, and I was angry. I thought the cop might be forcing her to perform some deviant sexual act for his own personal gratification. To this day, I am angry with myself for never bothering to ask her what he put her through.

This all was my fault. This whole sordid nightmare was a result of my bad judgment. I was a coward. I was shaking all over as I drove her home. It was a silent and shameful ride for both of us.

My inadequate response to this whole scenario is what I am most ashamed about. I have been ashamed with the way I dealt with this situation my whole life. I felt the need to confess these sins before I die.

I closed the door on our relationship. I would not speak to her. I didn't call her on the telephone anymore. Diana, the good girl who still was in love with me, actually came looking for me at the menswear shop, tears in her eyes, asking me, "Why don't you call me, Rich? Don't you want me anymore?" She was aching for an explanation. I gave her an inadequate answer, I am sure. All my life, I repressed this inadequacy of mine. It wrenches my guts writing this admission of guilt thirty-seven years after the fact.

I cut-and-ran on my dear friend. She was a friend who loved me. I tried to find her with my computer search recently, to no avail. If by some chance you read this miserable text of mine, Dear Diana, please forgive me for the heartless way I closed the door on you. You deserved so much better, than the likes of me.

THOUGHTS ON MY MORALITY—1972

My heart ached for Diana. I missed her terribly. I blanked her out of my mind. She didn't exist for me now, because of my shame. My sense of morality and doing the next right thing wasn't there.

Surely, I had intellectual, social, and physical growth, but my emotional and spiritual maturity were at a standstill. Maybe I had been abused too much as a child, in one-way or another. I regarded all people of religion as hypocrites. I hated "bible thumpers" and wide-eyed clerics. I couldn't accept big fat Irish Parish Priests, driving around in their Cadillacs, going to Europe a few times a year, drinking expensive scotch and smoking Cuban cigars. These clerics were phony. "Yes, my brethren, each family needs to contribute $500 to the church this Christmas." "Bullshit," I thought.

I remembered my family's poverty. I knew what it did to my dear brother. I was filled with resentment. I lived my life with a depression-era mentality. In regard to my work, I was always dedicated. I never missed a day. I was brought up to be responsible. I lived a hedonistic life, in regard to my play. I developed a me-against-the-world mentality. It served me well for many years. I vowed to climb the ladder of success. If I was forced to attend Mass for family celebration, I sat near or in the pews occupied by the sexiest young ladies. I methodically undressed them with my eyes during the church services. I loved women with well-developed breasts and short skirts. My unholy voyeurism allowed me to endure this agonizing pagan ritual called, the Mass. My mind was in conflict due to my Catholicism. A black dog and a white dog always were always in a ferocious battle. I tried to bury my Catholic guilt. I thought of myself as an Agnostic. This was my new theology now. When things got tough in my life, I resorted to "foxhole prayers".

When things were going good for me, God was forgotten. I was a product of the 1960's. I was part of the "Me" generation. "If it feels good, do it!" I was doing my own thing, not God's thing. I thought, "There will be plenty of time for religion when I'm an old man." I took a gamble that I wouldn't die for a very long time. I could manipulate and con people all my life, and then be forgiven by God at the last minute! I could amass money, without thinking about who I hurt to get it. Religion was for suckers. It was a dog-eat-dog world, and I was going to get mine. Later in life, my brother, Jim, told me, "Dick, we're both going to hell, but at least we'll be wearing expensive suits." It is hilarious to say, but this was what we both were all about. We came from a family with a long history of alcoholism. Both sides of our family suffered from the disease. I modeled myself in the image of my brother. He had a morality to him. I lost that somehow along the way. I suppose my lack of morals was a generational manifestation of an acceptance of the mores of my time. Jim continued to go to church and put family second, after money. Somehow, his behavior still exemplified a morality in some kind of skewed sense. I always put money and myself first. I believed in the holy trinity of "me, myself and I." This is how I lived my life.

MONDAY NIGHT FOOTBALL

ABC television launched the "greatest idea since sliced bread" in 1972. This phenomenon excited male audiences all over the United States of America! The show was a gala event, which featured Howard Cossell, "Dandy Don" Meredith, and last but not least, Alex Karas. The show had glitter and glamour and smacked of the testosterone-packed violence of ancient of Rome, where gladiators fought each other to the death!

Better yet, it had scantily-clad young girls, shaking their pom-poms. I couldn't wait for Monday nights. Customer flow was usually slow on Mondays at the menswear store. All day the salesmen bantered about the football match-up, and the bets were placed. The event we were to see that evening was prime time stuff! My brother Jim hosted this football game every week in his finished basement. I looked forward to a case of Stroh's fire-brewed beer in quarts, potato chips, pretzels, and little sandwich-type "thingies" made by his sweet little wife, Gracie.

It was male bonding time for my brother and me. Jim and I guffawed at the not-so-flattering remarks Alex Karas directed toward "straight man", Howard Cossell. Karas was hilarious. He depicted pro football players as "real men with smelly armpits and garlic on their breath." Cossell bantered endlessly about the game. He spoke endless diatribes. These were words, which were incomprehensible to 98% of the viewing audience.

This alone was hilarious, but added to the mix was the "down-home soliloquies", of Dandy Don. The TV audience had nothing less than a total mayhem of entertainment to enjoy for three whole hours! What made it even better, was it was just for us guys!

This male bonding ritual spread like wildfire throughout the United States. It surely ended many-a-marriage or relationship between loving males and females. It was a time for guys to drink, burp, fart, yell, and high five! We did all the primitive things that men love to do. The greatest thing about it was that we could actually get away with it!

By half time, Jimmie and I were so drunk we were half in the bag. He would drag out old letters I had written to him when he was doing his army basic training at Fort Leonard Wood in Missouri. I was only around 6 or 7 years old, way back then. It was hilarious for us to look at the crayon drawings and the kid stuff I used to write him. My brother had a great affection for me. I thought it was wonderful that he saved these little letters. They meant something to my big brother, and something to me as well.

We reminisced about the past during the half time show, until the second half of the game would begin. Jim and I drank a couple more quarts, and by the time Dandy Don sang, "Turn Out the Lights, the Party's Over," we'd be bleary eyed. We had full stomachs, and shit-eating grins on our faces. The game was over.

We trudged up the stairs, and every damned week, I'd about knock myself out by banging my noggin' on this filthy old deer head he had hanging on the wall. Banging my head happened every week like clockwork. Jim laughed until tears ran down his cheeks. He was a sadistic bastard, I thought. He took the greatest enjoyment in my pain, and wondered how I could be so stupid every week.

We hugged and shook hands, and did the things that brothers do when they say good-bye to each other. Jim always said to me, "Are you alright to drive home to Mom's house?" I said, "No problem, Jimbo! See yah Sunday." We did yard work and chores for Mom every Sunday afternoon. Then we pulled the old scotch bottle out from under the kitchen cabinet. We always had a couple for the road. Mom loved seeing her boys getting along so well together. It was only a few minutes drive to Mom's house from my brother's place in Evergreen Park. I always took Kedzie Avenue for the trip home. If I was seeing three lanes, I always drove in the "center" one. I loved Monday Night Football with my brother Jim.

MY FIRST APARTMENT IN CHICAGO — 1972

After graduation from college, I lived with my parents for about eight months. I had no problem with it, because everything was fine at home. I came and went as I pleased. My dad was getting a big kick out of borrowing my new clothes.

He went out proudly wearing my new sport coats and ties. If dad burnt an occasional tie or sport coat, or spilled some V.O. on them, I always was quick to forgive him. Dad was my role model for enjoying the nightlife. He loved to "put on the dog". That was his elderly vernacular for having a good time. I bought him outdated Arrow Shirts, and ties for pennies, using my employee discount. He loved every gift I brought home for him.

Even though things were well for me at home, I longed for the independence a young man gets from having his own place. Besides, I couldn't bring inebriated dolls home to play footsies with me at 3-in-the-morning at Mom and Dad's house. I knew this behavior would never be acceptable. Also, the combination of money spent on motel rooms, drinks, romantic dinners, and room and board were eating into my finances. I figured having my own place might be more cost effective. Money wasn't too much of an issue for me now. I continued to be the top salesman at the menswear shop. I had saved a nice nest egg. However, my dreams of graduate school were becoming less and less important to me.

I was now enamored of a life style which included a nice car, sharp clothes, and a thick wallet. This allowed me to date some very classy-looking women. I fell in love with the Chicago Nightlife Scene. I knew where all the action was. From card games to fast women, I had my finger on the pulse of all the happenings on the South Side. I could party, "high brow" or "low brow", depending on my wishes and whims. I enjoyed going out four or five nights a week. I dated a lot of different women.

Graduate school at Central Michigan University in Mount Pleasant Michigan was rapidly becoming as appealing to me about as much as a cell in Cook County Jail. I certainly didn't want to be a poverty-stricken graduate student, dating farm girls wearing flannel shirts.

I started my search for apartments by perusing the classified section of the Chicago Tribune. I found a nice two-bedroom apartment about six miles west of my mom and dad's house, in an ominous-sounding suburban town named Justice, Illinois. The apartment complex went by the name of Hickory Trace. The place had a reputation for being a swinging singles complex. High times were to be had here. Young, single adults flocked here to party, and live the Epicurean lifestyle.

So, I lugged all my things down the stairs, put them into a U-Haul, and headed out to the Western Suburbs. Among the things I moved was an old Gothic-style bedroom set. It was so old, it looked like something Count Dracula might have slept in out in Transylvania! My mom's parents owned this antique. It had a squeaky box spring, and all kinds of engravings on the huge headboard. I lied to all the girls who enjoyed frolicking with me, that the bed's headboard was an expensive antique. It worked every time! I moved my meager belongings into the elevator of the building. I took an apartment on the third floor. The apartment had a balcony and a beautiful view of a spacious courtyard and lake. I loved sitting out there in the summer time, drinking beer, and trying to pick up young girls, who were barbequing or playing Frisbee. We yelled at each other and set up dates.

The apartment had two bedrooms, so to defray my costs, I started advertising for a roommate I took on a nice, easy-going guy named Tom, to share the rent and utilities. The apartment was beautiful, until we put our gaudy, mismatched furniture inside. We didn't care. All we cared about was that we had a big color TV and a state-of-the-art stereo system. In those days, these two items put you over the top with any girl in her 20's. We started planning Friday night parties. I taught Tom the ropes on throwing successful parties! I learned my entertaining skills in Carbondale, and knew how to pack a room with lovely girls. We watched "Midnight Special" every Friday night. This popular show featured the best rock-and-roll and soul music of the times. The neat thing about this show was the new concept, called "simulcast". The TV show was simultaneously broadcast on FM stereo radio. The stereo radio cranked out music much louder and clearer than the television! Tom and I cranked up my stereo to full blast, and we experienced a spectacular rock concert. Add a big old pot of chili or order out for pizzas, (along with the cache of booze and grass), chips and dip, and other contraband which guys and girls brought in, and we had ourselves one hell of a party. Believe me when I tell you, these parties were better than anything Jerry and I ever engineered.

❦

It was springtime, and sales were picking up at the shop. I was doing a lot of business selling suits, shirts and ties for the Easter season. A lot of return customers were coming in to see me. I developed a sixth sense for sniffing out high-roller types who were going to buy a lot of merchandise. Life was grand!

FORGIVE ME JOANNE

She was a summer lover. We shared a short-lived romance.
I met her in a hallway as keys entered separate doors.
Shared cocktails, eventually led to more.
There was an easiness of manner about her. She was almost "ethereal".
Fine red hair, alabaster skin, a lithe thin body, and
Full lips which smiled broadly at me, when I amused her.
She was slightly older than I, and had a sister who no longer loved her husband.
We visited them and blessed our good fortune.
One day, while driving to work, Joanne suffered a brain aneurysm.
She survived the crash and died in the hospital the next day.
I never attended the wake or funeral.
At the very least, I owed her a few short minutes of my time,
To celebrate her memory:
That fine red hair, that alabaster skin, and especially those full red lips,
Which smiled at me, when I amused her. I carry my sin of omission, for all these years. I pray to thee Dear Joanne, forgive me.

SUMMER OF 1972

I now was 22 years old. I was pretty damned satisfied with what I had accomplished in just one short year. I established a position for myself in an upscale retail shop. I was respected and well liked by my employer, and fellow salesmen. My salary and commissions far exceeded my expectations. I had purchased a fine wardrobe for all the seasons of the year. The beautiful new Chrysler had replaced the old Ford. I proved my independence by taking on the responsibility of a new apartment, while contributing weekly to my growing savings account.

Yet, I remained unsatisfied. I realized that I had no medical insurance or profit sharing program. For me, this stark reality became a major concern. Other salesmen, who entered the shop to purchase clothing from me, recognized my native abilities. They prompted me to look for a more lucrative sales position. Many gave me business cards, and told me to mention their names if I decided to upgrade to a corporate sales position. I seriously started thinking of the benefits and possibilities, which might open up to me with a well-thought-out change of employment. I needed to secure a better future for myself.

Aside from all this, I was enjoying a great summer. My apartment complex was buzzing with activity for young people. We enjoyed a nice outdoor swimming pool. There were brand new Cabanas and fresh towels.

A short walk from the pool was a nice cocktail lounge / restaurant that served continental cuisine and exotic drinks.

During the day, the young ladies languished in the sun at the pool; later they sipped Margaritas or Daiquiris in the cocktail lounge. They filed in and sat at the fancy bar, showing off their soft and supple skin. Theirs was the beautiful skin of youth. The young ladies were fragrant with aphrodisiacs that stimulated my senses. I breathed in the moisturizers, aromatic perfumes, and suntan oils—enticing smells all very feminine and inviting. Their clinging summer outfits were multicolored. These women were beautiful flowers, waiting to be picked. They were to be placed in beautiful, ornate vases. These "flowers" were to be smelled and viewed with appreciation. They would be touched and fondled for a very short time. Finally, when their beauty faded and they drooped, they would be discarded in the garbage.

Their beauty would only last for a few moments. Sadly, this is a fact of life. This is the fate we all wait for.

BILL RETURNS FROM VIET NAM — 1972

Bill and I went to high school together. I loved his laugh and sense of humor. He was an excellent student who had multi-varied talents. He became my best friend when he moved to our neighborhood, from the "back of the yards" way back in 1963. We both attended St. Rita's and used to take the bus together every morning to start the day.

After school, I hung out at his house because he had three beautiful sisters! He thought that was my motivation. I genuinely thought he was a great guy—sisters or not. After a while, he came to believe me. However, I did have a hell-of-a-crush on his sister Penny. I always copied his math homework when I couldn't figure out my assignments. He played his six-string acoustic guitar for hours and he was the biggest Beatles fan I ever knew. He drew cartoons next to his lecture notes all the time in class. Sometimes, the Augustinian Fathers made him pay the price. He always beat me at ping- pong in his basement. He teased me and laughed so hard that I got red in the face with anger. I couldn't stand to lose to him. The damned guy beat me at just about everything! He always out-wrestled me, even though I was taller and heavier. This really made him laugh with animated glee. He beat me at chess most of the time, which really pissed me off! In spite of it all, he was my best friend.

Bill threw me a winning touchdown pass in a sandlot game after senior year in high school. When I slid into the end-zone area—a concrete sidewalk—the sparks were flying from the contact of my football spikes! It looked really cool because it was already dark outside. We beat a better team against all odds. Bill said it was a miracle! "What a catch, Rich!" We hugged, and high-fived each other, and just laughed and laughed at the other team. Their team captain couldn't believe we beat them. Billy and I had done it! We relished this victory for many years.

Bill and I gazed into the stars shimmering in the sky that summer. We dreamt about how it would be for us, each going to separate Universities. That summer was magical with dreams and goals to be attained. We shared our dreams, and hot dogs, and quarts of beer in Marquette Park on the bridge.

I called Bill when he came home from "Nam", a year and a half after I returned from college with my degree. Bill had been drafted. He didn't make "the cut" at DePaul University. The voice on the other end of the line was dull, as if interrupted by some other thoughts. It was a strange voice that didn't sound like my buddy's. Yet, I knew it was his. Bill lived only five minutes from my apartment complex. He was "entombed" in his parent's large, retirement "dream home". He didn't smile too much anymore. That was my first impression. His eyes didn't sparkle the way they used to when he laughed. He had seen too much, too soon in his young life. The changes weren't readily discernable to someone who didn't know him as intimately as I had. He now wore a green army fatigue jacket. His hair was long and had an unkempt look to it. He had grown a scraggly mustache, which looked like a Fu- Manchu type thing. Before he left for Viet Nam, his girlfriend said she would be "forever faithful". Bill said he was going to marry this girl. She didn't wait for him. She couldn't wait out the war.

Bill enjoyed drinking thirty-five-cent draft beers at Al's Hilltop Lounge in the afternoons. An old grandma shuffled slowly behind the bar, pulling cheap draft beers from the tap for us. Bill loved this old lady. He called her "Grandma" with the utmost respect. Grandma served us bowls of stale popcorn. Sometimes Bill liked to watch "Sanford and Son" with me at my apartment. He didn't speak too much about Viet Nam. He was quiet now, but he loved chuckling occasionally at the antics of Red Foxx. He sounded like his old self on these occasions, but soon he drew back into his cocoon. He inhaled the marijuana and Pall Mall smoke deeply into his lungs and asked me if I had another beer. Bill got a job as a Pizza deliveryman. He was so much better than that. Bill said he liked driving at night, all alone. He liked the solitude of it all.

When he was in Viet Nam, I wondered whether or not he could see the same stars that we were looking at here at home. It felt special to me, having my best friend Bill back home where he belonged.

"THE DECISION" — SEPTEMBER — 1972

Mr. "O" at the menswear shop had employed me over a year. I finally came to realize that it was a dead-end job for me. It was hard to hit it big in a small family-owned retail business.

Something happened in early September, which changed the direction of my life. Dad called me at work, excited as hell. My God, I thought Mom dropped dead! "Dad," I said, "slow down." I finally made some sense out of what he was trying to tell me. "I want you to come to the house after you finish work tonight", he said. "I have a great opportunity for you!" My heart sank. I envisioned another "horror show" of employment. It was going to be another replay of the shit job on Halsted Street, but I replied: "OK, Dad, see you around 6:30."

Dad and Mom and I sat at the kitchen table. Mom poured us cups of coffee, and put a tray of cookies in front of me. As she did this, her eyes were twinkling, and she had a big smile on her face. "Setting me up for the kill," I thought. They both looked so happy; my interest was piqued. I couldn't wait to hear the "good" news.

My dad started explaining the whole deal. "I served cocktails today to the President of Local #150, the International Union of Operating Engineers. He said that they were looking for bright young men for the Union Apprenticeship Program." It would take me four years, and I would own a Journeyman's Card. "There is nothing for you to worry about," Dad said. "The fix is in." Mr. Martin, the President of the Union, assured my father that he was going to take care of me. I would be sent to work right away. I was "In like Flynn", so to speak, if I wanted the job. I was to attend classes on Pershing Road one evening a week, and had to go out to the Machine-Training Site on Saturdays.

I told my Dad I needed time to think about this life-altering decision. Geez, I was freaking out! I graduated a Dean's List Scholar, with a degree in the Behavioral Sciences. For the last year, I had honed my conversational skills, and learned how to be a pretty-damned-good salesman. This new enterprise seemed to be a drastic turnabout, which required considerable thought. After all, I was doing all right on my own, and didn't want to screw things up!

I had lousy skills with tools and machines. I didn't like getting dirty working on cars and engine parts and all that stuff. I didn't even like adding oil to the engine of the Chrysler. That is what full-service gas stations were for! If the TV set wasn't working, I smacked it a couple of times. If that didn't do the trick, I threw it in the garbage and bought a new one. Someone else fixed every car I ever owned, or I ran 'em till they died.

Conversely, I realized that an opportunity to become a member of a trade union was offered only to a select few. Guys "killed" to get this job, and it was being handed to me on a silver platter. Clout was on my side, and Union Tradesmen made big money in Chicago. My fears about good medical and dental insurance would be eradicated by this employment. I was guaranteed a Federally Insured Pension to boot! I had one more stop to make before I made my important decision. I told my dad I'd let him know after I spoke with my brother, Jim.

Dad hit the roof! Dad said, "Whaddaya have to talk to him for?!" I expected to hear this response. As I rose from the table, I told my dad, "Be patient Pop. You will have my answer tonight. I just have to sort out a few things in my mind."

THE POW-WOW—JIM'S HOUSE

My brother, Jim, was entrepreneurial and I trusted his good business sense. He was one of the smartest guys I knew. Jim worked like a demon all his life. He worked hard since he was a young kid. He now managed one of the largest and most successful flower shops in the city of Chicago. He started out by sweeping floors at Kelly-Flynn when he was 8-years-old. Since that time he had learned every single aspect of the flower business. He eventually ended up owning this multi-million dollar enterprise. He was the man I needed to speak with before I made any rash decisions.

When I arrived at Jim's house in Evergreen Park, he was calmly sitting on his front porch with his West Hyland Terrier named "Tiger". Newspaper in his hand and a pipe in his mouth, he was enjoying the summer evening. After eating a fine meal made by my sister-in-law, Grace, he was unwinding from his busy day. The summer breezes were blowing gently and the sun was starting to set. Jim was in his prime at 35-years-of-age.

Here at my brother's house, I would get a straightforward, logical answer to any of my inquiries concerning the Union job.

My brother said, "Dick, you've attained a good liberal arts education, but if I were you, I would go for the money in the Trades. Remember, if you don't like it, you can always quit and go to graduate school. Think of all the plumbers and electricians you see driving around in Cadillacs and living in big homes." I called Dad and told him I'd be giving my notice to Mr. "O" at the menswear store the next day. I decided to go for the money. I was rolling the dice. I just hoped I wasn't rolling "snake-eyes".

SAYING GOODBYE

It's not easy to give notice and say goodbye to an elderly gentleman who treated you like a son. Mr. "O" was gracious in saying that I did a fine job for him and the firm. I was a valued employee and the store was going to miss me. If I wanted to start right away with my new job, he didn't need to hold me to my two-weeks notice. He also told me that the door was always open in case things didn't work out and I wanted to come back. So, that was that. I shook hands with my mentor. Both of us were smiling and getting a little misty. Leaving the door open for me was an act of a true gentleman. This was the way leaders reacted, like Mr. "O" and my brother, Jim.

I returned many times to visit the crew at the menswear store. I shopped there for all my clothes. I felt I owed the shop my business since Mr. "O" had been so kind to me.

I enjoyed these visits, and shared old stories and a special camaraderie with Mr. "O" and his family. We always laughed about the fast pace of men's retail during the holiday seasons. I learned much about hard work and perseverance. Most of all, I learned about respect and loyalty, and always being a man of your word.

A NEW JOB, A NEW LIFE

I was to find out there was a lot of pride in the men who wore the Union button of Local #150 on their bill caps. I began by putting my name on an "Out of Work List" in the Union Hall. I might have over a-thousand men ahead of me, but they didn't all have to be sent out to work before I got the call. You see, the more expertise I had on a variety of machines, the more employable I became. A versatile man didn't have much waiting time. A man who didn't care to learn the trade and preferred to sit on a bar stool, could wait a year or two. This demonstrated good-old American Capitalism at work. It was a "dog-eat-dog" world and only the strong survived and made a good living.

If a man was a "one-machine-wonder", he might sit in the union hall for a long time. I found out very early that I had to constantly learn the new things I was taught, and be vigilant about upgrading my skills.

Contractors liked guys who learned how to run a variety of machines. If a man had a bad reputation for incompetence, quitting jobs, or showing up drunk, he sat on the Out of Work List for a long time. We hated "scabs"—men who cut deals for less than Union scale. I felt through my whole career that these men were the scum of the earth. They undermined what past generations had fought for so dearly. I made sure that when I found them working on my job-site, they were reported to the Union. Sometimes, these scumbags went before a judiciary board and lost their Union Cards. These rats lacked honor and loyalty. They deserved being put back out on the street. A bad Union man never prospered around me.

There was a separate Out of Work List for apprentices. We made lower wages. The contractor got the benefit of paying lower, but had to "break in" a new Operator. If the company got a good man, this gamble paid off in big dividends. If the foreman got a bad one, he always found a way to release the guy. Some new guys in Local #150 would have twenty or thirty W-2 forms at the end of their first year! New guys were fired all the time. It was a demanding job, and contractors wanted their money's worth. Imagine the self-esteem issues a new man had to endure by being fired so many times. Not doing a good job can drive a man to drink, and often that was the case.

I went to the window of the Dispatch Office my very first day. I paid my initiation fees. Also I paid my quarterly dues as a first year apprentice. I had to carry a book with me and the contractor had to sign it, letting the Union Hall know if I had performed my job up to expectations.

I received all kinds of paperwork and a Union card showing I was a first-year apprentice. I received a pay-scale book listing all the rates of pay for a wide spectrum of various machines. There were binders with all kinds of information relating to rules and regulations. I received Insurance Benefit and Pension information. They gave me instructions on when-and-where to show up for training on machines at our site near the Illinois-Indiana border. I had to do classroom work at an old government building on Pershing Road, East of Western Avenue, on the South Side of Chicago. All the guys went to the tavern across the street after classes. I was most advanced in this area of expertise! We all were a hard-drinking lot from the start.

I was issued a hard-hat and grease gun. I was told what tools to carry in the trunk of my car. I had to buy flannel shirts, jeans, steel-toe boots, and heavy outdoor gear. I bought Carhart-brand coveralls, knit caps, wool socks, long underwear, and all kinds of stuff a soldier would wear if he were deployed to Antarctica. After all, it was September, and winter was coming! I was instructed to always have my vehicle in good working order. I sat with "bated breath" at my phone every morning from 7 to 10 a.m., and from 3 to 5 p.m. every afternoon. This was a must because the dispatch office called me with my new job between these hours. All of this stuff thrown my way was a lot of information to process. I felt as if I were being sent to a Marine boot camp, not to a new job. All of this was so alien to me it gave me a headache! I hoped that I had done the right thing. Only time would tell.

DYNAMIC PROFILE OF A HEAVY EQUIPMENT OPERATOR

I'm going to let the faithful readers of this Memoir in on a little secret! I spent 33 years as a heavy equipment operator, so I guess I'm knowledgeable enough to paint you a pretty accurate picture of our membership. I'm going to try and detail what we look like, the habits we have, and try to correct any misconceptions you may have about us. We might not be what you expected, so here goes...

The typical "Caterpillar" Bulldozer Operator wears a dusty, old bill cap. The bill is usually furled down at the ends in a sporty fashion. Sometimes the cap is worn in a cock-eyed way. The choices depend on the wishes and whims of the operator. There are many variegated styles. Some of these caps are so well loved by their owners, that the end of the bill becomes frayed from fingers constantly readjusting it. The Local Union Button is usually proudly displayed on the left side of the cap, so that when our Operator is driving home everyone who looks at his head knows that he is a proud member of Local #150.

The vehicle of choice, of course, is a pick-up truck—preferably a huge Dodge Ram, 3500 Diesel, with fancy diamond-plate boxes. The truck also has a bed liner, and "dualies" in the rear. (For the un-initiated, "dualies" are four off-road tires, mounted on the rear axle). The truck should have a nice bed liner and a ball or pindle hitch for hauling a huge bass boat for weekend fun at the fishing lake. The fishing boat has a huge Mercury engine, so the Operator can speed 100 mph to his favorite spot on the water in a "nanosecond". Our guy stands about 6'4" and weighs in at about 290 lbs. He carries a huge lunchbox onto his Bulldozer every day. He has enough coffee, sandwiches, and cold drinks on hand to feed an army. Our Operator has a red, unshaven face from being out in the sun and wind all his life. However, he does shave at least once a week on Sunday mornings, if he is a church-going man. These shaving instructions come from the "little woman" who is his wife.

Our man's eyes are red from dust, diesel smoke, and alcoholic drinks. The redness in the eyes is most noticeable on Monday mornings, after he spends quality time on Sundays watching NASCAR races or pro-football games on TV. These Sundays are spent with his buddies, who are also Operating Engineers. They all have a fine time in the tavern after church, drinking shots and beers.

✌

We always have a pack of smokes or some chewing tobacco stuffed in our flannel shirts. We wear thick leather belts with huge belt buckles depicting cowboys, bull's horns, skulls, bulldozers, or other man-type things immediately identifiable to members of our subculture.

We Machine Operators wear Levi's or Wrangler boot-cut jeans. The really cool guys wear Redwing or Laredo brand cowboy boots.

In the summertime we wear our Harley Davidson tank tops to work, so we can display our 16" biceps, which brandish assorted tattoos. This display allows us to multi-task. We work on our tans, while establishing ourselves as leaders in the "male pecking order". You are a leader if your arms are big enough, and if your "tats" are scary enough and multiple. A man never rides his spotless Harley to work, unless he can park it in a special place where it won't get dirty. This is a Cardinal Rule! An Operating Engineer is never foolish enough to drive his Harley to work, if there is any chance of rain or dirt! Real cool guys are 3rd-generation Operators, whose grandpa's came from Kentucky or Tennessee. These guys listen to Willie and Waylon and Travis Tritt on the country radio station. They can tear any engine down and put it back together with band-aids and bailing wire. After they are done, it purrs, sounding like a big tomcat after swallowing a canary. These Operators, after working all day on the machines, go home and farm all night. They all speak real slowly, and all of 'em have arms just like Popeye. They know everything there is to know about "ditching and dewatering", and moving dirt. City-folk think they are "rubes", but Lordy, watch out for them, 'cause they have calculating minds to go along with all their other skills. These so called "hillbilly" Operators have gun racks and Dixie flags proudly displayed in the rear window of their pick-up trucks.

✌

Most of us who are running heavy equipment have a variety of bumper stickers or decals supporting: Trade Unionism, The National Rifle Association, various tattoo parlors, country music radio stations, or our personal heroes on the NASCAR circuit.

All good Operators can read Blueprints and understand GPS Systems. We can calculate the weights of all materials to be hoisted by our cranes. The best of us take a lot of extra schooling at night in order to become Certified Crane Operators. Life and limb and big money is always involved. A guy has to have a lot of knowledge to run the big rigs. We usually work 6-days-a-week. 60 hours of labor a week is the norm. Some guys do this year-round. Most Operators who are involved in "dirt work" have time off in the winter, due to the mud, rain, and snow. A man can't dig in mud or slop, to make any money for the company. The "dirt operators", are usually laid off for a couple of months. The winter freeze goes deep into the soil, and it isn't possible to dig anymore. We all then went to the Unemployment Office to collect our "rockin' chair money". We live in smoky bars for a couple of months, waiting for the sunshine. By March, cabin fever sets in!

A good Operator who had paid his dues for 10 or 20 years in the Union can distinguish truth from bullshit right away. We demand total allegiance from our wives and kids. When we come home late at night from work or the bar, we want our dinners brought to us hot and fresh, no matter what time it is.

I always showered first, and "hit" the Lazy boy, with a cocktail in my hand. Wives had to adjust their schedules to our working situations, which were haphazard at best. If these women whined a lot and couldn't cut our lifestyle, we would have to "run them off". (We would divorce 'em.) High divorce rates and early deaths due to alcoholism, cigarette smoking, accidents, and other job-related maladies run rampant in our trade. Children were to be seen and not heard. The TV remote control is relinquished to our calloused hands immediately when we entered our dens.

An Operator worth his salt learns how to run as many machines as he can. A man always strives for expert proficiency. Being good at what we do makes us more employable. A man demands and receives respect when he has salable skills in this business. An expert Operator takes no crap from a Foreman, Developer, or Job Engineer. The owner of the company can be the recipient of a good Operator's wrath. "Knowledge" in this business is "Power"! If management gets in your face or disregards Union Rules, your Area Business Agent is always available to "crawl right up their ass", and set things right! This is how we "brother operators" protect ourselves. In the old days, we used to just wait for our enemies outside the gate, and "smack the hell out of them". Then, we walked off the job, call the Hall, and get a new place to work. Those days are long gone. I'm sorry they are, because things were settled more quickly and decisively back then.

This behavior doesn't "fly" anymore. These are the days of frivolous lawsuits, and political correctness. BAH! Guys my age, used to take care of business. Now we have a bunch of "Nancy's" whining and getting nothing done.

A good Union Man never crosses a picket line. We delivered pizzas, painted houses, tuned up cars, anything for our families, until the strike was settled. UNITED WE STAND!

In the wintertime we worked long shifts, even if we had no feeling in our frozen hands and feet. Many a time I sat running a machine, shivering and soaking wet, on a ten-hour shift. I remember cold days, with icicles hanging from my scraggly beard.

In the summer, we worked long shifts in the stifling heat. Dust blew in our eyes and stuck to the sweat on our arms and faces. My hands blistered and then calloused from the heat and friction of pulling levers on the machines. I always looked forward to consuming huge amounts of cold beer to get the dust out of my throat, when my day was done. Tavern time was my reward for suffering the elements.

Old timers like me are tough-as-nails. We were willing drones for our families. We worked our lives away. In reality, when I look back, I did it all for myself. I loved being a "cowboy operator". Ours is a selfish game. The love of it all gets in your blood. This chosen life becomes obsessive. Yes, we looked at ourselves as being "modern-day cowboys". We are the last of a dying breed.

Our machines didn't have those new-fangled enclosed cabs with heat and air-conditioning. We faced the elements, and didn't have the new hydraulic rigs. Our machines were mostly cable operated. We didn't have automatic transmissions in the beginning. It was rough going back in the 60's and early 70's.

So now, we old men tell our tall tales and lies. We re-create our Mythologies, so that young men in our trade can continue on in our Traditions. These are Traditions we hold very dear in our hearts. We will always be proud to be Operating Engineers until the day we die. When we retire, we are deaf from the roar of the diesels. We bark and scream as if we are still on the job. We hobble around looking for something to do, because we know that if we don't, the Reaper will get us all too soon. A lot of us die on a bar stool in a tavern. That isn't the legacy I want for my future grandchild. That's probably why I am writing this book, and painting pretty pictures, and working out at the gym. Drinking and smoking aren't an option for this old man anymore.

When our grandchildren come and sit in our laps, and we hug them with our gnarly hands, and we smile at them, we know it was all worthwhile. AMEN!

THE EARLY YEARS IN LOCAL #150

As a first-year Apprentice, I sat at my phone as instructed by the Union. I waited for the call that was to send me on my first job. It seemed to me like an eternity had passed. I waited for almost a full week. I was thinking that I had made a big mistake. Finally, I was dispatched to my first job.

My advice to all new Operators is to invest a few bucks in the newest edition of the Chicago Metropolitan-Area Roadmap. Get the laminated kind that doesn't show beer or coffee stains. Make sure it also has Suburban and State of Illinois Maps as well. This simple purchase saves a man many hours of anxiety and embarrassment. Believe me, I know! I learned the hard way. It isn't easy waking up with a hangover, not knowing where in the hell you are going first thing in the morning. It's best to plan ahead!

Anyhow, I found my first job, and I was on time, thank God! My duty was working on a huge crane, near Downtown Chicago. I had the job title of "Oiler". It sounded kind of like a dirty job to me. The crane was huge. It weighed 100 tons and had about 150 ft. of boom. It was one of those "Big Mamas" you see on crawler tracks. Believe me, I was amazed and overwhelmed. I was lucky that I had some experience doing this type of work in the summers when I wasn't attending college.

The Operator running the crane was named Jim Seeley. We shook hands and I immediately liked this guy. He had big, blue "twinkly" eyes, and a typical Irish face. He also had a whiskey nose and a potbelly.

Jim looked just like Santa Claus, but without the beard. He had a set of arms on him too! He ended up being a great friend, and more importantly, a great teacher.

OK, now here's the drill: My job consisted of checking the oil and fluid levels on the big diesel engine inside this monolith every morning. This activity was to be accomplished by me before the Operator arrived for work. An Oiler begins his shift a half-an-hour before the Operator. I "fired up" the engine every morning and got the cab nice and warm for Jim. I pulled various levers to loosen everything up and lifted the "headache" ball on the hoist cable up and down in order to dry out the brakes. I swung the massive boom from side-to-side carefully, then engaged the swing brake, and locked everything down. There is a master clutch, which has to be disengaged, above the Operator's seat. You don't want the damn thing in gear, so the crane, "runs wild". You can imagine what kind of damage a 100-ton machine could do if you didn't have your shit together. It has to be incapacitated by putting everything in neutral!

If it was summertime, I had to pull all the windows out. Let me tell you they were HEAVY! I secured these steel-framed monsters in a storage compartment, and threaded them down with wing nuts. Inside the house of the crane were open gears. Before I started the crane every day, I smeared a black, gooey, thick substance called Crater Compound on the open gears. I used an old stick or trowel for this purpose. The stuff was in a big old five-gallon can. The compound had to be spread evenly on all the open gears. A good Oiler knew just how much was enough. This came with experience. If a man smeared too much of the stuff on the gears, they threw grease all over the place when the crane ran at "full tilt". When I was a rookie, I'd be standing back there with this black shit all over me and everywhere else.

I'd end up on my hands and knees pouring solvent on the crap, scraping it up with trowels and rags. I gagged and coughed from the fumes. After I finished cleaning up the mess, I looked like a tar baby. I finally learned how to stay clean while doing this job. This is the earmark of a good Oiler. Every morning, I checked the radiator and battery cells for water. They both had to be filled to the brim. The windows of the crane must be kept crystal clear. I used Windex and paper towels. I wiped down the levers and seat, and made sure that the floor was clean under the Operator's feet. I wire-brushed any mud or dirt from under the brake pedals and de-accelerator. I swept it all into a dustpan with a whiskbroom. I was one fastidious Oiler!

I took great pride in this menial work. I wanted the inside of our crane to be as fresh and clean as my mom's kitchen. A good Operator, like Jim Seeley, appreciated my efforts. When the job didn't require the crane, he taught me how to run it. We call this "seat time". In our Union, this is how a new apprentice learns how to run the crane. I was quick to learn, and operated the crane for 3- or 4-hours-a-day. Jim didn't have to work so hard and I was gaining valuable experience!

If the Crane Operator you oiled for didn't like you, he "ran you off". In Union terminology, this was called, "being run down the road". Once your Operator was in his seat and everything was taken care of inside the cab, a good Oiler took his grease gun and greased all the fittings on the rollers of the tracks. The swing gears underneath the cab-house had to be greased as well. The big "bull gear" that the cab-house rotated on needed Crater Compound smeared on it. Picture the tracks on a tank, in your favorite Army Movie, and that's how this crawler crane looked.

A man didn't ever want to get pinched between the cab and the tracks. He could get cut in two. Yes, this does happen. It takes only a second for a guy to lose his focus on safety in this business. If he does, he ends up dead.

COFFEE TIME

An Oiler always carries "a million" rags in his pick-up truck. It's also smart for a guy to carry an extra grease gun and a twelve pack of grease. I call this "protecting my job". Always be prepared, just like a freakin' Boy Scout! Hanging out like a tail, I always had a rag tucked in the back pocket of my Levi's.

An hour before coffee time, it was my responsibility to collect money from the guys on the crew and write down their coffee orders. Guys wanted smokes, chewing tobacco, aspirin, and Alka-Seltzer for hangovers. They asked me to get waitresses' phone numbers, cotton gloves, sandwiches, and even coffee and donuts! Sheesh! I had to write down orders for up to twenty men sometimes. I got everything mixed up and brought back the wrong stuff sometimes. They bitched and screamed so I gave them the finger, and said, "Get it yourself next time, Asshole!" Jim Seeley rolled on the ground laughing. I wasn't about to take any shit from anyone, and he loved it! As time went on, I developed a system and became as proficient as a damned waitress in my order taking. I learned to over-charge these guys, so I would be compensated for my gas and get my breakfast for free!

If they complained about the prices I charged them, I said, "What's the matter, you got fish-hooks in your pockets, you damned cheapskates?" When some of the guys in the crew heard this coming from a young guy, they laughed! Guys in the trades respect men who don't take any crap from anyone. There is no room for "girlie-men" in the trades. I learned to stand my ground early because someone is always testing you. This is the way of men in a man's world.

At lunchtime, the Operator lowered the boom of the crane so I could grease it. Every day, an Oiler had to inspect the cable for "frays". I greased the shives at the tip of the boom. I greased the drum spool fittings. Where the cable wraps is on the spools or drums. I inspected the lay of the cable to make sure we were running right-and-true. Crushed cables means accidents and crushed bodies! After I had completed all these tasks, I "fired up" the monster and raised the boom. After the boom was up in the air, I got my chance to practice my crane operating skills. When the Operator goes back to work, an Oiler takes his lunch break.

I was proud to be a Local #150 man. The afternoons were easy. I joked with the other tradesmen on the job, and got coffee for them. I whistled at girls walking by our job site. My God, if I tried to do that today, I might end up in jail for sexual harassment. How the hell does a young man pick up girls these days? I sure didn't have any problems way back then. I closed up shop at the end of the night, and put all the windows back in the crane. I then put the plywood window guards on and fastened them down with wing nuts to guard against broken windows. After working hours, the neighborhood kids just loved playing with your construction equipment. Then it was off to the tavern with the crew. It was a hell of a good life for a young man!

MEANWHILE, BACK AT THE RANCH

I still leased the apartment with Tom, but I wasn't quite the party animal anymore. When I worked retail, I had more energy. I fell out of bed at nine in the morning, showered and suited up for work, showing up as fresh as a daisy by 10 a.m. I worked my eight hours, laughing and bantering the way sales people do, and arrived back at home by 6:30, still smelling good, with no dirt underneath my fingernails.

All of this changed, with my new life as a tradesman. I rolled out of bed at 4:30 a.m., half asleep, and made my lunch and a big thermos of coffee for the grueling day ahead. Sometimes, I had to drive forty or fifty miles to work. Job locations changed periodically and I had to relocate myself wherever the company sent my "gnarly" ass. If a contractor had a lot of work and deadlines to meet, I clocked 12- to 16-hour shifts. I was making some huge money! I was paid time-and-a-half after eight hours and also made time-and-a-half on Saturdays. Sometime, we worked Sundays, and I was paid double time! The men fondly called this the "double bubble". The contractors had to allow my attendance at apprenticeship school on Wednesday evenings, so they couldn't work me overtime on that night, per Union orders. We were learning mechanical systems, welding, hydraulics, blue print and grade stake reading. Of course, we also were learning heavy equipment operation and maintenance. The students were also learning about drinking shots and beers at the bar across the street!

After work, I stopped at a local tavern with the crew for cocktails and bullshit—a winning combination! These were fun times, full of fellowship and good humor. Drinking really pulls a crew together!

I felt it paved the way for better job execution and effort. A guy always carried his weight after hanging with his buddies in the tavern because he didn't want to let them down on the job.

Before leaving the tavern, I'd buy a six-pack to take home. I'd shower and order a pizza or pick up some fast food. After watching some television, my eyes started closing and I'd fall into the "rack" by 10 p.m. This was my new life. My soft hands were getting rough and calloused. My demeanor was changing as well. I no longer pranced around like some kind of "dandy". I was assimilating the language, and hard-boiled attitudes of my construction buddies. My "pencil neck" was getting thick, and my arms and back were getting muscular. I liked my new appearance. I became addicted to the lifestyle and the fast pace of it all. The construction business was mentally and physically demanding. It was life to the extreme. I liked the passion and danger of it all. The pay was great. I knew I had made the right decision to live this kind of life. I had no regrets about quitting the white-collar world. I told Tom, "The parties at night are over! I need it quiet around here. When I come home at night, I have to get a good night's sleep for work in the morning." When he disregarded my request, I glared at him. We were no longer on the same page. Partying during the week was going to get my roommate killed, and I was going to be the guy to do it to him! I made sure I pissed him off every chance I got. I needed to rid myself of him.

He moved out two short weeks later. I was glad to be alone. I had enough money now to pay all my bills. I was buying nice furniture and thinking about luxury apartments. I had more privacy and started entertaining some nice-looking girls on the weekends.

LAYOFF TIME — 1972-1973

I was relieved and elated when the layoff came in mid-December. Our crew was working anywhere from 50 to 70 hours a week. We were all exhausted. The company gave us the anticipated fifth of whiskey and one of those Butterball frozen turkeys. It was the kind with one of those plastic things that pops out to show you when the bird is cooked. Contractors today usually don't give a man anything anymore. Nowadays, money is the bottom line. Also, due to drunken driving accidents, Contractors are all afraid that their employees are going to go on the road, after drinking their Christmas bottle and run over some grandma. I can visualize her walker flying through the air, after being hit by that big Chevy Silverado. I imagine it's not a pretty sight, seeing those green tennis balls from granny's walker flying through the air!

There are too many lawsuits today, but in this case, the Contractors are right. Back in the old days, we kind of thought we knew our limits. We crept home really slowly, taking the back roads.

Anyway, after we all were laid-off, we went to the local tap and got pretty drunk. It always was a good old time around the Holidays. Half the guys always forgot their turkeys. Their wives would have to do without this year! The barkeep probably had to buy a meat locker to store the birds left behind by the construction workers! Most of the guys tucked away the unfinished fifth of whiskey behind the bench seats in their pick-up trucks. They went on their merry way down the road. Drunker than hell, they whistled Christmas songs full of warmth and good will towards all men!

I went to the Unemployment Office the next day with a pounding headache, a sour stomach, and cottonmouth. I stood in that damned line for eight hours, and never got to see anyone. The workers in that grim, gray office packed up their gear and started going home. One of them gave me a ticket with a number on it, and told me to come back tomorrow morning. God, I was pissed off! I stood in line for eight hours, and never got to see anyone about my claim. Damn bastards! I paid their wages out of my paychecks! I hated these lousy, bureaucratic, pieces of dung! I was so mad, that I felt the hair standing up on the back of my neck! I was hyperventilating as I told myself to calm down.

All of the sudden I heard some crashing noises, and saw this scuffling and yelling. I saw a big black guy fighting with security guards. The three security guards were losing at first, but finally got the cuffs on the poor guy. The man reached his breaking point and let all hell break loose in that unemployment office. In the 70's, this was an everyday occurrence. A lot of people were out of work due to our dear friend, Mr. Jimmy Carter. The poor black guy in the silver "bracelets" was crying and hollering. When the cops put him in the paddy wagon, he was spitting and kicking. I really felt sorry for him. "Chicago's Finest"—the Chicago Police; our boys in blue—were going to give this guy a nice escort to the local "tank". When he finally calmed down, he would realize his mistake. His poor wife would dejectedly receive his phone call. She would have to beg, borrow, or steal enough "dough" to bail him out. This is my beautiful Chicago! A large city of many wonders! The "dance" has been going on for a very long time. All working-class city dwellers know the ballroom!

❧

Thanking God the next morning for my patience, and feeling a whole lot better, I went back to the Unemployment Office and produced my ticket. The recipient was a morbidly obese, female bureaucrat, who disinterestedly processed my information. In a monotone voice she said, "The first check should come in 2 weeks. If you haven't received the check by the date stamped on your ID card, call this phone number or come back to this office." That was straightforward enough for me. I had no clue about the trials and tribulations I would have to face to get my money. This office screwed everything up for me. I got used to the "drill" over the years.

I was all set. My paperwork was finished and I figured that the "rocking chair money" should be rolling in soon. The Union had instructed us young guys to save our money for these hard times, so I had built up a nice little nest egg. I had the apartment to myself and enjoyed the solitude. My best friend, Viet-Nam Bill, and I met up with another South-Side neighborhood guy named Johnny. We drank beers together at Al's Hilltop Lounge almost every afternoon.

❧

We shot pool and pumped quarters into the jukebox, listening to The Allman Brothers, George Jones, and Merle Haggard. Billy loved "Silver Wings" by Merle Haggard. Over the years I heard a lot of sad country western songs. Johnny was a "professional" pizza deliveryman, just like Bill. I thought I might give this job a try if it paid cash. So, I found a pizza delivery job as well. Here we were, the three of us from the old neighborhood delivering pizzas 3- or 4-nights-a-week. We were always in the bar together around noon before our pizza shifts at 4 or 5 o'clock. We were three stooges, listening to the jukebox waiting to start our horseshit jobs. Life sure has some strange twists and turns!

I GOTTA GET A HOBBY

I was 23-years-old now. My life had always been structured. I never wasted my time. I never had huge chunks of time to blow. I was just sitting in the tavern all day long. This activity was getting old really fast. I began to read. I read Ernest Hemingway, Ann Rand, Upton Sinclair, Ralph Ellison, Jack Kerouac, and Robert Pirsig—mostly informative kind of stuff.

The "running boom" was starting to take off. I got "fired up" by watching some U.S. competitor in the Olympics. He won a race while wearing a raggedy painter's cap. Man, that was really cool! Imagine winning a Gold Medal! Common people need heroes like him. Regular folks, need something to strive for. I was hooked on the running phenomena. Running had a vice-grip hold on the country. I remember what joys running had given to me in times of stress and boredom. The next day, I bought myself a pair of Addidas running shoes, and a couple pair of sweats. I also bought some athletic socks and knit caps. I took off down the road, hacking and coughing like some kind of "tubercular precursor" to the now-famous Rocky Balboa.

My Lord, I was fat and out of shape from all the booze and smokes! I had a 2-pack-a-day habit. I smoked Marlboro Reds and was eating all kinds of crappy food. I cut my smokes to about a half-pack a day. I started buying "rabbit food" for my health from the grocery store. I liked grocery shopping because it was a great place to pick up girls! I lived and learned something new every day! I also started drinking light beer. I hated that crap, but got used to it as time went on.

I bought myself a ten-speed bicycle from some wide-eyed Hare Krishna-type guy, who advertised in the Sunday Tribune. I drove way up to the North Side of Chicago and made the purchase at some obscure Buddhist Temple. I got a great deal for my 80 bucks. My brother, Jim, knew everything about bicycles and told me to buy it because it was worth around $400. The bike was almost brand new. It was a racing bike that went by the name "Bottachia". It was an Italian racing bike. It had a hand-lugged and braised frame and a quick-release lever on the front wheel.

The bike also had brand new gum wall tires and an air pump mounted on the frame that supported an air gun. The fancy bike had a simplex derailleur, as well as toe clips and straps. This was one nice machine!

We brought it to my brother's house and he tore it down for me. He re-packed the wheel bearings, greased the headset, and fine-tuned and balanced the wheels. The bike was a work of art when my brother, Jimmie, was done with it. Jim had every tool you can imagine, and knew how to fix anything.

I bought a mileage meter that hooked up to the front wheel. I bought thick leather racing gloves. We bar taped the handlebars. These handlebars were something to behold. They were elegantly engraved with some beautiful inscriptions. I don't remember what the engraving said, but it was beautifully done. I bought a gel seat and seat cover for my fat Polack ass. A hobby cyclist needs comfort for long distance riding.

My brother Jim was such a "bike-nut", that he bought a set of rollers on a platform so he could ride his bike indoors in the wintertime. Jim and I talked about doing a 100-mile "Century" ride in the summer. There are some beautiful trails we were going to ride up in Wisconsin. We never got around to doing one together, and I regret this. The famous Wisconsin Bike Trail is supposed to be absolutely beautiful. If a bike rider does the "Century" in less than eight hours, he is in reasonably good shape.

Another thing I did to get back into shape was to pick up the old, rusty, 110-lb. weight set that sat collecting dust in Mom and Dad's basement. I used these old weights in high school, and was glad I didn't toss them like I did my baseball card collection. If these baseball cards were in my possession, I wouldn't need to write this book. I would be driving my Bentley on Rodeo Drive with the money from their sales.

Some people just have shit luck! Anyway, I started pumping iron again. I was planning on moving out of Hickory Trace Apartments. The rent was getting to be unmanageable with the lay-off. I moved back to the city, to a 3rd-floor walk up apartment on 73rd and Maplewood Avenue. The place was spacious and had a lot of windows. The kitchen was nice, and I still had 2 bedrooms, and a storage room for my bike on the back porch. My new roommate was the best part of the move. "Chicago Johnnie" moved in with me. He was my pizza-man buddy, whom I had known since grammar school. I always liked John. He was the easiest going guy I ever knew.

My move back to the city was a smart decision. I was only five minutes from Mom and Dad's house. Mom's home cooking was always there for me on Sundays. Dad was really ill from his diabetes. His feet were terribly ulcerated. He was a tough guy, and kept working at his bartending job eight-hours-a-day. He should have been in a hospital. He just kept going. Dad was a tough, old, South-Side-kind-of-guy. Mom gave him footbaths in Epson salts every night. She dried his poor feet with a towel, just like Mary Magdalene did for Jesus, except Mom was the real saint to me. She put salve on his feet, and covered them with gauze. Dad slowed down on his drinking now. He only went out about once a month and didn't stay out for 3 days at a time anymore. The "old itch" wasn't getting to him anymore. Age and pain helps with alcoholism.

I went home to cut the grass, trim the hedges, paint gutters, wash windows, clean the grease trap, pick up papers, and put the garbage out. I did all the things your elderly folks appreciate when they can't manage it for themselves anymore. It happens to all of us. The house you love starts overwhelming you when you get old and tired.

My brother Jim was always there for Mom and Dad as well. Jim did more than me because he was the first-born and had more of a sense of duty than me. He was one fine example of a responsible man. Jim always did the "lion's share" of work. This is the way our lives played out in regard to Mom and Dad at this period in time. Things changed later.

Mom rewarded us with huge, hot meals. We had dinner rolls, and deserts, and all kinds of good Polish-German food. Sometimes, Jim and I drank a few beers or whiskeys together when the work was done. Dad and I smoked cigarettes and talked about sports or the Union. Dad was really proud of himself, and proud of me. He loved the fact that he was the reason I was doing so well with the Union job. When I told him about the big money I was making, it made his eyes light up. I guess in his mind, this favor he did for me made up for all his shortcomings as a Dad. I forgave him, and loved him anyway. I knew I was going to stick with the Union. The layoff was going to be a long one. I wouldn't get back to work until the end of March. The coffers that once were filled were starting to look meager now.

SPRINGTIME 1973-WELCOME TO DIRT-WORK

Dirt work is a whole different animal than Building Trades work in Local #150. Crane Operating is done by the Union "Prima-Donnas". The guys who run the cranes have great minds for calculations and are quick to adapt to ever-changing situations. Their quick decision-making and knowledge can save life-and-limb. Their skill level is high caliber. I always felt that some of these men who got the high quality jobs are slugs who knew someone in the Union who had clout. Such is the way of the world, I suppose. Guys who do dirt work are just as intelligent, but this kind of work is "lower echelon". Operators who do "dirt-work" hunt for overtime jobs. A man has to work ten- to twelve-hours-a-day, five-days-a-week, as well as Saturdays to make good money in the dirt. A guy can't work after heavy downpours of rain. Rain is the enemy, and it keeps you sitting at home for a week or more. You can't work when the ground is in a deep freeze, so you lose a considerable amount of time to all of the elements. We get a lot of "blow" days in the dirt. Bulldozer Operators work most of the time, but rubber-tired equipment like the "Scrapers" sat for long periods of time after rain or snow. The Scraper is the lowest of the low, as far as status is concerned. If you are a good Scraper Operator, the excavating companies treat you like Gold. No one in his right mind wants to run one of these damned things. I ran 'em on-and-off for 20 years. I never claimed to have a brain in my head. A good Scraper Operator is hard to find, the same way a "hard man is good to find" in some circles. If an Operator learned proficiency on a Scraper, he learned how to stay comfortable on the machine. It wasn't such a bad day's work. This ability to have an easy day running a Scraper takes many years of pain and self-education. Scrapers bounce a man around something terrible. Your back and neck hurt like hell because you have to look over your shoulder all day long. When you load the dirt and dump it, your head is continuously looking over your right shoulder.

The only break a Scraper Operator gets from this hell is when he is driving to the dump or cut sites. It's really not much of a break! A man still has to bounce his ass off! Envision one of those toys where the little man is bouncing up-and-down, with a rubber band in the center of his head.

Yeah, you've got the idea now! This is brutal work. I was sent out of the Union Hall in March of 1973 to run one of these damn Scraper machines. I should have run away screaming and gone to Mt. Pleasant, Michigan for Graduate School, but I was D-U-M, dumb! You've seen these machines working as you've driven your car on the expressway. They are green or yellow and look like elongated grasshoppers. They have 2 engines, front and rear, which belch black smoke into the air and into the Operator's lungs. One engine sits right next to the Operator, and the other one is in the rear of the machine, directly over the rear tires.

They are scary machines. You had to travel up on these huge hills, dump your dirt, while the lanes on the huge stockpile kept getting narrower. My asshole used to "pucker up to the size of a pinhead" when the wheels were hanging off either side of the stockpile.

Guys who run these things their whole careers hobble around when they walk, and speak too loudly. They all need hearing aids from the deafness caused by the roar of the diesel engines.

On my first dirt job, all the machines were lined up neatly in a row. These things were huge and I was frightened to death. To a neophyte, every aspect of approaching his first dirt job is threatening. I sauntered over to the Foreman's pick-up truck, where all the men were congregating. I put on my best John Wayne-style strut. Rough men, with big belt buckles stared at me coldly—almost with disdain—as I signed up. I filled out my W-2 forms with collegiate knowledge. At least these hillbillies would know I could write and "cipher" with the best of them! They all were wearing these bill caps with Union buttons. These guys weren't as friendly as the crane guys I worked with before because they were pissed off that they were working in the dirt. I wished for the previous year in the Building Trades. I didn't feel the warm-fuzzies here. I said "Hello," but they purposely ignored me. "Am I freaking invisible," I thought? "What's all this non-recognition bullshit all about?"

These guys were "shit-kickers". They came from Arkansas, Kentucky, Tennessee, Missouri, and Southern Illinois. None of these guys ever stepped onto my old campus at S.I.U., unless they were cleaning toilets or doing some kind of landscaping work. They had faces that looked like shoe leather. I could see a "far-away look" in their eyes. It was as if they were longing for home or someplace else. That look they had was intense. It was a cold, steely look. It is hard to explain to the "uninitiated".

They had gnarled, calloused hands with veins popping out of them. Some of them chewed tobacco. They were chewing stuff like Redman and Copenhagen. The brown spittle ran down the sides of their mouths. It was disgusting. The spittle dried in the sun and the wind as the day wore on.

What the hell were these guys doing in "my" neighborhood? We were just 30 miles outside of Chicago. I felt like I was in Kentucky. A lot of the men rented cheap motel rooms together, and then drove home when it rained. When the job was shut down for a week, I suppose they went home to farm. I knew they didn't like me. I could feel them sizing me up. I knew how some innocent fellow must have felt when a guy with a white hood put the noose around his neck. These guys were going out of their way to treat me like shit. I was an outsider on my own turf. I felt like an alien. I thought to myself, "This is my town, you hillbilly pieces of shit! You guys are the interlopers! Don't you know that I'm a College Graduate? I'm a Dean's List Scholar and a Super Salesman!" They didn't see my big "S" on my Tee shirt, I suppose.

They couldn't care less about any of my academic or business accomplishments. They thought I was a stupid kid, and they were right! I was a city "feller". I had no business being out in that farm field with them. I was just a soft, pasty-faced kid, whose Daddy had gotten him a Union Card.

They thought I hadn't paid any dues in life. I was mistaken about them because this city boy never realized how hard these boys had to work to make good in the world. They knew poverty because they had to work dying farms. They knew hardships, long hours, desperation, and exhaustion caused by being outside in the elements all their natural lives. They knew the machines, how to run 'em, and how to fix 'em. They knew these things since they were little boys. Theirs was a fraternity of guts and hard work. I was really the "interloper". I was the object of their hate and fear.

I didn't understand their language at lunchtime. They talked of different kinds of machines, dirt spreads, blue-topping, pump-loading, draft arms, and Lord only knows what else!

I had no clue what the hell any of them were talking about. It tore my guts up inside because I was an educated man and none of them gave a "hoot" about anything I had to say. I sat with them anyway, hoping that maybe I might learn something. All I got from them was, "Y'all might catch on someday. Maybe y'all might be better off if you went back to school." I decided that I hated them as much as I hated the boys who stuffed dog shit in my baseball mitt, years ago.

Anyway, I ran this machine that scrapes up the dirt. When I have a huge pile of it, spilling over the sides of the box, the Dozer guy gets right behind my machine and rams the shit out of me! I know I have whiplash. The freakin' fillings are gonna' fall out of my teeth! I glare at him, and see him swearing at me. He's waving his arms at me menacingly. He's pissed off at me because I'm digging holes in his cut area instead of scraping the dirt, nice and flat, like an ice skating rink. My ineptitude makes his job an agony because he has to back over my holes and experience whiplash himself. Not only that, he has to fill my holes and get ready for the next idiot to push-load.

Off I go to dump the dirt. I'm bouncing my ass off, just like the little man with the rubber band in his head. I get to the dumpsite and instead of spreading the dirt nice and evenly, my machine "pukes" out these huge clumps "willy-nilly" all over the place. The other "cowboys" are laughing at me. I get stuck with a giant load under my machine, and instead of waiting for a push out from the dozer man in the dump, I'm spinning my tires. I'm valiantly fighting like hell to free my machine. The tires are spinning, burning up the transmissions in both engines. This Dozer guy at the dumpsite is livid. He comes flying at me in 3rd gear, arms waving, screaming at me to stop! His face is beet-red with anger. The veins are popping out of his neck, he's so mad. Then, BANG! He hits me so hard I'm seeing stars. Then, he steers me out of my self-generated hole.

My God, the pain in my spine is like some kind of electric bolt! I animatedly give him the finger and on the way back to the cut area, I'm so pissed off and nervous that I run over three Engineer's stakes. OOPS! Operators use these stakes to read the topography of the job site so that it co-ordinates with the blueprint. Without these pretty little stakes (with the lovely, pink, blue, and yellow ribbons), everyone is lost. You can't do the job without the stakes.

The foreman sees my atrocity, and throws his bill cap in the dirt. He kicks it with his cowboy boot, lofting it better than any place kicker I've ever seen in the NFL. I just wanted to crawl into a hole and die. My arms were so tired from pulling and pushing levers all day that I didn't think I could last until quitting time. My back ached from bouncing and getting hit in the "rear end" by bulldozers. My neck is sore and my legs feel like "toothaches" from mashing down on the throttle pedals, and brakes all day long.

This was my third day on the job, and just like it is on any baseball field in America: Three strikes and your out! I was fired that night. Nobody says goodbye. Nobody cares. They just get in their pick-up trucks and go home. The 5 or 6 guys remaining on the job are calmly drinking their beer. They're smoking their cigarettes, or chewing their tobacco. Some look over at me and shake their heads once in a while. I feel most hurt, when I see them laugh, as they look at me. I get in my car, smelling of sweat, diesel fuel, shame, and fear. I am ashamed and confused. I feel belittled. I vow to go to our training site in Lockport, Illinois and learn how to do a better job. I go home and shower. I drink a six-pack of beer, watching the last rays of sun peeking over the treetops. I hobble inside the apartment and set the alarm clock. I plan to visit the Union Hall early in the morning. I need to put my name on the Out of Work List.

THE PIPELINE JOB-SUMMER—1973

The next day, I drove back to the Union Hall with my tail between my legs. I told the dispatch office business agent my tale of horror and woe. He laughed, put his arm around my shoulders and said: "Son, you'd better get used to it. It happens all the time." He made me feel a hell of a lot better. I knew there were other "morons", just like me, screwing up their jobs. He said, "That's what the Union Hall is for, Kiddo! We will find you a job, that fits you right." Whew! It wasn't the end of the world after all.

I went out to the training site and practiced on dozers, scrapers, backhoes, and end loaders. I learned a lot, but the real quality learning comes from hands-on experience from the job. Whenever I was between jobs or got rained out, I always made it my business to head out to the training site.

I hired onto a few more dirt jobs that spring. I started to learn the machines and developed into a "pretty good hand". I don't know why, but the guys called a good Scraper Operator, a "Pull-Skinner". The nickname for a scraper is a "pull". The slang must have come from that old tune "Mule Skinner Blues". I don't know.

Early in June, I was dispatched to 51st Street and Oak Park Avenue to work as an Oiler on a Link Belt LS-58 Crane when who the hell do you think I see? Good old Jim Seeley is the Operator, my old boss. I knew right then and there, that everything was going to be fine on this job! We shook hands and he smiled that broad smile of his with those Irish eyes just twinkling. Jim said, "Good seeing you, Richie. We've got a good job this time! We're setting a 48" gas pipeline in the ground. The run goes all the way from Harlem Avenue to Cicero Avenue, down 51rst Street. We're working 10-hours-a-day, 5-days-a-week. There ain't going to be any rainout time or layoffs. This job is a 'peach'. You have your weekends free to chase girls and no layoff comes until December." I could have thrown my arms around old Jim and kissed him! I struck the Mother lode of jobs! Pipeline was great work!

We were going to be working a single-hoist line to make various "picks" to facilitate the job progress. Then we had to change over to a double-cable line for a "clamshell" bucket to dig what were called "bell holes" for the welders. They had to crawl under the sections of gas line to weld them airtight. The steel gas lines were jacked together by powerful hydraulic machines. The welders "laid a perfect bead" all around the circumference of the steel gas line. It was imperative that their welds had to be perfect. The job engineers x-rayed the pipe welds before we covered them with dirt. When a crew deals with gas, no mistakes can be made or...KABOOM! We hired the best Welders in the Continental United States for this job.

These gentlemen were mostly boys from the South. They wore multi-colored welder's caps. The welders were the most important guys on the job and they knew it! They only worked periodically, but were on the clock for a 50-hour workweek. The rest of the time, they lollygagged around, playing cards, drinking shots and beers in local taverns, or playing practical jokes on each other. When it was time to weld, they all were serious and sober. They lay under the shade trees along the route to stay cool. They reminded me of predator male lions, sleeping after a good meal.

On the lower echelon, were the pipeline laborers. They were rough-and-ready guys, who popped open their trunks or truck boxes every morning to suck down a few beers and shots of whiskey. Remember, these were the old days! Drinking on the job was no big deal as long as the work got done! The laborers worked like dogs. All day long, they played jokes on each other. This frivolity made the day fly by for us, observing the drama of their wonderful hijinx. Because of the good times, our job morale was high all the time. All the trades worked well together. In the 70's, Management's prevailing Philosophy was, "Out of sight, Out of Mind".

Jim Seeley taught me how to run the Link-Belt Crane. The "clamshell" works just like those you see in the glass cases at Amusement Parks. Instead of picking up stuffed animals, it picks up dirt, boulders, and other things. The levers in the cab control the cables and the jaws of the monster clam. The toy clamshell tries to hoist the dollies and teddy bears and swing them to the pay-off slot, where Dad delivers them happily to the arms of the darling kiddies. The booty is usually dropped and lost during the swinging process and Daddy has to reach into his pockets for another quarter. The real crane clamshells work much better. One cable hoists the bucket, while the other one closes the jaws. The load is hoisted up to a waiting dump truck. The Operator eases off the brake and the jaws open and dump the dirt. Hopefully it lands in the trailer box, otherwise you are looking for a new job.

If an Operator gets really good, he can easily pick up a beer can off the street with the massive jaws of the clamshell. We drove big wooden planks on either side of the pipe ditch with the clamshell, too. If we didn't have a chance to backfill the deep hole before quitting time, this would keep all the crazy neighborhood kids from falling in the ditch. Once the dirt covered the pipe, we could pull out all the planking material with the crane.

Before the dirt was put in the ditch, a rubber tired end loader sprinkled small-sized stone over the pipe, and then the dirt could be dumped in layers and compacted. The dirt had to be hard so the asphalt street wouldn't cave in later on. There are a lot of things to think about on each construction job. I often wonder if the general public thinks that we construction workers are just uneducated idiots. I suppose some people look at us this way, but believe me—each construction job needs men with great minds to accomplish all tasks, quickly and safely.

Many times a crane operator on the Pipeline has to work in the "blind". This means he can't see what he's doing and depends on a signalman for directions. The signalman has to be trustworthy and reliable. One false move and a man in the ditch could be hurt or killed. Conversely, the crane operator had to be observant of all the signals and proceed with the operation, slowly and safely. A good operator will "dog everything off" (stop doing everything) if he doesn't understand a signal. Sometimes the signalman is angered because of this, but better to understand the signal than kill someone and have to live with that reality for the rest of your life. Fatal errors are totally unacceptable. SAFETY FIRST!

After listening to Jim and watching him operate the crane for a couple of weeks, I was getting "seat time" in the rig, and learning how to operate it really well. Once I was really good at the job and had confidence, Jim took breaks and let me "carry the ball" for a few hours each day. He engendered confidence in me, the same way he had on the previous job. Jim was one of Local 150's best men, because he cared enough about the future of our Union to pass on knowledge to young men who were thirsting for it. Jim was always patient and kind to me. My self-esteem was high due to his tutelage. I was proud of my skills once again. Good money and fun times would be mine on that glorious summer!

SUMMER FUN — 1973

Working as Jim's Oiler was pure joy. So was "laying pipe" down 51st Street in the great city of Chicago. Most of the route was residential neighborhood, but some small factories and office buildings also proliferated along the street as we headed eastward toward Cicero Avenue. The absolute best thing the neighborhood had to offer was the abundance of ethnic taverns along the way. They all had their own special "flavor", and most of them offered a great menu of hot lunches. We looked forward to the cold beer and air-conditioning as well. Polish, Irish, Lithuanian, and German entrepreneurs owned most of these little "mom and pop" businesses. These were 2nd- and 3rd-generation families who owned these establishments. For a couple of bucks, all of the taverns without exception served wonderful homemade meals. The blue-collar guys who frequented these establishments at lunchtime, quickly gobbled down homemade polish sausage, oxtail soup, meatloaf, pot-roast, and corned beef and cabbage. Freshly cooked vegetables, potatoes, and fresh dinner rolls with plenty of butter accompanied all the meals.

This food was as good or better than the stuff your Mom served at home. Add to all of this a couple of frosty pitchers of ice cold beer, and it made it really tough to exit the gin-mill to meet the heat and humidity to finish the day's work. Hot Chicago air in my face, my belly full of good food and beer, and slits for eyes, the afternoon was always a tough animal to face. The whole crew was buzzed and we laughed and joked all afternoon. The pace slowed down. It was a great time for me to stand next to the crane—rag in hand—proudly polishing and cleaning its sparkling exterior. I did this with my shirt off, exposing my muscled chest, arms, and back to the sun. I enjoyed the fact that the Pipeline Company was paying me to work on my tan! I eyeballed all the pert young females walking down the street, and if they were smiling at me, initiated conversations with them. I relish the memories of being young, strong, male, and horny! My dad used to tell me these were the best days of my life!

The girls walking down 51st Street were beautiful. Their halter-tops, short shorts, and miniskirts, were a welcome distraction from the job. These lovely creatures made all my days totally enjoyable. The ultimate pay-off was the occasional phone number and hot date. My apartment was only ten minutes from the job, so the gals I met from the neighborhood were only a stones-throw from my bachelor pad.

By this time, money was coming into my bank account again, so I traded in the Chrysler for a really clean 1968 Oldsmobile Delmont 88 with I-beam suspension. It had a 400-cubic-inch V8 engine under the hood. The car sported a black power ragtop, and beautiful black leather bench seats. The car had a white body that was in mint condition. It had awesome-looking wire wheels and brand new tires. I added a high quality 8-track tape player with a powerful speaker system. The car had a heavy duty racing clutch with a manual-shift transmission. A tachometer was displayed in the instrument panel, so I knew when I was "red-lining" my baby. I brake-torqued this sweetheart and laid some smoking rubber off the line. The front end of the beast rose up and the girls just loved it! So did I, because this was a "righteous ride"! Men usually love their cars. I'm aware that it's probably a Freudian thing, but who cares! My penis always worked just fine. The ultimate pay-off was that my car was a super "babe-magnet". This was the mindset of guys in my generation. Right or wrong, this way of thinking seemed like a beautiful thing to me!

On the pipeline job, I always came to work looking clean. I was tan and fit from my winter exercise program. I wore muscleman tee shirts and red-tab, boot-cut Levi jeans. I always had a fancy pair of cowboy boots. I liked the alligator and snakeskin styles. After work, the pipeliners drooled when I brought various well-endowed young girls into the tavern. The men bought us drinks, desperately hoping we would stay for a long time. I guess these old-timers were reliving the days when they were "young, dumb, and full of cum" just like I was then. Lord only knows what cheap pornographies they ran through their minds. I am sure some strange sexual scenes were playing behind the leering eyes of these grizzled men with dirt under their fingernails. They "danced" their dance already and their ballroom days were over. I suppose the poor guys longed for the magic and passion of their youth.

I always made sure, to shuffle my girl out of there, before things would get nasty. I liked to take my dates back to my place for dinner. I was a pretty darned good cook. I learned from the recipes my mom gave me when she shipped me off to college. I always treated my girlfriends to a big pot of chili or spaghetti. I really knew how to make kick-ass gravy. Beef stew was another favorite of mine to prepare for these girls. These wonderful meals were pre-made, so all I had to do was warm them up. I always asked my date if she would tend to the meal, while I showered and freshened up for her. My game plan was to come out of my bedroom, shirtless and in a pair of cut-off jeans and sandals. I was fresh and clean and smelling good. I sauntered into the kitchen smiling at my little "meal tender" and put my arms around her waist. Usually, one thing led to another, and the meal ended up being burnt and sticking to the bottom of the pot, looking like a black hockey puck.

I smiled the next day as I "jack hammered" the burnt tomato sauce out of the big iron pot with my hammer and chisel. A little labor was always worth a whole lot of lovin' from a sweet little vixen!

THE BLUE FOX LOUNGE

My roommate, Chicago Johnny, and I got along just fine. John owned a "boss" reel-to-reel sound system, and sat in his lounge chair smoking reefer or cigarettes. When he was stoned, listening to his music, he smiled like a Cheshire cat. He was usually rocking to his tunes on Friday nights when I came home from work. He always had a bottle of beer next to him on the end table and a plastic bottle of Vick's nasal spray, which he constantly overused and abused. I'm amazed he never acquired a deviated septum from the many times he squeezed that damned solution up into his nasal cavities.

Johnny owned the best collection of blues music I had ever heard in my life. He was a simple man with modest aspirations. He knew what he wanted out of life and was willing to settle for less. He was calm, happy, and likeable. I felt he was an excellent choice for a friend and a roommate. John chose to be an individualist and aspire to nothing. I smile when I toss this fact about him around in my "brain-box". Another reason why we got along so famously was because his pizza shift ran from five p.m. till one-in-the-morning. Our paths rarely crossed, and that makes for a great relationship between men who share the same residence.

Most every Friday night on the weekends, Johnny, Viet Nam Billy, and I met up at The Blue Fox Lounge. This establishment was located on 55th Street, a couple of blocks West of Kedzie Avenue on Chicago's South side. The Blue Fox was a late night joint. It had some of the best "Do-Wop" music on the jukebox I had ever heard in my life. The lounge was dark and gothic. The bar was so long that it went on forever. The bar had red candles placed intermittently that flicked like seductive fingers, inviting me to sit on the garish red barstools. The owners had a five a.m. license, so most of the clientele started arriving around midnight. The women who came in the bar wore too much eye makeup and bizarre shades of lipstick and nail polish. Most of them wore short skirts with black nylons and high heels. The girls all had ratted hair or "falls". Some had beehive hair-do's for their "crowning glories".

These gals were a little on the trashy side, to say the very least. They clustered together like a bunch of hens, clucking a-mile-a-minute.

Their dark eyes were always darting this way and that. They looked around the bar furtively, almost desperately, sizing up everything. They appeared to be on some kind of do-or-die mission. These girls were a throw back to the late 50's. We just loved them!

The men who came in the bar wore gaudy banlon shirts, black leather jackets, sharkskin pants, and pointy black boots with zippers on the sides. Most of the guys looked like aging crooners, with greasy ducktails and pompadours. The general mood of the bar was one of danger and anticipation. Most of the music was soul-type stuff. All of it was sexually charged. A lot of dark lighting and slow dance songs made this bar "tops" with me. All that went on in the place was really sensual. Eye candy and auditory sexiness prevailed in this bar. I listened to Roy Orbison, Little Anthony and the Imperials, Curtis Mayfield, Santo and Johnny, The Platters, Sam and Dave, and Jerry Butler. They were all on the jukebox. This place was a real blast-from-the-past. I loved it, because it was so unique.

Bill and I were always half hammered by the time Johnny would arrive. The three of us drank and laughed and told tale tales while we checked out all the girls. When the time was right, we made our moves on them. If a "dolly" was stumbling around and smiling at you or inadvertently putting her breasts on the bar while ordering her whiskey, you knew the time was right to approach her.

These inebriated angels danced so closely to you, that thoughts of pre-pubescent basement parties always came to my mind. I thought of those little parties where I explored the wonderful intimacies of dry humping my dance partner and doing taboo things not to be seen in public. I felt the danger of being 14 once again!

For some odd reason, Viet Nam Bill always got lucky in this place. Maybe it was the sad look in his eyes. Maybe his luck was due to his war experiences, or not quite measuring up to the expectations of his anal-retentive, successful, sales executive father. Maybe a combination of these things put him in the drivers seat with these needy women.

Sometimes, I got lucky in there as well. It was always hit-or-miss with me. Poor Johnny couldn't get lucky in a whorehouse with a fistful of hundred-dollar bills. Maybe he smelled too much like pizza or Vick's nasal inhaler.

MY FIRST WIFE — THE BEGINNING

Her name was Nancy. She was a long-legged beauty—tall and regal—with ample breasts. I first layed eyes on her as she strut like a queen down Archer and Pulaski Avenues. I was 18, and cruising with Frank in his gold Pontiac. She had a girlfriend just as beautiful walking with her named Ellen. Nancy had big, dark brown eyes, and chestnut brown hair. Her hair was parted down the middle and flowed down to the center of her curvaceous back. She looked like a fertile earth mother in halter-top, bell-bottom jeans, and sandals.

This first sighting of the girl—who was to be my wife 5 or 6 years later—occurred on a sidewalk in front of the Mount Pindos, Greek Restaurant. The place is still there and it brings me back to the past when I see it. The Duke of Earl by Gene Chandler was playing on the radio in Frank's car. It was a summer of parties, fun, and romance. I felt better than a king when she held my hand. We went arm in arm, enjoying the passion of adolescent puppy love. She was a good Polish-Catholic Girl. She attended Lourdes High School on 55th Street. I think she was going into her junior year there.

I kissed her gently in Marquette Park and while we watched the double feature at the Double Drive In. I took her to the local White Castle Hamburger joint on Western Avenue afterwards. It was like a scene right out of the movie American Graffiti. I went off to college with promises to her of my never-ending love. I was totally devoted to her.

She came to visit me at S.I.U. in the fall. I put her up at Rich and Vera's house on Route 13 in Carbondale. It was a safe place. Rich and Vera were a gentle hippie couple who saw to it that no harm would come to My Precious One. Nancy and I listened to the "Surrealistic Pillow" Album, and drank wine. We kissed and listened to "Marianne Faithful", and "It's a Beautiful Day". Soon the weekend was gone.

As I waved goodbye to her, I had tears in my eyes. I saw her sad, pretty face framed in the train window. Part of my heart was heading North to Union Station in Chicago. God, I was homesick for her and my life back at Mom and Dad's house. My gut told me that she was lost forever. We wrote to each other for a while and then the letter exchanges between us became less frequent.

I found her again after graduating from college, while working on the pipeline job in the summer of '73. It had been five years. I think this chance meeting is what is called "serendipity". She was broken-hearted from a bad first marriage. She told me she was finally free. I was more than ready to re-kindle a romance, which I thought had been lost forever.

Yes, I met my childhood sweetheart once again. She was driving a sharp 1971 Camaro. She looked so fine! She wore a nice blouse and a mini-skirt. She still had those beautiful long legs and knockout figure. Her car was parked at a red light, next to my crane when I sighted her. I jumped four feet down to the pavement, off the tracks of the crane. Jim Seeley was smiling. He knew that the hound was after a fox once again! I had no clue at the time that this gorgeous woman was My Nancy.

Nancy and I, both beamed at each other with surprise. I stuck my head inside her car, begging for her phone number. She smiled in my eyes and wrote it down for me on the inside cover of a book of matches. I knew I was going to get lucky and start dating her again. Car horns started blaring at us, but we didn't care. Finally, I told her to pull over into a parking zone. The men working on the job were all smiling and making catcalls at us. They didn't realize that Nancy and I were once in love, a long time ago. I had her phone number in my wallet now, as she flashed me that familiar smile and drove off, waving me goodbye. This started another chapter in our lives. I will write more about Nancy and our fates later in the story.

DRILL RIGGING—WINTER—1974

The pipeline job finished for me in early December. I was laid-off again. I looked forward to some rest and recreation, and my "rockin' chair money". I called the Union Hall and amazingly they had a job for me. The business agent asked me if I wanted to be a helper on a Drill Rigging Crew, in McCook, Illinois. I said, "Hell, yes, but I've never done this type of work before. What do I have to do?"

The business agent said, "Nothing, son. The foreman said he will break you in." I said, "OK". The next morning, I'm out there with my lunch bucket and thermos of coffee. I'm prepared. I have the Carhart coveralls, thermal underwear, heavy wool gloves, stocking cap, hooded sweatshirt, grease gun, and everything but the kitchen sink, to keep me warm and dry. The wind is blowing around thirty-miles-an-hour from the West. It's fifteen degrees and snowing. It's freakin' cold man! I get in the foreman's truck, shivering. While I'm filling out my paperwork, I figure today will be a "blow day", and I'll soon be in the tavern. This big mountain of a foreman, named Russ smiles and says: "Don't worry about bein' a little bit chilly boy, in half-an-hour, you'll be sweatin' like a dog."

My heart sank into the pit of my gut. Jesus, I didn't want to work today! He was right—I was sweating my ass off in no time flat. I climbed and coughed and sweat. Guys on the Drill Rig were flying around, barking orders at me to get them this and that. I felt like a whirling dervish. Tough men do drill rigging. That's why they're called roughnecks. They drill for oil, and they drill for water. The work is backbreaking and dangerous. It is a team job. Any guy who doesn't pull his weight is fired on the spot.

My job was climbing a thirty-foot drill mast, to hook up new sections of drill steel. I climbed up and down that tower a million times on my first day. The wind kept blowing and it snowed all day long. My hands were numb and almost useless many times that day. I got breaks to warm them up next to a kerosene-fired "salamander". I greased the threads on each section of drill steel with a small hand-held mop. We had to keep the five-gallon bucket of grease next to the salamander to keep it from freezing. I tossed 100-lb. bags of bentonite and pulled compressor hose. I ran for anything that was needed by the drill deck crew. I was their monkey, running hither-and-yon. It was also my job to hook up propane tanks to the salamanders, so we didn't run out of heat. I had to take coffee orders and start the compressor when it was needed. I carried 5-gallon buckets of water to prime the water pump every freezing morning.

My favorite job was shoveling muck, mud, and snow. I had to sweep any debris off the residential streets every night before we went home. All day long, I had to climb up on a flatbed truck and jump down with various supplies in-hand for the drill deck. Sometimes, my Foreman, Russ, had me drive a White cab-over diesel truck with a trailer loaded with drill steel. I motored down old Route 66 to Springfield, Illinois. I did this job, after working an 11-hour shift. I drank black coffee while I drove and popped amphetamines to stay awake. When I was high as a kite and kickin' into overdrive, I was lovin' the life! I listened to all the outlaw southern rock bands on the eight-track player in the cab of the rig. I'd pull back into Kankakee, Illinois, at Russell's doublewide trailer around 5-in-the-morning. His wife, Elma, cooked me a hearty breakfast as we all laughed, talked, and drank good strong coffee. Russ told me I was a good hand for a city kid. He was a good boss to me. I liked the man a lot.

I slept in his pick-up truck all the way back to McCook, Illinois, on the mornings after my nocturnal trips. Then I worked another shift. Sometimes, I worked over 30 hours with a few hours of sleep here and there. It's great to be young and strong and pumped up on speed! After monster shifts like this, the men joked with me, asking me if I wanted to stop in the tavern with them to have "just one". I'd say "no" and go home and pass out with my dirty clothes still on my worn body. I'd then wake up at 5:30 A.M. to work another shift.

All of this work was done with pride. At the end of the day, we men were soaking wet with perspiration, mud, and grease. Concrete and mud covered our boots and coveralls. My arms and shoulders were so sore, I could barely pull off my work clothes at night. The Well Works Company laid off a lot of men. I saw them come and go. My foreman, Russ told me, "They ain't roughnecks like us, son". This made me really proud. Tears welled up in my eyes. I gutted it out and made the grade. These are important tests that real men must pass. Once you make the grade, nobody can ever take your pride away from you. A man's life is filled with many challenges. Your legacy is the memory of how you performed. A "real man" in my trade has no quit in him.

McCook is an industrial town, just West of Chicago. The taverns there are threadbare places for working men. They smell of smoke, puke, and urine. The crew sat in these depositories of human detritus, to drink whiskey and beer. The booze killed their physical and emotional pain. We lived a gray, bleak, existence.

The rewards are your ability to get the job done against all odds. We endured pain, to work in the snow and the rain. We accepted the soreness and arthritis that comes from the hard physical labor. The men on this job had vacant looks in their eyes. They sat on their barstools, looking sad and emotionless sometimes. We sat red-faced in our taverns. We laughed heartily, but underneath it all was a pervasive anger and resentment. A "hair trigger" of violence was an undercurrent inside each and every one of us. This work de-humanizes a man and takes away life's joy. A man learns not to cross anyone's personal boundaries. We don't share feelings in my business. As I began to know these men, they told me they followed these drill rigging jobs all over the country.

They sent their money home to some obscure country town, where a fat wife with three or four screaming kids existed in a "double-wide" trailer equipped with a satellite television dish. The men bunked together in cheap motel rooms while working on the road. They drank whiskey, played cards, and ate fast food. They laughed at the stories told of past jobs they had worked on together. They created mythologies to give them sustenance in their sad subculture

I couldn't believe this way of life was anybody's "American Dream". It certainly wasn't mine. After doing this work for a few months, I realized how lucky I was to have a good liberal arts education. Knowledge is the wealth that can't be lost once it is earned by one's mind.

When the job ended in March and Russ asked me if I wanted to work in Beaumont, Texas with top pay and living expenses, I respectfully declined. I noticed how strangely he looked at me as I turned down his offer. His, was a look of befuddlement and loss. I questioned a deep-rooted value system in him, which for generations is passed down from fathers to sons. I watched the big man hobble to his company truck. His right foot was crushed in a combine accident on his father's farm when he was a teenager. This happened to him in Central Missouri, way back in 1959. I knew I was going to miss this old warrior. I'm sorry I broke his damned heart.

TUNNEL WORK—1974-1975

During this time in the United States, things didn't look very good for labor. The economy was in flux. The big steel plants were shutting down and people were lining up for rationed gas. We now were importing our steel from the Japanese. We can thank the corporate and political cabal of evil men for the demise of the steel industry in America. These men were filling their pockets, and the middle class was paying for their greed. There was a growing anti-union movement gaining momentum in our country. It was the beginning of the end for my beautiful America. I believe our great country had reached its summit in the early 70's. We started helping the Middle East—Saudi Arabia in particular—to extract the "black gold" that lie underneath their deserts. Our factories were being disassembled. It all was a terrible mess and agonizingly painful to watch. America was a poor dying animal being pecked apart by a bunch of greedy vultures. Global free trade was finally becoming a reality.

The spring and summer work situation for me was spotty at best. In my trade at this time, I got all kinds of variety. One day, I worked a scraper, another day, a job oiling on a crane. Nobody had any work. A man was lucky to get two or three days of employment a week. Jobs lasted only a week or two and then I had to sign back up at the Union Hall. Sometimes there were big gaps between jobs and my only recourse was to go back on Unemployment Compensation. I did a lot of sitting in the tavern and tried to get side jobs for cash. I contracted painting jobs, tended bar, and delivered pizzas. I did tune ups and brake jobs on cars. I didn't worry about how dirty I got any more. It was a matter of survival. I did just about anything now to keep my head above water. Construction money wasn't available and I thank the government of Jimmy Carter for that. People see him as a humanitarian. My personal opinion deviates from that myth. I think he meant well, but he just didn't have the expertise and he listened to the wrong people in his cabinet. Everyone in the construction industry and manufacturing was tightening their belts. Local contractors were doing just about anything to keep their businesses open. It was a "sinking ship".

Some Federal money was available however, and a lot of it! The Deep Tunnel Project in Chicago and its surrounding suburbs was going to provide a lot of jobs. A lot of the guys in our Union didn't want to do this work. It was work for desperate men and apprentices like me who were willing to take a chance. The work was underground—way underground! Often I worked in confined areas with bad ventilation. I spent my days in a dimly lit tunnel, wearing a funky-looking yellow rain suit. I longed for a suit and tie again. We wore hard hats and steel-shank rubber boots. The boots provided for us by the contractors were cheap and were lousy support for our feet. The tunnels were dirty and dangerous. In all the rock tunnels I worked, water dripped on me all the time. My life was one rainy day after another. The dampness got right into my bones and sometimes I shivered all day long.

What kept us men on the job was the "big league" money we made. There was never a lay-off to worry about. We worked every day, rain or shine. If a man could stomach the lifestyle, tunnel work was a good gig.

When I received a call from the Union in September of '74 to work for a small tunnel outfit, I took the job. The outfit was based in Livonia, Michigan. It occurred to me at the time that I was designated by my local union to be a dirty-jobs kind-of-man.

FIRST DAY ON THE TUNNEL JOB

It's a lonely enterprise, driving to work early in the morning. I always hated driving in the dark, sipping coffee with slits for eyes. I was Eastbound on Interstate I-80, anxiously looking for the 394-exit that headed South for Joe Orr Road. The job was in Chicago Heights. My heart was palpitating in fear and anticipation. "I shouldn't let these new jobs affect me like this," I thought. It was my practice to always leave early for a job, because facing the embarrassment of being late on the first day is painful. I wanted to make a good impression. Making a bad one might play against me for the duration of my employment.

I pulled off at my exit and found the job site with time to spare. Trucks with lowboy trailers were lined up, all stacked with 60" concrete pipe. The diesels were idling with their throaty purr. The fumes gagged me as I walked toward the gate. I observed the company placard with the "safety first" signs. "That's bullshit," I thought. The equipment yard was filled with rusty machines, oil barrels, compressors, pick-up trucks, and various implements necessary for the job of mining clay. A few more steps and I saw what I needed most. There stood a portable "Johnny on the Spot" shitter. I opened the door, and as I gagged and held my breath, I dropped my pants. My butt cheeks hit the frosty seat, and I lit up a cigarette. I'd rather smell cigarette smoke than the aroma that was lurking under me. At 7:00 A.M., ten of us entered a steel man-cage, which was hoisted up into the sky by the big crane. The Operator gently swung us dead-center over the drop shaft. We were then gently lowered to the bottom where we would start our day's work. All my co-workers were grim and dirty. They had beard stubble, cigarettes dangling from their mouths, and hard hats decorated with stickers advertising mining tools and companies they had worked for in the past. These men were pretty much uncommunicative unless they wanted me to do something for them. They scowled and waved their arms around a lot. They yelled at me all the time. This tunnel was not a friendly place. I walked through the pipe up to where I was designated to work. I was to be the helper on the mining machine.

I met the Operator and put my hand out for him to shake. He just frowned at me. He looked me up and down and pretty much disregarded me. I understood his antipathy immediately. This guy was an asshole. I knew it would be a hateful relationship between us right from the start.

The gearbox that ran the mining machine was leaking oil, so I hauled in five-gallon cans of heavy 90-weight gear oil, all day long. This is backbreaking work, hauling in two-at-a-time, hunched over like one of the clay people on the Flash Gordon show. I also had to keep the conveyor belt greased and cleared of debris that accumulated underneath it. I shoveled clay into a boxcar while we were mining. I was sweating like hell, right away. If we hit big rocks we couldn't mine, I had to walk out of the tunnel, hunched over like "Quasimodo" to fetch the Bosch drill. I drilled a big enough hole in the rock for a stick of dynamite. The drilling was slow going. When I was finished with it, I had rock dust on my face, and looked like someone threw flour all over me. I was coughing up limestone powder while I was jamming dynamite in the hole of the rock that I was going to shoot. We'd all walk out of the tunnel and someone would scream, "Fire in the hole!" I'd push the plunger down on the box and blow the rock to smithereens. We sauntered back into the heading of the tunnel, breathing in all those "nice" fumes of dynamite smoke, and dust. The best part was the headache I got after breathing it all into my lungs. I pulled the chunks of rock out of the cutter wheel onto the conveyor belt, and we started mining again. The heat from the gearboxes made me sweat once again. We had to inspect the cutters on the machine a few times a day and replace the damaged ones.

This always involves a lot of hammering, cussing, and yelling. Time is money, and we were always in a hurry. We got pissed off and swore epitaphs at each other until all the work was professionally negotiated. Then we started mining again. There are all kinds of fun things to do in the tunnel. We had to install our dim lighting as we went along, pull heavy electrical power cables, and bend over in pain while we bolted rails together for the "dinky"—a battery-operated locomotive that hauls the clay out of the tunnel. Also, we got to hang plastic PVC pipe for our ventilation. It's nice to be able to breathe. The mining process is a non-stop, go-go-go job that works your ass off all damned day long, if you are a tunnel rat like me. My agony doesn't end till the next shift of "clay people" arrives to relieve me of my burden. At the end of the day, my head is still hurting from the dynamite powder. If you've ever experienced the torture of a migraine headache, you know what I mean. I think to myself, "This is all a bad dream, it will go away when I wake up." Not so. The real agony is knowing that the dream is reality, and it is happening to me. When the crane finally hoists the cage out of the hole at night, we all look like filth-encrusted zombies. The men head for the change house, to hang up the rain suits in their lockers. Everyone looks and feels like shit. This was my life until March of 1975. After seven months of abuse and anger directed my way, I didn't run scared anymore. I learned the ropes. I developed some more "swagger" and hard muscle. I even got a few smiles from that asshole Bobby, the mining machine operator.

One fateful day in March, he pushed me too far. I don't remember what he said to me. I remember throwing a grease gun at his head and running twenty feet to get him. I ran as fast as my feet could carry me. I saw the fear in his eyes as my thumbs squeezed his windpipe. I remember two big black laborers pulling me off him saying, "You're gonna' kill him Richie! It ain't worth it man!" The two black miners escorted me to the man cage, giggling and patting me on the back. I knew this was it for me. I was going to get my check. On the way up, the black guys smiled at me and said, "You got him good Richie. We were waiting for you to whoop his ass!" This was the only time these men ever smiled at me or talked to me. We shook hands and said goodbye. I was still pissed off as I went to the trailer to get my two paychecks. We call this "lay-off and payoff" when we are fired. Fighting on the job is never tolerated. Bobby never filed charges against me with the Union Hall. Neither did the Company. I guess everyone knew the bastard had it coming!

NANCY—1975-1978

Nancy was my drug. I couldn't get enough of her. I obsessed over this girl for years. I dated other women, but always came back to her arms. I tried to get inside her head in order to understand her, but failed miserably at every attempt. I suppose this was my pathology—trying to be her Psychiatrist! I don't know if it was her upbringing that caused Nancy to carry a lot of emotional baggage. I saw signs of it in a lot of instances. I knew she had an unsuccessful first marriage. I didn't care—I just wanted her for my wife. I was young and hoped that in time I could fix everything emotionally that was bothering her. Both of our families weren't exactly examples of "normalcy". The stress of my job, the long hours, and my layoffs, were always bones of contentions between us. In many other ways, we were a good couple.

We enjoyed what most young couples enjoy: family dinners, dancing, movies, and making love. I tried to sell the idea of marriage to her, and I sold it hard! What I willed for us was doomed from the beginning. A pervasive feeling always haunted me that the marriage I was proposing to Nancy was going to fail badly. In spite of our fears, we were married at City Hall in Chicago. Our Roman-Catholic families didn't view it as a real marriage. We eloped to the "Playboy Club" in Lake Geneva, Wisconsin. Now that I think of it, this was a bizarre place to take my young bride to for her honeymoon! I worked in Nancy's family business when I was laid off. I didn't like it at all. They wanted me to quit the union and work with them full time. Somehow, I knew if I gave up the Union, it would be a big mistake. I didn't want to lose my last trump card if I ended up out on the street. The marriage failed in three years, so I was right! There were many lay-offs and money problems for me. She only worked part time. I constantly nagged her about money and responsibility.

We bought a home, and then sold it for a better one. We worked and bought nice things, but neither of us was really happy. In the worst way, I wanted her to have a child. Nancy told me that she was emotionally incapable of accepting this responsibility. My heart was totally broken by her declaration. She wasn't ready to commit to a family with me after three years.

Then my father passed away. Six months after my dad died, I packed my bags and left her. I went to live with my mom back in Chicago. I left with meager items. I just wanted out. I left the new car and all the furniture. I didn't want anything but my freedom. I filed for the divorce. As usual, with two attorneys involved in the divorce proceedings, it was a long, drawn-out affair. I took a beating and had to sign a divorce document that made me sound like an abuser. Maybe I abused her psychologically. I don't know. I knew I drank too much, but always loved her and provided for her as well as I could, given my job situation. I never physically harmed her. I never would harm a hair on her pretty head. I thank God now that there were no children involved.

Mom was glad to have me back at home with her. She was lonely in that Chicago bungalow without Dad. I was 28-years-old and starting out all over again. I didn't have a dime.

THE HOUSE I LEFT

Nancy and I lived in a big old, drafty, stucco bungalow. It was built in the 1920's. It was one of those old Montgomery Ward Catalogue floor plan homes. This house was "stout". It had big thick 4" floor joists. A giant boiler, which provided us hot water heat, sat in the basement. We had clean and efficient heat in this old house. Upstairs, we had a beautiful foyer. The living room was spacious, with lovely crown molding. The house had wonderful oak hardwood floors. I did a lot of remodeling and repair when I wasn't working construction. Sometimes in the evening, if I wasn't too damned tired after dinner, I worked on our house. We decorated with beautiful and expensive Ethan Allen Furniture. I was turning our humble domicile into a beautiful country-style refuge.

The house sat on an acre of land. We had a nice long concrete driveway that led to a large, double door pole-barn. We had a lovely garden, and a rhubarb patch in the back of the house. Perennials popped up every spring and their colors and fragrances were lovely. We also had abundant, fragrant lilac bushes in the front yard. We lived in New Lenox, Illinois. Back in the mid-70's, there was little out there. I drove many miles now to get to work. I didn't complain, and enjoyed "God's Country" on my long drives to and from my construction jobs.

Two old spinster sisters lived in a little cottage next door. Lord only knows why these "cuties" never married. Both of the old ladies enjoyed our company. Nancy and I came to their place on Sunday afternoons. I serenaded them with my accordion. When I was a kid, my mom paid for 9 years of accordion lessons for me.

I was a pretty darned good musician. We sat in their kitchen, drinking coffee and eating homemade cookies. The sisters were well into their 80's and sang along to all the old standards I played for them. I always wondered why the floor was nicely smooth on one side of the basement and roughly scalloped near the boiler. The sisters told me that the farmer who owned my house fifty years ago, way back in the day, had to stop "bull floating" the new concrete that was poured so he could go rescue one of his cows. The poor animal was sinking somewhere in a bog. When he came back home, the concrete had set, so he just left it as it was. We all had a good laugh over this tale!

Across the road from our house was a huge cornfield interspersed with thistle patches. The man that owned the property had around ten acres. In November, I hunted rabbit in the thistle, and pheasant in the corn. After reading my Chicago Tribune and enjoying some good strong coffee and cigarettes, I enjoyed the fresh cold air on my face and in my lungs early in the morning. I owned a nice shotgun—a High Standard twelve-gauge automatic. They don't make 'em anymore. It shot really true, but I traded it in for the popular Remington Model-1100. This was a mistake. Shell casings always jammed in the breech when it was freezing outside.

Anyway, the farmer who owned the land was a really nice old man, named John. He let me hunt his land for free. I gave the birds and bunnies I shot to his wife, Nora. She cleaned them and then fixed us a feast. I always watched out for twelve gauge pellets so I wouldn't break any teeth. Pellets in your meat are one of the hazards of eating what you shoot!

John was a retired Electrician and he enjoyed sharing stories with me about the construction trades in the "old days". We sat on his porch drinking Jack Daniel's, viewing God's beautiful panorama, until the sun started going down over the corn on the horizon. My dear wife, Nancy, would be coming home soon from her Saturday shopping. I winced when I wondered, "How much money has she spent this time!" I enjoyed these Saturdays spent with the old man. I didn't look forward to the trek back to my house, stumbling through the corn. I saw my house getting closer and closer, as my breathing became heavier with every step I took. I knew I had to face the music. I knew she was gonna' smell the Jack Daniels on my breath.

EPIPHANY

In 1977, the winter was cold and we had more than average snowfall. This was to be my last winter with Nancy. I put in a good hard year with Plote Excavating and worked a lot of overtime. They laid me off sometime in early December.

I sat in the old house on gray winter days, sipping my coffee and watching the snowdrifts build on Cedar Road. Every day the wind played a song for me, blowing through the small cracks in the heavy front door. It was inviting me to the challenge of going outside. I knew my marriage was falling apart. My soul was redeemed by one solitary thing. This thing I could call mine, and only mine. I started running again. I quit the booze and cigarettes cold turkey. I started eating boiled chicken and tuna fish. I was eating "clean" again. Asparagus, spinach— all the rabbit food; the whole grains and yogurt became my life once again. I was motivated by anger, anxiety, and fear. Most of all, I ran to fill the hole in my broken heart.

Running raised my spirits. I laced up my old G.I. combat boots every day. I put on thermal underwear, sweats, a knit watch cap, old painters gloves, and a hooded sweatshirt. I bounded down the road, running through the snowdrifts and cornfields, smiling like a mad-hatter. I worked myself into great shape. I was addicted to running the same way a wide-eyed religious fundamentalist is addicted to Sweet Jesus. The running bug bit me so hard that I drove 60 miles into the city to get the newest issue of Runner's World Magazine. This was insanity, but my insanity had a purpose. Can you call this "rational insanity"? I think too much, that's why I have to run or pump iron!

Running became my salvation. It became my religion, my Zen. I ran the same route on most days. The halfway point was Pilcher Park in Joliet, Illinois. A beautiful path winded through the park. It brought me deep into the woods. Alongside the path flowed a babbling brook. During snowy days or rainstorms, there was nobody out there. I had the park all to myself. I loved it this way. I saw deer, raccoon, and winter flowers; I was totally at peace with the cosmos and myself. I listened to my footsteps, and breathed in cadence to each strike of my running shoes. I also repeated my mantra—something I had paid for to help me attain serenity—from my Transcendental Meditation Guru! I just floated away. There was no pain or exhaustion. I was high on adrenal morphine. Icicles hung from my beard and mustache, but I never was cold. I felt absolutely wonderful. I experienced Zen-type out-of-body experiences sometimes, when the runner's high really kicked in for me. My body's endorphins made all negativity in my life disappear. I was truly focused when I was running.

I saw lovely rainbows of prairie flowers. They existed defiantly in the snow. Pansies popped their proud little heads out of the snow. They sure weren't Pansies to me, in this rough weather. I wonder how they got their name? They were tough little flowers! On these treks, my running distance varied between 7 to 12 miles. I tried to run hard one day and easy the next. This is the Bill Bowerman method. He was a famous running coach from Oregon, the running state.

This running lifestyle is too glorious for words. Only distance runners know the secrets of the joys of running. Being totally in touch with my inner being, and feeling the glow inside of me all day long, saved my sanity...and my life.

I ate low-calorie meals every day. At that time we were led to believe by the exercise physiologists, that a diet of complex carbohydrates, fruits, and vegetables was the key to running fitness. These days, weight training and protein consumption are stressed more. Fitness has come a long way since 1977 when I first saw Rocky Balboa doing his training. I gave up eating meat because I felt that it sapped my strength. I felt my energy levels increase as a result of this denial.

My weight dropped from 195 lbs. to a mean, lean 168 lbs. in four short months. In the spring I ran between 60 to 70 miles a week and sometimes more.

I looked in running magazines for local 10-kilometer races, and enjoyed the adrenalin rush I got from the competing against other runners. Every Sunday, I woke up at the crack-of-dawn and drove all the way to the North Side of Chicago. I ran at Riess Park on Fullerton and Narragansett Avenues. We had use of the Field House, and the best runners in the Chicago land area competed at the park. Soon, I met the famous Dick King, who had run over 100 marathons and was still running sub four-hour marathons in his 70's. I also met Dr. George Sheehan, the Physician who wrote books on the spiritual aspects of running. George was a wonderful man, and my running Guru. I felt at home here, so I joined the Riess Park Striders Running Club. Everyone

I knew thought that I had finally gone round the bend, mentally. Somehow, they accepted me, but thought I was saner when I was a fat, cigarette-smoking alcoholic. Hmmm, go figure that one out! Nancy was really sure I had finally lost my mind.

To become a good distance runner requires three things:

1. Racing in running events and quarter miles on the track. A runner has to do speed work to increase his racing fitness and race times.

2. A distance runner training for the marathon (26.2 miles), has to run a lot of mileage during the week and do a long run on Sundays.

3. All distance runners need plenty of sleep and good nutrition. No cigarettes are allowed, but minimal alcohol—preferably beer—is good for its carbohydrate value.

A runner has to run quarter miles. I had to run as fast as my little legs could carry me. I took jogging breaks to recover. This trains my body for speed and gives my mind the ability to endure pain. I decided to train for the Marathon. I read a lot about the Boston Marathon and its past heroes. The 26.2-mile race is the ultimate test for the serious runner. Some of us "nuts" even run Ultra-marathons through deserts, mountains, and other weird conditions. These are the extreme athletes. I read all about the "feared wall" that a runner hits at about 20 miles into the Marathon race. This wall comes to you when your body's glycogen supplies are depleted and your legs become "lead weights". Your pace falls off and you run in agony. Even though you try and maintain your form and stride, it becomes an exercise in futility. This is where the sheer will of the mind separates the winners from the losers. I wanted this test. I wanted to know how I measured up in this personal quest for the Holy Grail.

By April I was running 80 miles a week. Every Sunday I ran 20 miles. My first Marathon was to be held in Milwaukee. The date for the event was May 28th, 1978. I moved into Mom's house in April with a few boxes of stuff and a couple of beat-up suitcases. Of course, I brought her a duffel bag full of dirty laundry. She smiled that wonderful smile, and hugged me tight, saying, "Oh, Dickie, it's so good to have you back home! Let me start the laundry for you. I made you Oxtail soup for tonight!" That day I blew my diet. I had to, because Mom's Oxtail soup was as close to heaven as one human being can get. The tears welled up in my eyes as I felt the weight of the world being lifted from my shoulders. It was good to be home. I looked forward to training at good old Marquette Park. I had my life back again.

MY SISTER, JUDY

My "sis" was always my pal when I was a little kid. I remember sitting on the front porch with her on hot summer nights. We listened to rock-and-roll on the radio. She smoked cigarettes, and my mom and dad used to yell at her, because she was only sixteen-years-old. They were concerned about "what the neighbors would think"! Judy taught me how to dance when she came home in the afternoons after her classes at Maria High School. I was in first grade at the time at St. Adrian Catholic Grammar School. Every afternoon after school, we watched American Bandstand on TV.

She took me to the Marquette Theatre on 63rd and Kedzie Avenue on the weekends to see the latest horror films. I loved these grade "B" movies. If she had a date with a nerdy guy, she always insisted that she bring me along so she could sit me in between them. We used to laugh about this a lot! We saw The Fly, The Incredible Shrinking Man, The Thing, The Blob, Rodan, The Beginning of the End, and The Creature from the Black Lagoon. For a kid 6- or 7-years-old, this was great fun!

Judy always bought me my favorite treats. I remember them all as if it was yesterday. I loved milk duds, root beer barrels, fire sticks, and that soft-serve ice cream in safety cones. I had twelve cavities every time Mom took me to Dr. Caruso, our family dentist! Everyone at the show always threw their empty popcorn boxes up in the air, like flying saucers, at the end of every movie. All the kids whistled loudly, clapped and screamed and stomped their feet if the movie stopped due to a malfunction. If a reel broke, we screamed, "We want the show, we want the show!" Teenagers always took the seats way up in the last two rows in the balcony, to make out and French kiss.

Going to the movie show in those days was a participatory event. It was hilarious! People seemed more expressive way back then in the late 50's. When my sister, Judy, attended Maria High School, it was a punitive, grim, Roman-Catholic Girls Academy run by Lithuanian nuns. Judy was always in trouble there because of her rebel ways. I remember my sis as a wild girl who possessed a heart of gold. She was constantly at odds with authority figures. She wasn't a slut by any means. She walked home many times from Marquette Park, if some guy tried putting his hands on her while she was kissing him in his car. Judy was a good girl.

My brother, Jim, was constantly on her trail, looking out for her. He vigilantly policed her every move. He "blew the whistle" on her all the time, telling Mom and Dad about the people she was hanging around with and the things they were doing. Judy and Jim were always at odds. I remember the tears, the threats, and recriminations at the dinner table.

Most of the time the arguments ended with Sis running to her room, and slamming the door. I heard her sobbing her "teenage tears" in there every time my parents grounded her. Any family that has a teenage girl hanging around knows this familiar teenager lament. Ours was a typical, normal American family in 1957.

When Sis was 19-years-old, she met a handsome Mexican man who was considerably older than her. Lou Gutierrez was 25-years-old. They met at the "Club Tiny" Polka Club on Western Avenue. They fell in love and married after a very short while. Horrors! In the 50's, this was considered an inter-racial marriage. Thankfully, we've come a long way since then. Most people in the neighborhood were horrified by my sister's lack of good judgment. Mom and Dad accepted Lou into our family with open arms. God bless our lovely parents! As it turned out, my Brother-In-Law, Lou, was a good guy and a hard worker. His whole life, he did the best he could to take care of his family. Sis and Lou had three lovely children and lived in a little "ranch" house in Crestwood, Illinois. They never had a lot of money, but there was an unlimited amount of joy and love in that household.

Lou came from a large family, and every weekend on Saturday mornings he swept out the garage while listening to Mexican music and drinking an Old Style beer. It was hilarious! He knew people would be coming over for a party in the afternoon. They all partied until well-past midnight. My sister made tortillas, burritos, hamburgers, and hot dogs. Lou set up chairs and tables in the garage for the feast. Everyone drank and ate their fill and then danced. We laughed and ate way too much food. The children also were totally involved in all the fun every weekend. They played catch, a variety of games, and drank pop, and ate potato chips and cake. Everyone enjoyed the family party and festivities that were held every week! Poor people really know how to have fun!

The older generation of Mexicans loved the Spanish Radio Station, but the younger ones wanted Rock-and-Roll. We German-Danish-Polack's didn't care either way, as long as we could drink another cool one or down another shot of whiskey! I thought the merging of our two families was a combination made in heaven! I learned how to be Mexican, in my heart!

Later on in our lives, Judy and I loved drinking scotch whiskey together. We were both crazy simply because we shared Dad's DNA. Judy and I always had more than a few drinks together. Once the party started with Judy and me, watch out! In my mid-to-late 20's, I remember sleeping on her couch a lot. She never let me drive home drunk. She always cooked me a big breakfast on Sunday morning to soak up the booze in my belly. I remember in particular a beautiful sunny Saturday afternoon in the fall. My sister drove out in her big, red Buick Electra Convertible to see me in my home in New Lenox, Illinois. The top was down and she eased out of that big car with that endearing smile of hers. She had a devilish twinkle in those big blue eyes. As she came up my stairs, she proudly displayed a big expensive bottle of Single Malt Scotch. Yum! It was our favorite! Laughing like the Devil, I waved at her to come inside the house. We proceeded to the kitchen table to unplug that bottle and do what we did best!

Nancy wasn't home yet, but Judy and I started drinking anyway. We told stories and our minds traveled to the past. We laughed together until our sides were hurting. When Nancy came home, she wasn't angry. She loved my sister Judy as much as I did. Everyone loved Judy. She had this special aura of joy around her. I wanted to attach myself to it and never let it go.

When our party of two was over and Nancy got a meal into us, we asked Judy if she could make it home all right. Judy gave us the "thumbs-up" and down the road she flew, just like James Dean. She was flying like hell, but straight as an arrow. Nancy looked concerned. I said, "Don't worry about her; she's driving just like Richard Petty."

Many times on Saturday nights, the whole family drove out to Judy's house, to watch the Carol Burnett Show. We laughed and ate like kings. Judy always put on a big spread for us. She always had that big old bottle of scotch just for us to enjoy. Mom used to shake her head and say, "You two are just like your father". Judy and I looked at each other and laughed. We knew Mom was right. My sister lived her life to the "max". The Beatles sang, "Hey, Jude. Take a sad song, and make it better." My sister loved the joy in this song, but unbeknownst to her, the "dark" was coming for her.

MY FIRST WEEK AT MOM'S HOUSE

Nancy and I said our sad goodbyes. I was committed to the divorce, but we both cried and hugged each other anyway. I got in my cheap work car and headed to the city. I wanted a clean break from our marriage. For years, Nancy and I vacillated back and forth. We couldn't live with or without each other. Our relationship was tearing my heart out, and I was finally through with this kind of suffering. I left her with conviction this time and never looked back.

I moved back into the old house with Mom on 73rd and Homan Avenue. Our house was only three blocks from Marquette Park. It was the month was April and the weather was absolutely lovely. Spring was in the air. I longed for the smell of fresh topsoil in the morning. It was time to go back to work and move dirt. Plote Excavating called me back to work on a huge job way up in Glenview, Illinois. Plote had a million yards of dirt to move for a big housing development. The job was scheduled to last for two years. I had it made! We worked twelve-hour days and eight on Saturdays. We could turn down the Saturdays if we wanted a two-day weekend. Since I was a young guy I loved the option. I was assigned to operate a brand new Caterpillar 627-B Scraper. When I first got in the cab of the mammoth machine, the factory plastic was still on the seat. It was an awesome machine and that had the latest technology. It was comfortable for an operator's body, which was a real plus for me! Ray Plote, the owner of the company, purchased three of these "Cats" and assigned them to his best Scraper Operators.

I was really happy to be back to work with old friends and have the honor of being assigned to one of the new machines. The crew worked every day, from 6:00 in the morning until 6:30 in the evening. I left Mom's house at 4:30 in the morning so I could enjoy my coffee with the boys. I liked to get to work at least a-half-an-hour before starting time. At 6:00 a.m. sharp, we fired up the Big Cats for a day of moving dirt. At 6:30 p.m., I parked my rig and fought traffic on I-294 and then again on Route 55 to my Exit on Pulaski Avenue. I was dirty and tired, but happy. I bought a brand new CJ-7 jeep, and it was a "honey" with four-wheel drive and a stick shift. The Jeep had one of those fancy fiberglass tops that I could pop off and leave at home when the weather was nice. It had a nice stereo system so I enjoyed the long drives to and from work. I usually made it back to Chicago by 7:30 p.m.

When I got home, I'd race into the house and give my mom a big hug and kiss. I showered right away to get all the dust and dirt from my workday swirling down the drain. Throwing on my running shorts and shoes, I flew out the front door to do my ten-mile run. As I ran to the park, I waved to all the neighbors sitting on their front porches. They could count on me like clockwork every evening to run to Marquette Park. I was known as "The Runner" in the neighborhood. Rain or shine, I had to get my training run in every night.

The neighbors, who knew me since I was a little boy, cheered me on. They shouted, "Have a good run!" or "Looking good, kid!" or "When are going to run the Marathon?!" I always enjoyed talking with them. They were good neighbors. I had known them all my life. Back in those days, people stayed put. Most people in Chicago lived in the same house for decades. Some died in the same homes that they were born in. Friendship in the neighborhood was as solid as a rock. We had an unspoken solidarity. People cared about one another. The doors weren't locked at night. We were rooted in our little bungalows. Everybody drank in the same taverns and shopped at the same grocery stores. The loving arms of the neighborhood embraced a Chicago resident.

Today, the goal of making money moves a family all over the place. There isn't much loyalty shown between neighbors anymore. Some people never bother to meet their neighbors anymore. People look at their homes as investments and don't stay in one place for more than a couple of years. I often wonder what this does to the children of the family. Nowadays, doors are locked and people are afraid. This is not the Chicago I knew and loved in the 60's and 70's. It has changed for the worse.

In the late 70's, Marquette Park was verdant green. It was beautiful. On my runs, I watched people playing ball, taking walks, and young lovers kissing while sitting on the park benches together. Today I would be taking a big risk walking or running through that park. "Gang Bangers" rule the park now, and at sunset it is closed. When we were teenagers, we parked there and gazed at the moon. We listened to romantic songs on the radio and kissed our girlfriends in our junk cars. People barbequed various delicacies in the park. The smells of their food entered my nostrils and made me quicken my pace. I longed to get back home to Mom's house to enjoy the meal she had ready for me. I loved my run at night. I did four loops around the park. Four loops measured out to be just around ten miles. Every inch of the park brought back childhood memories. On hot summer nights, I drank from the park's water fountains. The fountains were interspersed through the park along the asphalt paths and the cold Lake Michigan water was fresh and pure.

I never needed to carry a squeeze bottle or Gatorade. I drank a quart of that stuff when I got back home. Back in the old days, we runners didn't listen to any music when we ran. We didn't have the luxury of an Ipod. Somehow, listening to music detracted from the total running experience for me. I liked to hear the birds, the sound of wind in the big trees, and my rhythmic breathing. I liked the sounds of my foot strikes on the pavement. This was my time to meditate. I released all the garbage in my mind. This running time was mine to own. All extraneous matters became less important to me. The "running mind" I possessed was an ethereal blessing.

A few blocks before I returned to Mom's house, I started cooling down. I jogged slowly and stretched before I entered her front door. I accomplished my day's goals. I worked twelve hours and ran ten miles. It was wonderful to accomplish so much in a day. Mom put my dinner in front of me, and we sat at the kitchen table with the little twelve-inch and black-and-white television set.

We talked about old times and about how our days went. She made me liver and onions sometimes, per my request. I guess the poor-folks food that I was raised on never gets out of my system.

Mom was my angel now. We needed each other. She was lonely without Dad, and I was lonely without Nancy. What a perfect pair we were now! No one can love you more than your Mom.

A PARALYZING EVENT

I was living at Mom's house for about five days while happily preparing for a running event. On Saturday at Caldwell Woods, I was going to participate in a race with some top-notch distance runners from all over the Chicago-Land area. The Windy-City-Striders Running Club sponsored the event. If my memory serves me properly, I think that the "Striders" were affiliated with the Leaning Tower YMCA, in Niles, Illinois. This race was a big event. Since it was a "15-miler", I thought it would be a good tune-up race for the Milwaukee Marathon.

I had the pre-race jitters after coming home from work on Friday. I decided to go to Bruno's Tap and kick back with a glass of orange juice. Maybe I would shoot a few games of pool and meet a decent looking girl. The chances of that were slim in this scum bucket bar, but hey! A guy never knows when luck is going to come his way! As it turned out, Bruno's bar was a horrible idea. The cigarette smoke was suffocating, and the affronts I endured from the regulars who laughed at me and my orange juice precipitated my early exit for home and a good night's sleep.

Driving home to Mom's, I smiled as I pondered what I had accomplished in the past year. My body was racing fit at 164 lbs. I had some lean, solid muscle on my 5'10" frame. The running magazines that I was buying all the time informed me that when my friends and relatives took me to the side and inquired about my health, I would be in good running shape. A lot of people came up to me and asked me if I had cancer or some other dreadful disease. When this happened to me time after time, I was totally shocked and amused! The running magazines were right! A runner's thin body and hollow cheeks can bring back memories of Holocaust survivors to the general population. My body fat composition was really low and people were freaking out about the way I looked. All their doom-and-gloom provided me with hours of amusement!

Mom was happy to see me when I arrived home early from the bar that Friday evening. She informed me that Judy was taking her shopping in the morning. Since Dad died, my sister always took Mom out on Saturday. This excursion was Mom's favorite time of the week. I told her I was setting my clock for 5:00 a.m. and would try and be quiet when I tiptoed out the door for my race in the morning. I kissed and hugged her goodnight and she smiled at me and said, "Good luck,

Dickie! You go get 'em tomorrow!" I went to my room for a good night's sleep, and as I drifted off, I visualized victory.

It was cold and blustery on race day. The wind blew the snow and sleet sideways. At the starting line, needles of ice and freezing rain attacked my face. My beard was freezing up and icicles were forming. "It's a great day for racing," I thought! I loved the harsh elements. This separates the men from the boys! Two hundred of the finest runners in Chicago were out there, flapping their arms like strange birds to stay warm. We stomped our feet and blew into our cotton gloves to keep our fingers from going numb. Everyone was feeling the adrenaline rush and pre-race jitters. We were "skitterish" racehorses ready to explode out of the starting gates.

The gun went off and we all were off like lightning! I went out fast to warm up my frozen body. I sucked in wind and pushed my lungs to their limit. My lungs heaved in the oxygen and I started rationalizing that a "jack-rabbit" strategy might be a fatal mistake for me in the later miles of this race. I didn't want to "die" at the 13-mile mark and finish with a hobble. I was running faster than any of my fastest training runs. I just felt really good on this day, so I decided to go for it. I was running 6-minute miles, which was way over my head in regard to my ability. At mile 12, I sighted the two lead runners. The pack was way behind me now. This became a race of three men. I was gaining on them, but couldn't reel them in. I finished this race with a 3rd place ribbon. I still have it in an old shoebox in my closet.

I was amazed at my own performance. This was a proud moment for me, to place so well in a race with a distinguished field of athletes. My fellow runners from the Riess Park Striders were hugging and congratulating me. People driving by in the slush and freezing rain must have thought we had lost our minds! A bunch of grown men in what looked like underwear, wearing knit caps, hugging and high-fiving, must have fired the car drivers' imaginations! We were cheering the "stragglers" to the finish line (every one of them a winner) to finish the 15-mile challenge! We drank beer and ate sweet rolls at ten-in-the-morning! "It doesn't get any better than this," I thought!

I was frozen stiff. When I got into my jeep, I turned the heater on full blast, and it stayed that way all the way home. Hypothermia isn't fun! I had my rock-and-roll tunes on full blast and sang them victoriously at the top of my lungs. I couldn't wait to show my 3rd place ribbon to Mom and Judy! I wanted to impress them with tales of my pain, strategies, and ultimate victory!

With a big smile on my face, I parked the Jeep in front of the house. I bounded up the stairs of the front porch and rushed into the living room. I heard activity in the back of the house, so I headed back to the kitchen. Sitting there were my mom and Mrs. Danber, our next-door neighbor. Their faces were somber. I knew something was dreadfully wrong. I looked incredulously at their pale "death masks". Mrs. Danber was the first to speak. She said, "Dickie, you'd better sit down." My stomach felt sick and I felt goose bumps come up all over my skin.

I never saw my mom look like this before, even after my father had passed away. Her eyes were red and wet. Her face was pale and lifeless. She said to me, "Oh, Dickie, Judy is dead!"

JUDY'S DEATH

At first, I denied the fact of my dear sister's death with every fiber of my being. I imagine my immediate reaction of denial is typically human. I suppose the feeling is some type of psychological defense mechanism. We all have this in our DNA, to protect us from despair or madness. All I could do on this horrible Saturday afternoon was cradle my mom in my arms and sob. I put a whiskey bottle out on the kitchen table. I prompted Mom to have a little bit of Sherry. We both had our hearts broken by this horrific cruelty. We sat together and tried to numb our pain.

My brother got the call from Lou, my sister's husband. Sometime after midnight while we were all sleeping, Judy pulled the Buick Convertible into her garage. She pressed the automatic garage door opener, closing the door. This simple pressing of a button sealed her fate.

Wedged between the bumper of her car and the garage door, Lou found Judy the next morning. The engine of the car was still running. Maybe she tried to get out in a last desperate moment. Maybe she didn't want to get out, but changed her mind all too late. I can't imagine Lou's horror, finding Judy—the mother of his children, his lover, and his wife—sardonically posed in the final act of her life.

Being a simple man of few words and being overwhelmed by his gruesome discovery, Lou called my brother Jim. The ever-dependable Jim always seemed to get the hard tasks in our family. Jim had to leave the flower shop to break the news to my Mother. I can't imagine what must have been going through his mind to make it easier on her. He had a very difficult task. Somehow, Jim gathered the strength and the words. Recently, Jim told me that this was the hardest thing he ever had to do in his life.

Mom reacted in utter disbelief. She said, "Oh, no, you're lying! Judy and I are going shopping today." Jim stayed for a while and called Mrs. Danber, our next-door neighbor, to stay with her until I got home from my race. Jim had to get back to run the flower shop. Lou had the job of calling the police, taking care of the children, and making the funeral arrangements.

The death was entered on the certificate as being accidental. Death is death, but the losses that bother all of mankind are the ones that are unnecessary. This horror had to be preventable! I just couldn't accept the fact that my family was being inflicted with such pain. The deaths that bother me the most are the ones that happen to young people. Judy was only 38-years-old. I was angry.

I felt cheated. I miss her so much, even today. She and I were supposed to grow old together. She had too much to drink. I wanted to believe that all of this was some sort of freak accident exacerbated by alcohol. The idea of suicide keeps coming into my mind. I ran all the scenarios in my head over and over again for many years. It never ends. It only slows down over the years. I try and digest all the particulars, just like a detective, and always come up empty. The answers can never be trusted. This senseless re-run in my head, over and over again just makes me more insane. I play the movie less these days—after all it has been thirty years. The pain in my heart has healed over, leaving scar tissue. I learned how to live with a damaged heart.

SATURDAY EVENING

That evening, I took Mom to Queen of the Universe Catholic Church for Confession, Mass, and Holy Communion. I held her fragile hand through the whole service. I stole sidelong glances at my mom and watched her agony. I wanted to protect her from any more harm, real or imagined. I took her to a nice restaurant for a meal, but she didn't eat much. I brought her home. She didn't say too much on the way home. Some of our dear neighbor ladies came over to the house to be with her. I'm kind of fuzzy in my mind now as to who they were. I was grateful that evening for their presence. I pulled out some bottles of whiskey and sherry to calm our nerves. I offered drinks, sandwiches, and cookies to all who were in our house comforting Mom. I put on a pot of strong coffee. I went to the local grocery store to buy some deli items for the occasion.

I felt this pervasive numbness inside of myself. I just went through all the motions because they had to be done by someone. I had no runner's high anymore. I just felt weary. I hadn't had an alcoholic drink for six months, but today was different. I thought I would celebrate my race with a couple of beers and that would be it for me. I was wrong. I was drinking alcoholically today to kill my pain, but I wasn't getting drunk. At around 8:00 p.m., Mom said, "Dickie, I'm OK. You're a young man and you should go out and forget this thing tonight. You're a good son and you've done all you can do for me. I have the neighbors here with me to keep me company."

I'm glad Mom said this, because I couldn't take being there anymore. I felt as if I was going to explode at any minute. I got in my car and pulled into Marquette Park and started sobbing uncontrollably. I cried for a long time. The cry I had made me feel much better. I blew my nose, dried my eyes, and regained my composure. I drove to a dark tavern on 71st Street and proceeded to get good and drunk.

THE FUNERAL

Judy's wake was held at the Thomas-Kuenstler Funeral Home, on 95th and Central Avenue in Oak Lawn, Illinois. Her corpse didn't look right to me. I think the effects of the carbon monoxide poisoning couldn't be hidden by any amount of makeup the morticians put on her cold, dead body. Her skin had a purplish, blotchy cast to it. Her face and hands were bloated and swollen. It was terrible. I wished Lou had made the decision for a closed-coffin funeral. I thought of my poor nieces and nephew viewing this monstrosity who used to be their beautiful mother. It just didn't seem fair.

I mean no disrespect to Lou or my nieces and nephew by writing this way. Nor am I trying to be ghoulish in my style. These are just observations that are indelibly marked in my mind. I remember all of this with crystal clarity. I wish I remembered all the good times with the same amount of clarity. Such is life. At least writing about my last good-byes to her provides me some sort of cathartic release in my old age.

People never get over the pain of losing someone dear to them. In this case, the real agony is seeing the emotional turmoil the children have to endure, and the husband who is left to deal with the terrible reality. All had to cope with life without Mom. Lou had to cope with life without his wife and do the best to raise three young children. I tried to spend a lot of time with their family to accommodate them for their loss. I could never fill the void, but wanted to be available for them. All of this is brutally sad.

Judy was interred at St. Mary's Cemetery, in Evergreen Park, Illinois. She rests near my dad. I never visit gravesites. I think maybe I took Mom there a few times, but never, ever would go by myself. The dead are always in my prayers. I think that is enough. I like to remember all the good things they left me. This is how I honor their memories. Judy's best friend, Rosemary, hosted the funeral brunch on Chicago's South Side in the basement of her humble home. The brunch was the typical affair with a lot of good food, too much liquor, and plenty of strong coffee. I poured the whiskey freely to dull my senses. Drinking and working and running ten-miles-a-day became my "prescription" for the soul sickness that afflicted me. All types of women—and sex with them—were added to the mix. None of it did me any good, except for the working and running. This helped me minimally.

In one year, I had lost my father to a stroke and my sister to a horrible "accident". All of this happened while I suffered separation anxiety from not being with my dear Nancy. I constantly worried about the upcoming divorce proceedings. It was not the best of times.

DAD'S DEMISE AND MOM'S LOVING CARE

He could have been so much more. I guess that is a fitting epitaph for my father. Grandpa sat Dad in an office chair at the Armour Company. Dad responded to this marvelous opportunity by "blowing it". This was Dad's chance for an Executive position with all the perks that go along with the job. Dad chose a life of bartending, drunkenness, and bad behavior. Dad quit the Armour job after a few months.

Dad never had two nickels to rub together after his bad choice of careers. If he got lucky at the racetrack or at some poker game in the back room of a seedy tavern, he headed out to Cicero, Illinois, for a three-day bender. He came home stinking of whisky. I always saw him after these interludes. He usually was dirty, tired, and broke.

At Christmas, Dad always started celebrating early. Christmas was an ominous time for me, because I remember my mother's tears. Dad sometimes drank himself into a diabetic coma, so Christmas meant visiting him in the hospital. Mom salvaged the whole sordid affair with her indominitable smile, an unsinkable faith in God, Christmas decorations, good food, and her indefatigable spirit. She was quite a gal, my mom.

In his later years, my father's body finally shut down on him, due to his excesses. At the age of 62, his feet were badly ulcerated from his Diabetes. He continued to smoke three packages of Chesterfield cigarettes every day. He slowed down on the drinking, because I guess it became too painful. Once in a while, the Devil got a hold on him and he went out for a night of debauchery. Now, in his old age, these instances were few and far between. A man who is an alcoholic binge drinker gets to the point where finally the cravings for alcohol cannot overcome the pain that comes from physical debilitation.

Dad worked a day shift at the restaurant-cocktail lounge. When he came home from tending bar, Mom prepared him a footbath of Epsom salts. I still remember the old beige aluminum pan. Dad's pitiful feet took their much-needed rest in warm water. After the soak, my mom tenderly dried Dad's ravaged feet. She applied a special antibiotic salve to the open wounds and put Father's soft, white socks on for him.

Mom then dumped the water, cleaned the pan, and served my father his dinner and coffee on a TV tray in the living room where he watched mindless shows and chain-smoked his cigarettes. He was still the king of the house, barking orders, and expecting immediate results. I never said a word. I watched this perversity for years. In the later years, Mom ate her dinner alone in the kitchen, like some kind of servant. She carried all of Dad's dishes to the sink and hand washed and dried them with a clean towel. She sang happy songs while she performed every single task.

Mom attended to all these duties, even after working a full eight-hour-day as a secretary at the Sommer and Maca Glass Company, in Cicero, Illinois. Mom was a very bright woman with impeccable diction, spelling skills, and perfect penmanship. She excelled in all her secretarial skills. She learned all of these things in business school as a very young woman. Mom walked four blocks to the bus stop to go to work. She lugged shopping bags home at night. Her workday never ended. She did all of these things, day in, day out, rain or shine. She trudged through the snow in her old-lady boots while enduring the freezing cold. Unflinchingly, she did all these things at sixty-six-years-of-age. Mom was a heroine. She did it all with a smile and no regrets. She worked at the Glass Company for over twenty years and would have worked longer, but they asked her to retire. I guess she wasn't as pretty in a skirt anymore. A younger, prettier, dumber girl took her job. Mom never complained about this. Mom would have worked well into her 80's at the company. This is the kind of woman I had for a mother. She cooked and cleaned for us all, and her weekends were spent vacuuming the carpets, washing windows, and scrubbing sinks and tubs. She did laundry and went shopping for groceries. The list goes on and on.

My mom was a dynamo. She started her own bank account many years ago. She managed to put aside some money every week from her meager paychecks. Every Sunday morning she walked a mile to attend Mass. After Mass, she walked a few blocks further, and returned home with a bag in each hand filled with groceries for Dad. She stopped every so often to rest. Sometimes a kind neighbor picked her up and brought her home. Mom made the Church and grocery trip well into her 80's. She smiled at everyone she met on the street.

Ultimately, my father lost his gangrenous leg. The next year, the other leg had to be amputated. I credit my Dad for being courageous through the whole ordeal. He never complained, and when he came home from the surgeries, started treating Mom well. He started thanking her for her attention and loving care. My mother ate it all up! Dad always had a smile for her when she came home from work. He tried to do the household chores for her, and kept things clean so she didn't have to work so hard. Towards the end of his life, I think he and Mom were really happy together. Old age is sometimes a blessing.

Finally, Dad was diagnosed with colon cancer. Now his drinking completely came to a halt. Dad gave up the cigarettes for a few months, but finally surrendered to the addiction once again by saying, "What the hell, I have to have something to enjoy! I like to have a smoke with my coffee." So for Dad, it was smokes and coffee until Mom came home from work one night. She found him slumped over next to the little black-and-white TV on the kitchen table. His head was on the table and a cigarette was still burning in the ashtray. Dad had suffered a cerebral hemorrhage. He was still breathing. The cigarette was his final statement. It sat like a handgun, next to his mindless body. Mom called for the ambulance and our family gathered at Christ Community Hospital in Oak Lawn, Illinois, after we received the bad news. The plug was pulled the next day. He was 67-years-old.

LIFE AFTER JUDY

What can I say? I just had to pick up the pieces, carry on with my life, and hope for the best. I worked twelve-hours-a-day, and ran ten miles every night. That left little time for drinking myself to death. It was tough to come home at night and see my mother so heartbroken. I can't imagine the pain of losing a child. My mom endured a lot of pain in her life. How could I respond to her needs? I tried to make her feel better, but felt inadequate and inept in this regard.

The Marathon date was approaching quickly. I was hill training and doing speed work on the cinder track in Marquette Park. I did my long runs from 18 to 21 miles every Sunday. The books on Marathon running suggested six long distance runs, measuring from 18 to 20 miles before the race. I used my anger and sadness to push myself harder every day. I quit working Saturdays, so I could have more training time for the big race. I wasn't running anymore on Friday evenings. Instead, I went nightclubbing, looking for girls. I was drinking too much, and generally tearing it up pretty good.

On Saturday mornings, I ran my distance runs with some God-awful hangovers. A sure cure for a hangover is to run a sub-seventy-minute ten-mile distance. After doing this, I hit the shower and then filled my belly with some greasy breakfast. I felt like a champ! After drinking all night on Saturday nights, I managed to do my 20-mile runs on Sundays, but they were taking an awful toll on my body. The booze and exhaustion from work were breaking me down.

I used to go to a late night bar on Saturday nights to pick up older women. The name of the joint was "The Scotch and Soda". It was on 95th Street near Harlem Avenue, in Oak Lawn, Illinois. The place had a 5-o'clock license. The women were in this dark lounge, looking for young guys. It was easy "pickins". It usually took me an hour or so to get them liquored up and horny. I then took them in and out of some cheap motel. I had no morals anymore. Nothing mattered to me anymore. I wasn't the same guy I was after the divorce and after Judy's death.

After my long run on Sunday morning, I sat in the neighborhood tavern with the old crew once again. I usually drank beer or wine till 5-in-the-afternoon. I cut myself off at this point; otherwise I would be useless at work on Monday morning. My mom knew I was going downhill. If I didn't cut myself off, I would continue to drink sometimes until midnight. I was unfair to my mom, leaving her alone at home for hours on end.

I really got hammered one night in Chicago Ridge, Illinois. My buddy was the doorman and bouncer in this bar. I'd known him since we were 6-years-old. He was my neighbor from the old neighborhood. We boxed and played baseball together for years. He was a tough Italian guy. He introduced me to all the "sluts" in the bar. He made sure his old pal had free drinks and he introduced me to various women until closing time. I weaved down Cicero Avenue on the way home. I fell asleep at the wheel and ended up knocking over one of those brand-new halogen street lamps in Oak Lawn, Illinois. Luckily, the lamp landed on the parkway and not on another car. I came to my senses and saw the Mars lights on the cop car behind me. I was in my beater car, (this was before I purchased the new Jeep). My 1975 Mustang "four banger" was totaled-out. Luckily, I didn't have a scratch. I had the luck of "fools and drunks", eh? I spent the night in the lockup of the Oak Lawn Police Station. The policemen who wrote me up were kind to me. I drank coffee with them and told them about how my life was falling apart. They started liking me and we shared a few laughs. I guess they were bored in the wee hours of their shift. They could have written me up for a DUI, but I got lucky and only got a citation for ruining the streetlight. They let me sleep it off for a few hours on a cot. They even gave me a blanket and a pillow for the cot in my cell. I called Viet Nam Bill to come and pick me up. We went to his Uncle Wally's Auto Rebuilding Shop and I had him tow my demolished Mustang into the junkyard.

Wally fixed me up with a "beater"—an old, red Ford Maverick. It had a million miles on it, bald tires, but only cost me a-hundred bucks. You can't be too choosey when you're desperate. A couple of weeks later, I received a bill for towing, and a nice bill from the Village of Oak Lawn for about $800 to replace the street lamp. I really got off easy. It was a lot cheaper than a drunken driving charge.

The Marathon Race in Milwaukee was in a week. I had to drive up there in this "clunker". It had a noisy muffler, a shimmy in the front end, and all kinds of other problems that scared the shit out of me! Anyway, I had transportation for work. It would only be a couple of weeks until I scraped up enough money for a down payment on the new Jeep CJ-7.

The day before the Marathon, I drove the piece of junk up to Milwaukee and booked myself a room at the Howard Johnson's. The motel was only a couple of blocks from the starting line. I received the "special runners discount". They probably jacked up the room price twenty bucks so they could make an extra ten, by providing the runners with the so-called discount. I know I'd do that if I owned the motel! The race was all that mattered to me now. I did a helluva lot of work. I had to stay focused now.

THE MILWAUKEE MAYFAIR MARATHON — 1978

The week preceding a Marathon is brutal for a runner. All the advice I read about the last week before race day demands that I rest and relax. I was wound up so tightly that I was ready to blow a gasket. The week before the race, a runner is forced to cut down his training mileage to a meager couple of miles a day. No more "runner's high", no more escape from fear or anger. It sucked! If I ran at all, it had to be just a mile or two to loosen up, going at an agonizing snails pace. What really drove me insane was that I couldn't drink any alcohol. Alcoholic beverages dehydrate a runner too much in an endurance event. I had to be happy with a couple of beers a night. I was flipping out! These were dark days for sure, but my body had to rest, energize, and heal itself for race day.

Not only is the pre-race anxiety extremely high, but a runner usually gains about 5 lbs., too. I wasn't running extreme mileage anymore, so my body retained water from all the carbohydrates I was eating. My weight gains "blew my mind". Every time I looked in the mirror, I saw Fatty Arbuckle staring back at me. I reassured myself, "Not to worry. This is nothing more than a harmless hallucinogenic phenomenon, common to all anorexic marathon runners."

The experts say that all this pre-race agony is a necessary part of the "process". I had to believe them and dutifully follow all their advice. I suffered all this pain and agony training for this event and worrying about it! I thought, "I'm suffering and I haven't even run the damned race yet!" I really started to doubt my sanity.

I took Friday and Saturday off from my construction job to do this crazy thing. I figured I would lose somewhere around $600 bucks considering the overtime. If this wasn't crazy, I don't know what is! At least my foreman assured me that my job would still be waiting for me when I returned to work on Monday.

On Friday afternoon, I drove the beater car in the right hand lane, at a 50-mph turtle's pace. I experienced much anxiety from people "flying" past me, beeping their horns, and giving me the finger. This is just what I needed before the race to bolster my confidence. I checked into the Howard Johnson's in the City of Wauwatosa, Wisconsin. I opened the door to my room expecting to see an Indian blanket on the bed and a set of bull's horns over the headboard. To my relief, I encountered a conventional, cheap motel room. I went to race headquarters, pre-registered, and received my race number, which was supposed to be safety-pinned to the front of my racing singlet. I supposed, "The real reason for these numbers is for the Paramedics to identify my body." The numbers help the Physician signing my death certificate if I happen to expire during the race. My source of origin, phone numbers of next-of-kin, and other salient information had to be included in the registration forms I signed when I paid my fee for the race. Release forms, in case of tragedy, also have to be signed by the runner. The race promoters had their legal culpability covered!

I knocked around the town—all three blocks of it. I bought a six-pack of beer and went back to the motel restaurant. I ate spaghetti and cheese pizza with the other nervous runners. I never saw so much nervous fidgeting in my life! I felt like I was dining with methamphetamine addicts who were in treatment for their first day of detox. All the runners had dark, sunken eyes furtively looking left and right. They all had hollow cheeks and anorexic bodies! Holy Jesus! I couldn't believe these were healthy people! I knew in my heart-of-hearts that we were all insane.

I thought, "All will be well tomorrow at the sound of the gun." I got back to my room and drank a couple of beers. I lay on the bed and tried to visualize peaceful scenes. I chanted a mantra given to me by some yogic female. I think I met her in some obscure bar on the North Side of Chicago. Short of Voodoo, I did all kinds of things to quell my nervousness and get to sleep. I tossed and turned for a couple of hours until sweet dreams came to me in my cheap motel room.

I informed the front desk the night before to give me an early wake up call. Just in case this didn't work, I brought my trusty mechanical alarm clock. If the front desk forgot about me or if by some strange chance the power in the motel went out, I had all my ducks in a row for making it to the starting line on time!

RACE DAY PREPARATION

Believe it or not, the front desk called me bright-and-early, as promised. I hit the alarm button on my clock so I wouldn't have to hear the aggravating sounds that woke me up for work every morning. Immediately, I turned on the TV to get the weather report. The news was bad. The temperature was expected to hit the mid-90's. It was going to be hot and humid—an armpit of a day. Weather like this is deadly to a long-distance runner. I vowed to drink plenty of fluids before and during my race. I dressed myself and wandered over to the motel dining room for breakfast. I ordered a small bowl of granola and fat-free milk. I ate two bananas for potassium. My body was going to need a lot of electrolytes. I drank three cups of strong coffee with sugar and ordered another one in a to-go cup for my motel room.

It's important for an endurance runner to eliminate everything from his or her bowels before a race. I didn't have the luxury or the time to stop at a portable toilet during the race. A runner never wants to waste any time. Coffee has a dual role: It's a natural laxative, plus it has been shown through scientific study to increase a runner's stamina and performance. I knew all the Runner's World Magazines I purchased would pay off for me in the long run! (No pun intended).

Now it was time for race preparation. To begin, I take a nice hot shower to relax my mind and loosen my muscles. I dry off and apply "gobs" of Vaseline to my inner thighs, where the friction from my running shorts may burn my skin. Twenty-six miles is a long way to run with chafed inner thighs. I've experienced them before in shorter races, and believe me it's not fun! Next, I put on a clean pair of old jockey shorts. Well-worn underwear wont cut off circulation or irritate my skin. New elastic around the waistband or leg bands can be brutal to a runner. New jockey shorts aggravate my skin. Next, I put on my most comfortable pair of running shorts. I don't care what the hell they look like, as long as they're comfortable. This isn't a fashion show!

The most important application is the two band-aids I put on my nipples. Tee shirts wet with perspiration abrade my nipples and make them bleed. I already went through this agony in other distance races and didn't want to tie-dye my tee shirt with my own blood. It's good for a runner to invest in a few pair of expensive, soft running socks with heavy duty cushioning in the heel and toe areas. I lightly Vaseline my feet and then slip my socks on. I make sure to clip my toenails a week before the race. This gives my toes a week to get used to the toe box of my running shoes. Freshly clipped toenails mean bloody feet on race day.

I never wore new running shoes in an endurance race. They are sure to torture me, if I haven't broken them in. My feet and body weight have to make a nice cushion inside of my shoes. Conversely, old shoes can throw my foot plant all out of whack. When heels wear out on old shoes, they cause my muscular-skeletal system to get "jazzed-up", and extreme pain or injury results.

I always break in a new pair of running shoes at least 3 to 4 weeks prior to any important distance race. For a marathon, I safety pin a little bag of raisins and aspirin (no bigger than a tea bag) on one side of my running shorts close to the waistband. I also pin a little bag of Vaseline somewhere on my clothes just in case I get friction burns somewhere. This is a "thinking man's" sport! For hot weather running, I wear a super lightweight, light-colored cotton baseball cap. I make sure it has holes in it for ventilation. The cap keeps me cooled down and protects my head from the hot rays of the sun. I NEVER wear a dark colored cap. Dark colors absorb—rather than reflect—the rays of the sun. Heatstroke becomes a reality for those who make the mistake of wearing dark colors! While I'm running, I saturate my cap with water to keep me cool. I take great care never to splash any water on my feet. Wet feet means blisters, and blisters are "the enemy". I use a high-quality, high-numbered sunscreen on all exposed skin. I make sure my body is tan before I race in the heat. I don't need sunburn. Remember, I'm going to be out there between 3 to 4 hours. This is pain enough without sunburn!

When lacing up my shoes, I make sure they are moderately tight. I jump up and down, jog a bit, and then re-tie them. I don't want my feet "swimming" in my shoes, but I don't need the laces so tight that they cut off my circulation.

Now I'm ready. I grab a quart of Gatorade and a bottle of water. I head to the starting line. I'm already feeling the adrenaline rush!

THE RACE

I wander to the starting line. It's fifteen minutes before the gun. I get in line to use one of the portable toilets. There are only about 20 of them, but this is an adequate number. The marathon has only 455 participants. Remember, this is way back in 1978. Today, this race probably would have 15,000 participants. It's mind-boggling to me how popular the sport has become! What really disgusts me is how abysmally unprepared a lot of modern-day runners are for the race. Runners in my day were serious athletes and they never disrespected themselves or the race. We did the necessary training and came prepared.

I drank my Gatorade then evacuated my bladder. I carried my plastic bottle of water as an insurance policy against heat stroke. I watched the three-ring-circus of runners doing "wind sprints", wasting needed energy they were going to need to race in the heat. Geez! Don't they know its 90 degrees? It's 8:00 in the morning, and it's already terribly hot and humid. I'm sure we're all going to die out there! A little jogging and stretching is enough for me. Maybe I should say a prayer or two to my personal deity to protect me from harm!

The gun goes off and humanity moves. My game plan is to run a steady seven-minute-per-mile pace. I plan to run by the clock and abandon any foolish ideas of starting out with six-minute miles. I respect this heat too much! Besides that fact, I have never run further than 21 miles.

I reach the 3-mile aid station and my sports watch shows my time at 18:49. I'm running way too fast! I drink three cups of water, walk a bit and wet my baseball cap. I start running again. At every aid station, I'm going to have to drink water and wet my baseball cap. The racecourse is absolutely beautiful. I see many lovely flowers and shade trees, but there are barren stretches that seem to wear my resolve. Here, the brutal sun is beating down on my head. The tough parts of a race test my spirit. At mile ten, I'm looking good with a time of 68:00. I'm slightly ahead of my pace, and running "within" myself. I'm feeling good. I've always been a good hot-weather runner. I think working in the heat all day in my trade acclimates me and gives me an advantage over people who work indoors. Plus, running ten miles at night after working in the heat all day toughens my physical reserves and teaches my mind to endure pain.

I reach mile 15 and I'm in "the zone". This is the place where a runner feels invincible. I'm feeling way too good for the conditions. This really scares the hell out of me! My good vibes might just be a false sense of security. I'm hoping I remain this "juiced-up". Sometimes, fatigue and pain lies waiting for me right around the corner. I remind myself again to stay with my race plan.

Amazingly, at mile 18, I'm passing all kinds of people. They either went out too fast or fell to heat exhaustion. Some just didn't put in the necessary training. I see them lying under shade trees. Their faces are flushed or pale. Some are on all fours. Some are throwing up. Others are flat on their backs, being tended to by medical personnel.

At mile 19, an overly excited teen-aged girl tries to pour water on my head. She has a glass bottle and conks me on my crown. "My God! I hope I'm not bleeding!" I drink water, pull off my cap, and ask some dude if my head looks all right. He gives me the go-ahead, so I keep on running. "Thanks," I say as I look for my attacker. She has run away in embarrassment. Her moronic teenage friends chortle and laugh at my misfortune and her heinous crime. This was just the kind of help I need at mile 19! I was pissed off. If I only had a gun!

I was waiting to hit the famous "wall", but it wasn't happening. I started to wonder if it even existed or if it was just some type of folklore meant to scare novice runners. I was passing runners left and right. Feeling an adrenaline rush, I picked up my pace. The WALL hit me with full force at mile 24. My quadriceps muscles tightened up, as did my calf muscles. The small of my back was in extreme pain. I needed glycogen to negate the build up of lactic acid in my muscles, so I ate my raisins and took my aspirin with a few cups of water. I took time to walk and stretch a bit, but only for a minute or two. "Ah, so this is the 'wall'," I thought. It was just like they said. I was in agony. This is the circumstance where I had to learn to run on "mind" alone. A runner learns to focus and negate the pain. I willed my body to finish this marathon. I tried to maintain some semblance of what used to be my form. I ran mile 24 in 8 minutes. "Not too bad," I thought. I was pleased. I had put some minutes "in the bank" earlier in the race. Mile 25 was an 8:15 minute mile. Only a little more than a mile to go, and I knew deep within me that I was going to make it! The crowds were lined up deep on either side of the street now and they were going crazy! I cannot describe how good this feels with them cheering you on, clapping and screaming.

The last mile is joyous. I forget about my pain. I pick up my pace to finish strong. I was finally going to be a "marathoner". I thought, "No matter what has happened to me in my life or what was to come in the future, I'm going to own this moment as mine for the rest of my life." I could see the time clock now at the finish line.

I was crying tears of joy. Mentally, I was having some sort of "spiritual" experience. I can't describe it to you. Only other people who have done this thing can comprehend the joy and the pain.

I crossed the finish line, my arms raised in victory. I felt like the first marathoner, Philipedes. He was the ancient Greek who ran the first Marathon. He died bringing news of the war. We celebrate his feat and honor the human spirit!

My race time was 3 hours, 28 minutes, and 35 seconds. I did this in 95-degree heat with high humidity. I finished 135th out of a field of 455 runners. I thought it was a respectable time. I had just joined an elite fraternity. I was a Marathoner.

THE TEQUILA MOCKINGBIRD

The marathon was a success! I rambled back to Chicago in the beater car. I arrived at Bruno's bar, all smiles, ready to drink huge amounts of beer. Marathon training was officially over now. Drinking and celebrating my success were going to take over my life for a while. Slowly, I was recovering from the sadness of losing my sister. I felt my life was going to get better...and it did!

My inept divorce attorney finally informed me that the divorce papers were ready for my signature. Better yet, the realtor whom Nancy and I had hired finally sold our old house in New Lenox. The divorce papers, by the way, made me out to be an abusive and twisted individual. I couldn't believe what I was signing! I know how an innocent victim accused of a heinous crime must feel after days of interrogation. He finally signs the papers indicting him, to end the pain, whether the charges are real or just fabrications made up by the long arm of the law. No matter, I signed the damn legal papers to get my settlement check.

I was ecstatic! Now, I could purchase the CJ-7 Jeep with the big V8 and four-wheel drive. This baby came with a detachable fiberglass top, air-conditioning, 8-track and stereo radio, a 400-cubic-inch engine, and an in-cab device to change over to four-wheel drive. It had huge off-road tires, and a three-speed manual transmission with a heavy-duty clutch. I imagine, you must have guessed by now, that I like my cars!

My brother knew a couple of guys with this Jeep dealership on 76th and Western Avenue, so I got a good deal on the vehicle. I paid cash for it and couldn't wait to pull up on the construction job. The guys were going to be green with envy! This was one, bad-boy car! Cruising in my new Jeep a week later, I spotted a new nightclub near the Chicago Lawn Police Station on 63rd and St. Louis Avenue. The name of the bar was Tequila Mockingbird. "A cute play on words," I thought. I had to see what this place was all about, so I pulled over and parked my Jeep in a safe place. I pulled open the big door and walked into the bar.

The nightclub had 2 levels. Upstairs was this huge disco. Multicolored lights glowed underneath the thick Plexiglas dance floor. Above me was one of those stylish revolving disco balls with little mirrors all over the sphere. The sound system was state-of-the-art. I was hearing Donna Summer, Gloria Gaynor, The Village People, and Wild Cherry— all the latest disco music that was transversing the country like "wild fire". The bar had strobe lights, fog machines, and a colossal DJ booth. I just fell in love with this lounge! The house was packed with beautiful, young women! I knew right away, I was going to trade in my denim jeans and cowboy boots for platform shoes. I was going to be wearing silk shirts open to the waist, and gold chains! A man does what he has to do, to meet those little ladies! I decided that this glorious place was going to be my new hangout.

I realized that if I wanted to meet these disco-girls, I was going to have to forget about Elvis Presley and the Rolling Stones. I forced myself to learn the new dances and practiced for hours in front of a mirror. With a lot of effort, I ended up looking just like a blonde-and-bearded John Travolta appearing in my own version of Saturday Night Fever.

On the lower level of this big club was a blues bar. I loved the music downstairs, but the action definitely was upstairs in this establishment. The guy who owned this place covered all the angles. He devised two separate venues to pack them in.

About two weeks after first walking into this joint, I'm sitting at the bar. I'm cleaned up from work and ready to party because it's Friday night. One of the three bartenders gets into a huge argument with the owner. The owner is this ruddy-faced Irishman who is yelling at the bartender in his native brogue. I feel sorry for the owner. He looks like a hard-working man with big hands and a red face just like mine! Anyway, his "whiney" bartender walks off the job. The owner is just livid, screaming at the other bartenders, "How the hell are we going to keep up with the crowds tonight?!"

I see opportunity knocking on my door, so I grab his arm and say to him, "I'm a professional bartender. I can work for you tonight!" Without a second thought the owner looks at me and says, "Jump back there, Laddie, and get to work! You're hired!" I had tended bar in the past, but mostly in shot-and-beer joints. I had no clue how to make most mixed drinks, especially the ones that the fancy ladies were ordering for themselves. I was quick on the uptake and learned quickly that night with the help of the other two bartenders. These fellows really looked slick and knew their trade. They were nice guys, but they knew I was a phony. They knew I wasn't a real bartender. All was good for me however, because they appreciated the extra hands, especially when it was time to replace the empty kegs with full ones. The other two bartenders didn't want to muscle full kegs and get beer all over their fancy clothes.

One of the bartenders was a young fellow, about 22-years-old. His name was John. He was a ladies man for sure! The women flocked around him and he knew how to play them! I liked this young guy immediately. He had a great smile and personality. The other fellow was more businesslike. He was a burly sort-of-man in his 30's. His name was Carlos. He was a Mexican with an Afro-style hairdo and full beard. The guy looked like he could take care of himself. He was helpful, instructing me how to make specialty drinks, and explaining where things were around the bar. He knew right away that I was a ham-and-egger behind the bar. He'd definitely been around the block a few times! After sizing up Carlos, I knew I was going to lose this new job.

At the end of the night, O'Reilly, the owner, asked Carlos how I did. Carlos saved my ass by saying, "He worked hard, John, but he doesn't know the drinks." O'Reilly says, "That's alright, Carlos, you can break him in." Carlos scowled and walked away. O'Reilly looked at me and asked in his Irish brogue, "Can you work Friday and Saturday nights?" Impulsively, I said, "Sure, Mr. O'Reilly. No problem." He said, "Call me John, Lad!" He smiled at me and pressed a couple of 20-dollar bills in my hand. He looked me up and down and said, "You work construction." I said to him, "How do you know that, sir?" O'Reilly said, "I can tell, because you have hands like a man, not girlie hands." We both laughed and he told me about all the construction work he did back in Ireland. This man built homes and bought real estate. He was old-school and we liked each other right away. He still built homes; the bar was just a tax write off or something of that nature for John. He came up the hard way, just like me, and trusted a workingman. I knew I had it made.

Not only did I get the forty bucks that O'Reilly shoved in my hand, but about thirty-five in tips, after a three-way split. This was a good night for me. I made seventy-five bucks and drank free drinks behind the bar. I also managed to get a couple of phone numbers from a few comely young ladies. I figured that my chances of scoring with women could be exponentially elevated by working this new job. The women had to come to me for their drinks, and I was young, tan, and in shape. I also had a good Union job, and a brand new Jeep. Life was looking good!

ONE-NIGHT STANDS

I fell right into the groove of the disco scene. I thought the dancing and the music were quite romantic and beautiful. In my mind, the whole scene was reminiscent of those wonderful Fred Astaire and Ginger Rogers days. I remember my mom and dad telling me about the Willowbrook Ballroom and the Trianon in Chicago. In their vernacular, they spoke about dressing to the "9's" and dancing the night away. My parents certainly enjoyed their memories. From what I saw of noir (black and white) movies, I loved the elegance possessed by the women and men of that era. They had an aesthetic style way back in the 30's and 40's. No blue jeans with holes in the knees for my mom and dad's generation!

I gave up Bruno's bar, my bill cap, flannel shirts, and jeans. I looked slick now. I wore my Grandpa's diamond pinky ring. It was a full carat with little diamonds set elegantly next to the big stone. The ring was 18-carat gold. Everything surrounding the disco scene was glitzy and glamorous. I bought shiny shoes and fitted silk shirts. I applied deodorant under my arms and splashed on cologne. I never had to do this in Bruno's! I wore tight, flared polyester slacks. I wanted to be a "shark" in the pool of this little subculture.

One evening at the club, a group of pretty girls shared a table, and raised their glasses to a special girl. Some type of celebration was going on. I was making eye contact all evening with this "special girl". She was beyond lovely. I asked her to dance with me and she agreed, smiling at me while looking into my eyes. She moved her body provocatively. She had beautiful, soft brown hair that went down to the middle of her back. She had large brown eyes. She wore silver stars in her pierced ears. Her figure was absolutely astounding! She was Aphrodite! I thought she was worth more than a few bucks. Her clothes were high fashion and her nails and makeup were done with impeccable style. I mean to tell you, everything about this girl was top shelf! She wore clothes and jewelry that were tasteful, sexy and expensive.

This lovely woman stared deeply into my eyes. We were locked into each other. I instinctively knew, that she was all about being romanced this night. I felt chemistry, a wonderful eroticism between us. It was electric for both of us. I took the night off because I had to have this girl! Both bartenders said if they were getting this kind of play, they would do the same! I took her to a beautiful cocktail lounge, which actually was a revolving room that overlooked the city of Chicago and its skyline. She was an educated woman and a marvelous conversationalist with a wonderful sense of humor. I couldn't believe my good luck! We had a few drinks and she asked me if I wanted to drive her home. She guided me to an expensive town home in Lincoln Park. She lived in one of those "ultra-hip" neighborhoods. Little shops, bakeries, flower shops, and pubs were tastefully scattered throughout her neighborhood.

Her living space was large. It was minimally decorated with lovely, expensive leather furniture, and tasteful original artwork on the walls. She had romantic lighting, a nice bar, and a modern stereo system. She asked me what I wanted to drink, and put on some music for our mood. She moved with elegance and she seductively started unbuttoning her blouse.

She turned the dimmer switch to low. She smiled and pressed her body next to mine. She undid the buttons on my silk shirt. She undressed herself as she was undressing me. It was erotic and beautiful. We made love all night long and into the early morning hours.

We went to a little café for breakfast. It was a wonderful little place with a bountiful menu. We ate and smiled at one another. At the end of the meal, she informed me she wouldn't be seeing me anymore. The interlude, enjoyed by us both, was the high point of her bachelorette party. Wow! My jaw about dropped to the floor! The way my mind works, I figured she got the low-down on her fiancé's bachelor party. He might have been a bad, bad boy! She probably figured, "What's good for the goose is certainly good for the gander."

I was amused but also very disappointed. I gazed into those beautiful eyes and said, "Thank you, Darling. I'm certainly glad you picked me to be your party boy." I quickly said, "If you happen to change your mind about your wedding, here's my phone number." What more could I say? She took my phone number and smiled. I'm sure it ended up in her art-deco garbage can. She kissed me on the cheek and smiled a devilish grin. Out the door she went, my eyes following her shapely derrière.

I smiled all the way back home. The next day, I called my brother at the flower shop and had him send her a dozen long-stemmed roses. I don't remember what I wrote on the card. I would bet that she wore a gorgeous white wedding gown, complete with a beautiful veil. Her husband kept his dirty little secret and she kept hers. People are capable of the most Machiavellian behaviors.

On another occasion, the disco threw a magnificent costume party. An exotic-looking Oriental girl sat at my bar. She had lovely dark eyes, and beautiful red lips. She looked like a China Doll. She wore a nun's habit and a black frock, complete with a long knotted cord that cinched her little waist. I noticed high-heeled stiletto boots under the costume. She had lovely, long red fingernails. I was intrigued. A large silver crucifix rested on her ample breasts. She seductively smiled at me as I walked back-and-forth behind the bar. I thought, "The nuns at Queen of the Universe Grammar School never looked this good!" The religious implications turned me on and made this woman even more desirable.

Her sexy, mascara-laden eyes followed me as I poured drinks. She made sure I saw her sucking the juice out of the maraschino cherries that adorned her drinks. Being an All-American male, I made sure she had plenty of those cherries! She was making me really horny! She sat on that bar stool until closing time, denying all offers from a multitude of gentlemen asking her to dance. She never said a word to me all night long. She just ordered her drinks until the bright bar lights came on signifying closing time.

She asked me if I would give her a ride back to her home, somewhere in Chinatown near Archer Avenue and Canal Streets. She said, "We could have a nightcap together. If not," she continued, "Would you please call me a taxi-cab since I have no other way home?" She knew what my answer was going to be. "YES!! I will drive you home!"

It must have been a strange sight for people on the street. Here was a sexy nun, tongue kissing a guy in a leather jacket while she was being chauffeured in a sporty-looking Jeep on Archer Avenue around three in the morning!

The next day, a wrinkled Chinese woman rudely awakened me. She was beating me with a broom while screaming epitaphs at me in a foreign language. I'm falling, and laughing as I try to pull my pants up. My Chinese lover is also laughing hysterically. She's saying things like, "I'm so sorry, Darling. My grandmother discovered us! Don't forget to call me! My phone number is in your leather jacket!" Grandma finally calmed down now and was just muttering to herself. I'm hoping she doesn't put some type of Chinese curse on me. Grandma leaves in a huff, and slams the bedroom door. I kiss my laughing China Doll goodbye and run down the creaky stairs of the 3rd floor apartment. I gingerly skip down Archer Avenue, slipping and sliding through ice and snow in my platform shoes. I enter the Jeep, laughing my ass off!

I always made sure to call my mom before I stayed out all night on these escapades. I used to tell her that I was staying at a friend's house. She never minded that I called her in the wee-hours of the morning. I'm sure she worried about me anyway. I sure didn't want to cause my mom extra anxiety. She had enough of that with Dad and Judy.

Waitresses came and went at the "Mockingbird". O'Reilly leered at these beauties during the interviewing process, I am sure. He hired some of the most fetching girls that my young eyes had ever seen! Too bad half of them spilled the drinks before they got them to the customers. A lot of them had trouble figuring out the bills and making change. It was a price we men were willing to pay! These buxom beauties brought in the drinking clientele. They were a goldmine to O'Reilly. He certainly was one smart Irishman!

Sometimes, I asked a new girl to breakfast after counting the night's receipts and balancing the books. My hopes were always geared toward a breakfast that lasted well into Sunday evening! I didn't need to work my Local #150 job anymore on Saturdays. Sometimes, a few of the guys from my crew came out to the disco to visit me. They all went away saying, "You have it made, Rich! We had no idea why you were giving up Saturdays and overtime! Now we know!" Yes, I knew I had it made. When I considered the taxman, I made more money tending bar, drinking, and meeting women. I kept running during the week to stay in shape and to keep myself far away from the throes of alcoholism. I never drank during the week, but pounded them down on the weekends. I was the "weekend warrior" with the drinks. My routine was much like the old college days, only better! I had money to burn, and the world was mine for the taking. These were pre-HIV days, so I was quite lascivious in regard to my behavior with women. There were many romantic adventures in my life. We got away with multiple partners without the "deadly consequences". The only chance I might have to face might have been an irate husband putting a loaded gun in my face. The AIDS epidemic was soon to change my partying ways.

WINTER LAYOFF — 1978

We were still moving dirt on the job in Glenview in early December, but the year was winding down. I pulled the floor plate from my machine with my socket wrenches, so that the hot engine air from the big Caterpillar warmed my frozen feet. I wore all my cold weather gear now, and it still wasn't enough.

It was damned cold. I never minded working in the heat all that much. I could always drink plenty of water, find some shade under a tree, and be cooled by a breeze sometimes. Cold just flat-assed hurt you! It was more dangerous than the heat. We wrapped our machines up in canvas, so any heat from the engine wouldn't have a chance to escape. The more "expert" a man became in this task, the warmer he stayed throughout his workday. I put cardboard on the front of my big Cat's radiator, to keep the hot air blowing back toward me. I did anything I thought right, to keep the deadly freeze and cold wind off my body. The dreary days of winter brutalize a man's body and mind. Running a machine while maintaining one's personal comfort, without an enclosed cab, is an exercise in pain and futility. Nowadays, most of the kids in the trade have heaters and air conditioners. They still whine though. We old hands always say, "They should have worked in our day." Each generation voices how tough it was in their day. It's part of the natural aging process, I guess. The severe conditions wore us down. We all sat in our trucks at coffee break and at lunchtime. Our heaters were turned on full blast for the entire break. I drank a lot of hot coffee. I always changed my woolen socks and felt boot liners to keep my feet dry and warm. I discarded the wet socks and massaged my frozen feet. Perspiration freezes a man's feet. I learned to change my socks at noontime from an old-timer who knew how to survive outdoors. Men, who don't keep a complete extra set of winter gear in their trucks have to pay a heavy price. Shit happens, so always be prepared! A man never knows when he is going to get muddy or wet in this business! As I got older and wiser in Local #150, I began to understand what "paying one's dues" was all about. No matter what a man does in the cold, his daily fatigue accumulates and he longs for the winter layoff. In this cold weather, the crew doesn't joke around too much anymore. Most of us are sullen all the time. Nobody wants to be out there, but we do the time for the money. Eventually the freeze comes, and we are all thankful to be laid off. We say our goodbyes in the local bars, and vow to see each other in order to go hunting or snowmobiling during the winter. Generally, this never happens. We put our names on the Out-of-Work List, once again.

I'm still tending bar at the disco every weekend, and meet this lovely girl named "Katie". She is a great dancer. I watch her on the dance floor. She doesn't speak with me very much, but smiles at me all the time. My interest is piqued by her coquettishness. I dance with her once in a while. We smile and laugh together. Soon, after a period of time, her body moves next to mine during the slow songs. We start holding hands, and hug and kiss quite a bit. Then, for some odd reason, she disappears! I can't figure it out! She goes through this odd procedure a number of times before I can confront her and ask her for her phone number. I begin to think of her as my "mystery lady".

All of the sudden, she quits coming into the bar. The phone number she gave me was a phony. I can't stop thinking about her. No one in the bar seems to know who she is or where she came from. She will come back into my life later on. That chapter in my life needs many words, but now isn't the time.

NIGHTMARE ON RUSH STREET

In mid-December, the snow was flying in Chicago. My trusty 4-wheel-drive Jeep was up to the task. I had all kinds of fun speeding down Chicago's main arteries and passing other vehicles. People crept along in their beaters, and I blew by them as if they were standing still. I was not a very considerate young man, but I sure had a lot of fun in the snow! I truly believe my brain didn't develop from an adolescent mindset until I was in my early 50's. My wife agrees with me, although this statement is up to conjecture.

I loved doing "donuts" in parking lots with my Jeep. The summer before this snowy period, my little nephew and I went 4-wheeling through a muddy area next to the Cal-Sag River near Route 83 and 127th Street. We found some great off-road trails. Little Lou and I maneuvered the Jeep through all kinds of ruts and mud. He bounced so high that sometimes that he hit his little "noggin" on the fiberglass top of the Jeep. "Geez, kid," I would say. "I thought you had your damned seat belt connected." He loved every minute of it. When he looked at me with those 13-year-old little-boy eyes, my heart always melted. He smiled at me forgetting about the tragedy of his mother for a few moments. I'd rub his head and say, "We're the kings of the world now, Louie! Just you and me!" He missed his mom. I found out from his dad that Lou slept with her bathrobe so that he could smell her perfume and feel she were near him. It broke my heart to hear about all of this, so I spent more time with the boy and his sisters. It was hard for them to realize that she was gone for good and was never coming back. I taught little Lou how to shoot my twelve-gauge shotgun. It about knocked him over the first time he pulled the trigger.

It left a hell of a bruise, but Lou was a game kid and "sucked up" the pain. I loved this kid. He always washed the Jeep after our four-wheeling adventures. He surprised me with a job well done, every time! I told him I needed a clean ride for the ladies at night. He smiled at me and said, "Don't worry, Uncle Dick. It will be really clean for you." Lou's friends helped him as he washed down the Jeep. Little Louis and his friends were in those pubescent years when girls and cars were becoming the most important things in their lives. Ah, those are such sweet memories!

While all of this was going on, I visited with my nieces, Irene and

Julie. I asked them how they were getting on in school. I hugged them, and let them know I loved them. I told them if they needed anything from me that I was always there for them. I just hope I did enough for those kids. In those days, I sat with my brother-in-law many a Saturday and shared a few beers. There were no more garage parties. When his kids weren't around to see his misery, he cried many tears. Every time I went there, we ended up crying about our loss. It was really tough for big Lou to be without my sister. He was a good man and he raised those kids alone until he re-married. Big Lou married his sister-in-law after his brother passed away and raised her kids, as well as his own. He was a good man in every aspect of his life.

Excuse me, but my mind is drifting again. Let's get back to winter. I figured there wasn't going to be any work, so I would be able to nestle in the warm house with my rocking-chair money from the Unemployment Compensation Office. I'd stay warm and drink in the bars. Once again, Local #150 had other ideas about my vacation time. They called me with a job I couldn't refuse. The dispatch office wanted a man who would run a "bobcat" for a few days. A bobcat is a little rubber-tired end-loader. Contractors use it in tight spots because it is small and versatile. I was asked to spread stone in the basement of a high-rise building being built on Rush Street. The stone is to serve as a base for the concrete pour, which finishes the floor of the underground parking garage. This job was estimated to last a few weeks and I was lucky enough to be working the day shift.

I took the job. This employment opportunity was right up my alley, because a lot of the hip bars on the near North Side of Chicago are on Rush Street. I remember drinking at Butch McGuire's on Division Street many years ago. It probably was the most famous Rush Street bar. Most of the women who drank in these near North Side bars were either professionals or well-to-do types. What's not to like about that? These beauties could provide me with better opportunities for satisfying relationships than the drunken blue-collar chicks at Bruno's tap who sat on their tattered bar stools on the South Side. That fact was a no-brainer for me.

Yes, the big-time bars at the time on Rush were Butch McGuire's, Mother's, Limelight, and maybe Lolly's. I can't recall for sure right now, but I drank in them all at one time or another.

I was going to have a ball! A building trades job like this paid premium money. A man gets double-time after eight hours, and this was an overtime job. I figured I was going to make some big paychecks. I met all the guys on the crew and the general superintendent. All was well because they liked my work. Plus, they were all party animals. Many of these building tradesmen loved to drink after work in those fabulous haunts on Rush. After a couple of days on the job, they took me to their favorite "watering holes".

I don't remember where we went, but I do remember the inside of the bar. It was a handsome place with a lot of wood. The bar was a magnificent, old one, with great antique mirrors and light fixtures from the 20's. Little multi-colored Christmas lights were artfully hung around the mirrors and just about everywhere else. The crowd had a "Chicago" feel to it. The holidays were quickly approaching and everyone was in a celebratory mood. I enjoyed top-shelf Chivas Regal scotch with a Drambuie float. I believe this cocktail is called a Rusty Nail. If you drink too many of these "babies", they nail you in your coffin sooner than you think! This drink knocked my lights out in no time flat!

As the evening progressed, the bar was hopping. I got drunker by the minute. One of the Operators on my crew knew I was in trouble. He asked me if I wanted to bunk at his place down the street. I could put my Jeep in the construction-job parking lot. This certainly was the rational thing to do, but I declined his offer. I told him I was sober enough to drive home. In hindsight, I wish he had hit me in the head and locked me up somewhere. Before I left the bar, I was in an alcoholic blackout. All I remember in the last moments at the bar was that damned Billy Joel song, "The Piano Man". Customers kept feeding the jukebox, playing it over and over again. How apropos! It was a song about wasted lives and drunks in a bar being sung to by a "piano man". It was the horrible foretelling of what was to become of me that evening.

I stumbled out of the bar, "falling down drunk". I fumbled for the right key while weaving to-and-fro like we drunks do after our debauches. I entered my Jeep and proceeded to drive in a blackout down Interstate 55, past my Exit on Pulaski Avenue. I came to my senses momentarily and made my Exit on Central Avenue, heading South, about a mile west of where I supposed to get off. Asleep at the wheel, I engaged another vehicle in a head-on collision.

Vietnam Bill told me at his Uncle's body shop that if my door hadn't sprung open, I wouldn't have made it. The leaf springs of the Jeep were up against the frame of the windshield. All the glass was missing. The hospital staff told me that I went bouncing down the road and was found by the police, a-hundred-or-so feet from the scene of the accident. All of the policemen and hospital staff were amazed that I survived this accident.

Knocked out "colder than a mackerel", I woke up in the emergency room while a physician was stitching up what used to be my face. I tried to get off the gurney, informing the emergency room staff that I had to go to work in the morning. They told me that I wasn't going anywhere. They lashed my arms and legs down to the table and proceeded to shoot me up with a sedative. It was lights-out for me until the next day. Jesus, I hate thinking of that next day!

REMORSE AND CONSEQUENCES

I woke up the next morning with no memory of what had happened to me. My mom was crying next to my hospital bed. She informed me that I was involved in a terrible automobile accident. My boss called our house earlier in the morning, wondering why I hadn't come to work.

I called the company from my hospital bed. I told the General Superintendent of my situation. He was a nice guy about the whole horrible mess. He told me he figured something was wrong, because the men told him I was really "hammered" the night before. They feared the worst for me and thought I was too drunk to drive home. I lost my job because of this debacle. I'm lucky I didn't lose my life.

Seeing my mother cry after my bad behavior was horrible and humiliating for me. I didn't need to put her through this agony. She already had been through enough heartache this past year. I put her through yet another unnecessary nightmare. Being my mother, she loved me anyway. My mother's strength and capacity for love were without limits. I felt like the scum-of-the-earth. When I finally hobbled out of my hospital bed and summoned enough courage to look in the mirror, I didn't like what I saw. I had two black eyes and an ugly pattern of stitches in my forehead. Between my eyes, I had a lovely bunch of gouges and scars. The doctors told me I needed plastic surgery, so they gave me the phone number and address of a Physician located in Evergreen Park, Illinois. My forehead turned out fine, but the plastic surgery done between my eyes required more work. I decided not to have it done. I wanted to punish myself and use these scars between my eyes as a reminder of my mistake. I wanted to wear these scars for the rest of my life. This was to be my penance for the pain I caused two innocent people. These people had to suffer because of my drunkenness.

The people I hurt in the other car had leg injuries. I sublimated all the information I received about these poor people. I put it all in the back of my mind as if it never happened. Having this knowledge, I couldn't live with myself. I wanted my mind to bury the horrible mistake in a place where I could never remember it ever again. Guilt precipitated a defense mechanism in me, which made it easier for my mind to forget these horrible crimes. I learned how to deny. It became my survival mechanism for many years. I was too much of a coward to accept the results of my crime. The memories were too painful for me to live with all my life.

My comprehensive auto insurance took care of all the damages to both vehicles. Union Medical Insurance took care of all my hospital bills. Nothing repaired the minds of three damaged individuals. Two of the victims were innocent. I was the negligent perpetrator and I deserved the mental pain. Everyday, I pay for what I did.

I think God has forgiven me for these sins. I've learned to let things go and have put everything in God's hands. A year after the accident I was broke, so my victims' attorney advised them not to sue me for any more money in civil court. My limits of liability were up around one hundred thousand dollars. My victims were paid every penny of that, and they deserved much more, I am sure. All I know is that I still pay for this accident—in my mind—everyday.

When I was released from the hospital, I went back to running in Marquette Park. I needed to heal my soul. These were some of the darkest days in my life. I gave up drinking and was invited to a twelve-step meeting by a fellow runner who had been sober for a long time. He understood my story. He said meetings with other drunks had allowed him to put his life back together and suggested that I might give it a try for myself. I entered my first meeting on Chicago's South Side with great apprehension. I went into a church basement and was greeted by the smells of strong coffee and clouds of cigarette smoke. I looked around and saw all these old "B" girls, with too much eye makeup and gravely voices. They were smoking cigarettes and laughing it up. The old guys at the meeting were yucking it up as well. The men looked just like the old timers I had seen on construction jobs. The faces—both male and female—looked like "ten miles of bad road" to me. They had been through some hard times, but they had big-old smiles on their haggard faces. Instead of whiskey, they were drinking coffee...and a lot of it! Every one of them seemed like they were having the time of their lives! I thought they were either insane or on some kind of drug! Maybe they were crazy from having wet brains or something of that nature.

They treated me as if I was the guest of honor. Every one of them was bending over backwards to make me comfortable and at ease. I had a gut feeling that this was going to be a bad scene. What the hell did they want from me? I figured it must be some kind of "cult", but I stayed a while, dismissed my fears, and tried to be pleasant. Finally, I saw my chance to escape and got the hell out of there! I knew this wasn't for me! I stayed sober for about two weeks on my own. I hated every minute of it. How the hell does a guy live without the joys given to him by a few drinks? My mind started to forget the pain and soon my facial scars began to heal. I promised myself that from now on I would drink more responsibly. To replace my Jeep, I bought a beat-up, yellow Ford from a neighborhood guy for around $100 bucks. The car had bald tires and no brakes. I said a prayer to St. Augustine every time I got into that damned car for a trip to Bruno's tap or to work. I couldn't wait for my insurance money to come in so I could purchase a new car.

CHICAGO WINTERS — REYNOLDS ALUMINUM — 1979

In Chicago, the Winter of '79 had almost a record snow. The only winter in Chicago that had this one beat in terms of snow accumulation was the famous snow of 1967. We were lambasted back then by 27" of the white stuff. My spirits were really low. I hated my life! I hated Chicago! I hated everything! I had cabin fever, by God. I couldn't go out and run through this deep snow and slush. I ran in my mom's house. I ran up and down the stairs from the kitchen to the basement. I ran endless circles in the basement just like some kind of prisoner in lockdown, or rat in a cage. I even pumped those old rusty weights I'd had since high school. I did just about anything to ease my fevered mind. Boredom was my enemy now! I couldn't chance driving that piece-of-shit, yellow Ford down the Chicago side streets.

If you've lived in Chicago in the wintertime and you dare to drive your car after a snowstorm, you learn the game of..."RIDING THE ICY RUTS". These ruts are made by a "million" tires transversing the side streets. You hope your car's underbody doesn't bottom out as you journey out into the unknown. Cars are parked on either side of the side streets as you drive, and there is no place to go except into the "grooves of horror".

When two cars face each other at an impasse, the drivers of the "iron monsters" sit and look at each other in disgust, daring each other to take the first chance. The driver who has the "balls" to drive around the other car has to "goose" his engine to escape the ruts. His car usually goes into an uncontrollable "power slide" and he ends up sideswiping a brand new Cadillac.

The owner of the damaged new "Caddy" always sees the transgression. He is always sitting in his easy chair by the front window. There he lurks, drinking hot coffee and reading his Chicago Tribune. He has the radio on and is listening to Wally Phillips on WGN radio. The guy who owns this Caddy has a job to do. He stays by the window all day, if necessary, to be ever vigilant so he can alert the Chicago Police Department if there is any damage done to his car. At any malfeasance, he calls his Alderman to "chew his ass out" for the lack of city services and salt trucks with snow plows. This is a Chicago tradition. It has been going on for many a year.

All Chicago residents shovel their walks and parking areas in front of their apartments and homes. After the shoveling is completed, the parking area is declared off-limits to all but the owner of the space. Two ratty chairs are placed at either side of the space. Boards of various lengths transverse the middle of the space and are placed firmly on the seats of each chair.

Anyone who would ever be so brazen as to remove these sacred items from the area are dealt with harshly! Torture or death would never be questioned by the authorities. The offender always has it coming to him! The ownership of the space is clear! It is unspoken "Chicago Law"! All Chicagoans understand this law and abide by it!

I wasn't going to risk another car accident. That shitty, yellow car I was driving was going to sit in "MY" cleared off parking area in front of Mom's house. So I laced up my combat boots, put on my heavy winter coat, knit cap, gloves, and trudged the mile-and-a-half to Bruno's bar. Walking this kind of distance in Chicago during the month of January while enduring a 30-mile-an-hour wind and temperatures of 15 degrees isn't for the faint-hearted. The only people that are tough enough for this journey are fools and drunks. When I arrived at Bruno's after my march through a foot of snow, it was like being in heaven! I felt the warm, rancid air hit my face. "Ah," I thought, "I'm home!"

I smoked cigarettes and shared lies with toothless, old retired guys in raggedy jackets. I drank shots of Rock and Rye with my draft beer. I'd tell the old timers my tales of the marathon and how I was going to get back in shape. I did all of this between long drags on my Marlboro cigarettes, while sucking down shots. It was a lovable lunacy! I enjoyed every minute of this bullshit! The frozen Tombstone Pizzas we shared really tasted good on these freezing winter afternoons. It didn't matter that they were three years old and freezer burned. The booze made a guy hungry. If I had a good buzz going on, a Slim-Jim tasted like prime rib to me!

In January, I got a call from dispatch to go to work at the Reynolds Aluminum Plant on 47th Street and First Avenue in McCook, Illinois. This was a Federal job, and it was going to last for the rest of the winter. I drove my pukey-looking yellow Ford to work for about a week, holding my breath for each trip. Every time I hit the brakes, I heard grinding metal sounds. My foot was flat against the floorboards of that old-whore-of-a-car. Sometimes I thought I was going to have a heart attack when I almost rear-ended some expensive car in front of me. "Jesus, Lord, save me!" Luckily, my money came in from the car insurance company and I bought myself a brand new 1979 Pontiac Catalina. The car was beautiful. It was silver with red pin striping. It had beautiful red, fabric bench seats. The car was loaded with all the goodies. I never saved any money; it all went to girls, booze, and cars! I thought this was the way it was supposed to be!

Somehow a new car gives a man a new outlook on life. I knew I was down on my luck, but I was enjoying this dishonest feeling of self-importance! "Who cares? Screw 'em all!" It's a nice to feel like a "million bucks", even if you're only worth two cents. I drove my new "baby" to the job with great care. I damned the snow and ice every day. I sure didn't want to wreck this damn car!

I made the drive anyway, because I had it made on the job. I was an Oiler on a big "Lima Backhoe". The Operator running it was really laid back. After I prepared the machine in the morning, he let me go to the lunchroom so I could smoke cigarettes, drink coffee, and play poker all day long with the other tradesmen. These men were on call to do various little jobs. We were all making big money. I kind of liked this arrangement! These Federal jobs are called "cup cake" jobs.

The laborers who worked outside in all the snow and slop trudged in at noon in their muddy boots. We all smiled at them. We were all warm and comfy and greeted them for lunch every day. They all looked pissed off, with their red faces and muddy clothes. They scowled as they greeted us sarcastically by saying, "How's it going, 'Easy Money'?" We all said, "Just fine boys. How's your beautiful day going so far?" I loved all this bullshit. I hung on to this job for about a month. It was enough time to get a "grub stake" and head out to Las Vegas. My brother Jim said he would store my new Pontiac in his garage for me until I came back home. I left the gray skies of Chicago for the "glittering lights" of world-famous Las Vegas, commonly known as the "Disneyland for Adults"! I swore to myself I wasn't coming home until springtime, when it was warm and the flowers were blooming!

LAS VEGAS

One day, while I was at work at the Reynolds job, one of my old friends called my mom. He somehow had heard about my divorce and the passings of both my sister and dad. He wanted to talk to me. My mom told him I was at work, but she would relay the message to me when I came home from work that night. This was my good-old buddy, Frank. We had been friends since grammar school, and together had attended Southern Illinois University. We had some good times together back in Carbondale.

In high school, we cruised around in his Pontiac. He was the fellow who was with me the night I met Nancy. He was one hell of a character for sure. Frank was a big, good-looking guy with curly blond hair. The women just loved him! We drank a lot of beer and smoked a lot of weed together back in the college days. Mom wrote down his Las Vegas telephone number for me. He was especially nice to my mom with his sympathy and regards. This I greatly appreciated. Later, when I returned from my day at work, I called him.

It was great to talk about old times, and he lifted my spirits with his condolences. Frank was in Las Vegas temporarily doing a short-term job. He was trying to sell his home in Chula Vista, California. He was an Officer in the United States Navy and had decided to go to a corporate-type employment rather than making the service his lifetime career. I believe he was stationed out in Long Beach California. He was living in a huge luxury apartment out in Las Vegas. It was within walking distance from the "strip" with all its casinos and nightlife. He told me that his apartment complex had a nice swimming pool and fitness center, which he said was abundant with all kinds of good-looking girls. This appealed to me right away! He invited me to come out, forget my troubles, and take a well-deserved vacation. Frank must have heard about my run of bad luck from one of the neighborhood guys. I imagine he felt sorry for his old pal. No matter, I knew right away that I wanted to go out there! The winter was terribly depressing and I hadn't had a vacation in a long time.

I booked a round-trip flight on United Airlines. My departure time was 7:00 p.m. from O'Hare International Airport. I was so hyped-up for this trip that I arrived three hours early and settled in on the nearest bar stool near my boarding area. I started drinking Jack Daniels on the rocks at one of those depressing airport kiosks. You might remember them if you're my age. They serve three-day-old plastic sandwiches at inflated prices. They pour measured shots. There is no free pouring in these antiseptic, rip-off airport cubicles. I longed for Bruno's tavern so I could enjoy a real gentleman's drink at a fair price.

I wiled away my time at the airport striking up conversations with unreceptive young ladies. Nursing the watered-down drinks, I smoked a "million" cigarettes. After what seemed to be an eternity, I finally boarded the airplane. I was lucky enough to be seated right next to a bunch of drunken drill-riggers from Australia. I told them I had done some drill rigging and they welcomed me as a fellow "roughneck".

Naturally, we got along famously. They offered me pulls off a bottle of whiskey that they smuggled on the plane. We laughed and told jokes and stories of our adventures. We were all loaded to the gills when we landed in Las Vegas. These men bid me farewell saying, "Good luck, Yank! It was a pleasure makin' your acquaintance!"

I left them with a drunken, shit-eating grin on my face. Waving my goodbyes, I weaved my way to the baggage pickup. I couldn't believe all the lights, bells, and glorious sounds coming from the slot machines. I had a belly full of whiskey and I imagined scenarios of good times to come! I walked with confidence in my smart-looking clothes. Way in the distance, I saw good-old Frank waving at me. There's a working girl on each one of his arms, and an unbroken fifth of Jack Daniel's bourbon in his fist. God bless the man! He was going to make sure that I was already on a roll with an "unbeatable pair"!

LATER THAT EVENING

Frank and I got through all the perfunctory hellos and high fives and male- gesturing that old buddies do when they haven't seen one another for a long time. It was eight years since the good-old college days. Frank looked great! He still was the good-looking guy I remembered from what seemed eons past. He was well dressed and groomed and in great physical shape. He flashed that winning smile of his. Those pearly whites just sparkled! He looked like a country club kind-of-man. He appeared to be the type of fellow that a father wants his daughter to bring home to dinner. This merely was Frank's outer veneer. Inside, the old boy was a "player" who loved to chase women and drink booze. The man was a hound, just like me. The hookers were getting a big kick out of our reunion. I sure didn't want to leave them out of all our levity, by any means! I groped the merchandise they had to offer and started kidding them about what we were going to be doing in an hour or two. I played with them by saying, "You girls should be doing us for free, because we're good looking, buff, and young!" They both adamantly and immediately opposed this idea! Frank and I laughed and went on with more joking to put them at ease.

I just love hookers. For me it's like going to confession. The parish priest always listens to grave stories of my sins with genuine concern. He listens to my tales of hardship and pain, and all the bad things I have done. All of humanity wants forgiveness and hope. Hookers give absolution much in the same way as the priest, except I don't have to say three Our Father's, three Hail Mary's, and three Glory Be's. Hookers are wonderful and very forgiving. They give a man more warmth, love, and compassion than a confessional booth...and they even smell better! All a guy has to do is put the money on the table and light up a cigarette after the service is rendered. No prayer is required, just hard cash. Amen.

One thing I am sure of is that the hookers with us that night were sure happy that they didn't have to do a couple of fat, bald guys in their 60's. On the way to Franks place, I had both of the girls in the back seat, playing "grab-ass". I was having a ball! The girls were squealing and purring as I joked with them. I was enjoying taking in the sights and sounds of the Casinos and the street people. The whole carnival atmosphere of Las Vegas elated me and was a much-needed distraction, considering what had been happening in my life.

It blew my mind when old Frank told me he didn't want one of the hookers. This wasn't the old Frank I knew back in college. He told me the girls were his gift to me. His wife was back in Chicago looking at real estate and he was declining any extramarital amorous adventures. I knew his wife from the old neighborhood, and she was a total sweetheart. I give Frank credit for his fidelity. I'm sure that's a main reason why they are still together today. Well, I was single and this was a gift I was going to enjoy. It was a doubleheader for me! I was ready! I remember Ernie Banks of the old Chicago Cubs exclaiming, "Let's play two!" Right on Ernie! I'm ready to play!

MUCH LATER THAT EVENING

Frank's apartment was top shelf. I looked through the big plate-glass windows and saw miles of Las Vegas lights. I enjoyed his penthouse view. It was absolutely beautiful. I sat with both of the girls on a leather sofa in his well-appointed living room. Frank sipped whiskey in his lazy boy chair, enjoying the cavorting that was going on between the girls and me. We were all watching some ancient porno movie on this "amazing new invention". This box Frank had connected to his television set was called a Beta-Max. I never saw one of these video recorders, but vowed to buy one as soon as I got back home. The contraption amazed me! Wow! Movies right in my own home...even porno-movies! New technology for the working class was something I could relate to!

The hookers were young and beautiful. One was a tall, statuesque blonde. She had a sexy, British accent, which really turned me on. The other girl was dark haired. She was petite and more intelligent than the "Brit". The smaller girl was drop-dead gorgeous! Not only that, she was gifted with wonderful conversational skills and a great sense of humor! I took both of them to a dimly lit bedroom, which was beautifully prepared for us. I enjoyed the dim lights and burning candles. All my carnal dreams were served quite adequately on this magic evening. I knew I was going to hell but thought I could do one kind act, just in case I passed away that night.

I sent the women happily on their way with two crisp hundred-dollar bills. A C- note for each of the ladies prompted them to titter like a couple of schoolgirls. They each dishonestly professed their undying love and affection for me. "Please call us again before you leave for Chicago, because we had a great time with you tonight!" They were enjoying the fine treatment and an unexpected extra couple of hundred bucks! The erotic part of the evening was gone, but thoroughly enjoyed by me. I imagine the hookers thought it was just another night at the office.

Now that the lovely ladies of the evening were dispatched on to new adventures, Frank and I settled in at the kitchen table for some conversation and serious drinking. He told me how sorry he was about my losses. I told him what was happening in my life, and I shed a few tears. He put his arm around my shoulders and said, "Rich, you're going to be alright. Just let it go man." We talked about our families and the old neighborhood. We talked about our careers and just about everything under the sun. This was what I really needed to do. I didn't need booze or hookers, cigarettes or reefer. I needed that special camaraderie from an old friend, and Frank supplied that for me. Time just flew by into the wee hours of the morning. Finally, Frank said, "I have to rack out for a couple of hours, because when the sun comes up I have to go to into the office."

I remember passing out with a smile on my face, hearing the "Sultans of Swing" by the new group "Dire Straits" playing in the background.

THE NEXT DAY

The sun assaulted my eyes. Not knowing where I was, I sat up quickly and a "dagger" of pain hit the frontal lobes of my brain. I knew what this agony was. I had felt it many times before. It was the pain of "the morning after". Soon, everything in my mind came together. I trudged off to the toilet, not daring to look at my face in the mirror.

I opened my suitcase and dumped every thing out of it on the bed. I fished out a pair of jockey shorts and my raggedy toothbrush.

I stood in the shower for a long time, letting the hot water soothe my aching head. I brushed the rancidness out of my mouth. My sour stomach remained until I forced down the first "shot" of the day.

All alcoholics know that the first "eye-opener" of the day is always the toughest. Once the first one goes down and you're lucky enough not to barf it up, the rest of them are going to comfort you. Frank left a note informing me as to where I could find a 1.75-liter of cheap vodka. He also had a two-quart plastic pitcher in the cabinets. In-or-around the area of the refrigerator were other necessary items. I found tomato and orange juice, Lee-and Perrins Worcestershire Sauce, celery salt, tabasco sauce, and all the items a drunk needs to manufacture a Bloody Mary in order to "get well".

My buddy Frank also left me an extra key for the apartment, a pool pass, and a card to get me into the fitness room. I visualized him laughing as he lay the fitness center card down for me on the kitchen table! His note also said that I was allowed to carry my pitcher of "medicine" down to the pool area, without fear of any danger of harassment or prosecution by security guards. I thought the pitcher of Bloody Marys would be a great way for me to break the ice with neighbors and guests! Frank was a taking care of me in style! He finished his note by saying, "Enjoy your day, Asshole. Tonight, I'm taking you to Good-Time Charlie's." He finished the note by writing, "I'll be back home at five o'clock."

With all the preparations made, I got into my swim trunks and sandals, threw on a muscle man tee shirt, and forced down a couple of shots. I then sauntered down to the pool area and found a nice lounge chair with a table. I was blissfully loaded in half an hour, enjoying lean, tan female bodies in skimpy bikinis. They frolicked in the sun, laughing and enjoying this beautiful day. They were probably waitresses, hookers, dealers, showgirls—all of them some type of nighttime employees in this magic town. It's amazing how quickly things can change! Just a couple of hours ago, I felt like I was going to die; now I was in a blissful state!

As the day progressed, I ingratiated myself with just about everyone around the swimming pool. I poured cocktails for all the guys and girls I met, and had them laughing while telling them tales of my past adventures. The salesman was always ready to pop out of me! Once again, I was enjoying the warmth of the sun.

I worked on my youthful tan, never thinking that someday, my tight, supple skin was going to turn against me. I would be reduced to a "prune-like" state, by the age of fifty. Don't worry about these things! Live your freaking life! Enjoy your tan, because life is too damned short anyway!

Frank came back, needing a drink as badly as I had earlier in the morning. We laughed like hell at his situation! He looked at me and said, "You're plowed already, you idiot! How are you going to score any women tonight?" I told him, "You wish that you felt as good as me. Don't worry about the women! I procured a few phone numbers already." He laughed at this, and we both headed to Good-Time Charlie's.

GOOD TIME CHARLIES

Good Time Charlie's is a great watering hole. From four to seven p.m., Monday thru Friday they advertised a "happy hour". Happy hour in this Las Vegas establishment, allowed a guy to buy two-for-one Chivas Regal scotches for a mere pittance of a buck-and-a-half. This is top shelf scotch man! The buffet they set up was plentiful and free! The buffet included all kinds of lunchmeats, hot Swedish meatballs, and prime cuts of hot beef. The smiling chef carved hefty portions for me from a huge hunk of cow. Breads, potatoes, desserts, and all kinds of other delicacies were displayed on the serving table, with artistic flair.

I thought that, maybe the great artist Picasso was "slinging hash" in their kitchen! What a gorgeous canvas of food! I remember crashing weddings that didn't have a spread like this one! I was starving. I hadn't eaten anything since the plastic sandwich at O'Hare airport, and only ate peanuts and junk food at Frank's place the night before. I ate huge platefuls of everything that evening.

"Charlie's" had comfortable sofas and chairs scattered throughout the place to rest my weary, drunken bones. The lounge had a beautiful bar with two huge saltwater fish tanks. A cylindrical tube connected the tanks. The tube was about four feet long, and eight inches in diameter. A patron could sip his drink at the bar and languidly watch the brightly colored salt-water fish swim from one tank to the other. The booze and beautiful fish helped create this wonderful, relaxed, hypnotic solitude in me. My mind drifted to some non-existent, ethereal beach in the Caribbean. I feared that if I relaxed too much, I might end up with my head on the bar. I guarded against this possibility; by reminding myself of what shame I would feel being ejected hastily some large, ruddy-faced bartender.

The hookers in this bar were plentiful, and friendly as hell! This bar was way off the strip, and these girls weren't "Triple—A", but as the night progressed they all started looking pretty damned good to me! The old adage, "The girls always look prettier at closing time", holds true! If a guy played his cards right, he could bargain them down for sexual favors. Played-out-hookers always welcome bargain basement prices late in the evening. That first evening, Frank and I were really tired after stuffing ourselves with the buffet. We both went home early and hit the sack. I vowed to go back and party at this good old bar named: "Good Time Charlie's".

A man can't beat a place where he can get drunk on top shelf booze for pennies, eat a variegated, tasty buffet for free, and get laid, all for under a hundred bucks. I loved Las-Vegas, with all my heart! What wasn't there to love about a place like this? I was in my element!

PARTYING IN LAS VEGAS

I'm not much of a gambling man, but I do know one thing for sure: the odds are always in favor of the house. If you want to gamble and do well, I suggest you gravitate toward Blackjack or Poker. You can do well if you possess a good memory for the cards that have been dealt. A good understanding of odds and mathematics is a must! Stay away from the slots and the Roulette table. Slots are for fat, old ladies and other individuals who make trailers their homes. Roulette is for the wealthy. Guys like David Niven or girls like Audrey Hepburn look good playing roulette in the movies, but believe me, have no delusions of grandeur about making any money in this endeavor, no matter how romantic it appears. Roulette is a bad game for a working slob like me. Losing money quickly is a painful experience at best. I never have gotten an adrenaline rush from gambling, thank God! I have enough addictions in my life already. These have to be dealt with every day of my life, and it isn't easy for me to have more than I can handle! Fortunately, I never developed an affinity for gambling. I think that my father's bad luck with cards and the horses probably influenced me in this regard.

One cardinal rule I follow is, "Never bet more than you can afford to lose." Believe me, this is sound advice. If I follow this golden rule, I always end up having a pretty good time in Las Vegas. In 1979, Las Vegas was a town for adults. It was called "Sin-City". It wasn't the "Disney-esque" family oriented circus it is today. I liked the old Vegas with Frank Sinatra, Elvis Presley, Red Foxx, Joey Bishop, Sammy Davis, Don Rickles, and Wayne Newton. I liked the old hotels and casinos. I had good times in the Dunes, the Sands, the Frontier, the Silver Slipper, and the Landmark. I loved the dollar breakfasts, free drinks, and cheap whores. I have no need for Cirque de Soleil or Sigfried and Roy. If I need to go to the circus, I can buy tickets for Ringling Brothers-Barnum and Bailey when they are in town in Chicago. I say, "Leave the peanut eating at the big top." I don't want to see guys spinning dinner plates on six-foot long rods. I saw enough of this on the Ed Sullivan show as a kid. I feel that the new Las Vegas is hypocritical. It's cleaned up its act for the almighty family. I don't want "Wally World". I don't believe that, "What happens in Vegas, stays in Vegas." What a line of bullshit! The Vegas advertising minds had the "balls" to steal that saying from A.A. meetings. Talk about the bastardization of something good. Believe me that money is still the bottom line there. Maybe legalized gambling in other states is "hurting their play". In spite of all that I say, I still like the City of Las Vegas. I just prefer it the way it was.

Anyway, I had a great time the month I stayed there in 1979. I dated a girl named Chris who worked for the Howard Hughes Conglomerate known as Summa Corporation. Chris had "juice" in this town. She knew all the right people. "Juice" is power. I couldn't tip a maitre d' when I accompanied her. They wouldn't take my money. Everything was complimentary, because I was her guest. We received ringside seats — the best seats in the house—at every show or nightclub we entered together. She was a great girl. She called me in Chicago a number of times after I left town, to see how I was doing. She loved to dance, and we did the discos together. She always had a shoulder for me to cry on. She was a true friend to me in a town known for its callousness. Good people can be found in the strangest situations or environments.

I left this town with plenty of money in my pocket. Not many people accomplish that feat. The last thing I saw in the airport was a guy who looked alot like Flip Wilson holding a Bloody Mary to his forehead. He smiled at me and said, "Hello". This was the Vegas I knew and loved.

PACIFIC OCEAN BEACH

San Diego by jet plane is a short flight from Las Vegas. I checked into a seedy motel on Pacific Ocean Beach—a disheveled community down on its luck. This place was to be my home for the next six weeks. The motel efficiency apartment had a small color TV, a single-sized bed with a stained mattress, and a small kitchenette reminiscent of the 50's. The kitchen also had an old electric range and a small refrigerator. The place was adequate enough for my needs.

I paid cash in advance to an elderly woman. She sternly looked at me and in a voice filled with conviction told me, "The destruction of furniture, or loud parties, will not be tolerated by the management." As long as I abided by these two rules, I had carte blanche to do whatever my little heart desired. I thought this was a fair deal and looked forward to my stay. Besides, the price was right.

I struck up a friendship with the young girl who cleaned my apartment every day. After a short time, she introduced me to her boyfriend. He had long hair, tattoos, and was skinny as a beanpole. He also was a really nice guy. After I gained his trust he introduced me to some great bars. He also introduced me to the strange crowd he partied with in the local dives.

I liked that my apartment had a private entrance. I came and went as I pleased. I didn't have to worry about any hotel clerks with curiosities about my behavior. Most of the desk clerks were "kinkier" than me! Their interference never caused me any grief. I could entertain anyone I wished to bring over to the place. The motel was located right smack-dab on the boardwalk. If I opened my door to go outside, I was immediately enveloped by the majesty of the Pacific Ocean. The great waves were a mere hundred yards from where I stood.

In the morning I'd buy a newspaper and venture out to a dilapidated café for a few cups of good, strong coffee. I usually woke up early, as was my custom. Sometimes I slept late if I was carousing into the wee hours of the morning. I loved to sit in the sand with the wind in my face and hair. I listened to the shriek of the gulls and watched the surfers paddle out to the horizon to challenge the new day.

Every morning, I threw on my jogging shoes and ran along the beach. I filled my lungs with fresh Pacific Ocean air. I felt the bloat and excess of Las Vegas leaving my body. The boardwalk was abundant with old hippies, panhandlers, and drug addicts. Cultural diversity proliferated here on Pacific Ocean Beach. Always the student of human behavior, I was entertained by the colorful boardwalk life.

Female roller skaters in short shorts zoomed by me, followed by Venice Beach type muscle men in hot pursuit. Poets, intellectuals, doomsayers, and eccentrics were all there. This was the flotsam and jetsam of life. This ebb and flow of boardwalk-type humanity was a far cry from Mission Bay. I saw Mission Bay in all of its elegance. There were gigantic homes there, right on the waterfront.

I couldn't believe my eyes. Enormous wealth proliferated in Mission Bay, right next to the poverty of the boardwalk where I existed. The people of Mission Bay parked their hundred-foot yachts in garages underneath their mansions. I wondered, "Who are these people?" I could see them, but couldn't touch or talk to them. They lived in a gated waterfront community. Their beaches were inaccessible to regular people like me. There were gates and guards all around them. What were they hiding? Did they choose to be incarcerated? I was free, by God! These wealthy people lived in a contrived reality. I saw their lives pretty much as being a vanilla sort-of-existence. Self-imposed strangulation by way of a lack of cultural diversity is often the fate of the wealthy.

Balboa Park and the beautiful San Diego Zoo were not far from my humble abode. I loved walking there shirtless, in cut-off-jeans and sandals, feeling the warmth of the sun on Sunday afternoons. I was recharging my batteries. For me, this was a time to get well physically and mentally.

I was still grieving, but didn't realize it. I couldn't understand why I was so lonely. People whose company I enjoyed didn't make my sadness any better for me. I felt the ever-present hole in my heart. Nothing could fill the abyss inside of me. I listened to vacant barroom laughter. Vapid painted women, who took me to their breasts, couldn't repair what was broken inside of me.

I enjoyed being a "voyeur". I did a lot of "research" in my isolation. I traveled to National City and saw human dereliction at its worst. I talked to a variety of tough-looking women and men in those seedy bars. They were not much different than the uptown-types who drank martinis at the Drake or Four Seasons Hotels in Chicago. If anything, the down-and-outers were more honest. They didn't try and hide their dirty little secrets with contrived civilities. The poor folk didn't possess the aptitude to carry on with their indiscretions without having them discovered. The poor and uneducated are more honest in their depravities and are definitely more vulnerable to the pain caused by them.

On Pacific Ocean Beach, I rocked to the sounds of Van Halen at the Roxy Auditorium. Every afternoon, I played Backgammon with new friends on the beach. At night, we smoked joints saturated with hash oil. I drank shots of tequila and bottles of beer at Jose Murphy's bar. I didn't care to see the City of San Diego in all its glory. I squandered that opportunity. I was too busy in my own little world, enjoying high times with the detritus of society. I can't really say if this was a mistake. People and places, are pretty much the same after a while. I'm glad I gave a sweet little motel maid and her nice boyfriend a hundred dollar bill for being my friends. They asked nothing from me but offered much. They were generous and kind to me, a total stranger. They drove me to San Diego Airport in their "beater" car. I'll never forget their faces and tears, as we hugged and said our goodbyes.

BACK TO VEGAS

I arrived feeling fit and tan. Frank noticed I had lost the fat around my middle. I dropped around ten pounds of my Vegas bloat in California. The constant eating and boozing I did the last time in that wild party town didn't do me any good. I stuck around Las Vegas for a week this time. I saw Chris a lot. She continued to enjoy the new dance routines I taught her at the discos we haunted. We had a really nice time together.

I started thinking about going home, and whether or not I would still have a job at the Mockingbird. I doubted it. Jobs like that don't stay available for a very long time. I left O'Reilly without giving him adequate notice. I really needed to get out of town, so such is life!

I kissed Chris goodbye, and started preparing my things for the trip home. I always made sure I checked in with my mom a couple of times a week during this vacation. When I called Mom to let her know I was coming back, she was delighted. She told me the weather was warming up and it looked like an early spring in Chicago. Local #150 would be calling me soon, as soon as I let them know I was available again. I was chomping at the bit to get back to work. I always liked to work, and long vacations are no good for a strong young man. I thought it must have been a long, lonely winter for Mom without me around.

The last night in Las Vegas, I really got "hammered". I felt poorly at the airport the next day. All the money I had in my pocket was three silver dollars. I had my boarding pass, a pack of cigarettes, and an empty wallet. I knew I couldn't get rid of this horrible hangover with three silver dollars, so I slammed them in the nearest slot machine, pulled the arm and hoped for the best. It paid me off big time! I filled my carry-on bag with a mess of silver dollars. The "gods" were with me this time! Now I could fix my hangover. I boarded the plane with a big grin on my haggard face. I drank Chivas Regal scotch all the way home. I took my brother-in-law and Mom out for steaks at some fancy restaurant after they picked me up at O'Hare. It felt good to be home!

HOMECOMING

It was great to be back home again! Mom and our house on 73rd Street was a sight for sore eyes! Mom provided me with strength and purpose in my life. I tried to be strong for her as well. It was always nice to smell her homemade Polish food cooking in the kitchen. I grew up in this big old bungalow, and it held many memories for me. Mom and Dad and my brother and sister nurtured me in this house since I was a 6-year-old boy. Somehow, even though I was a grown man, the house still seemed to keep me safe. I don't think there should be shame in such an admission. It's good for a person to have a feeling of belonging, and some sense of history. Although I was 29-years-old at this period in my life, I never would admit to saying something this corny. I had a lot to learn about life. Being old makes me more humble, and gives me more clarity of thought.

The nice weather went sour with more rain and snow. The excavating company I was working with gave me my pink slip. In a few days, the Union Hall called me to run a crane for a steel-erecting outfit in Des Plaines, Illinois. I was pretty damned proficient at running the "big rigs" now. The machine they had for me was a thirty-ton mobile hydraulic crane. It had outriggers for stabilization when I jacked it up off its rubber tires. The crane operators with this company were radio dispatched all over the Chicago Metropolitan Area. The job paid big money and benefits. I took great care to get to bed early, and never to overindulge in alcohol the night before I went to work. Crane work is dangerous, and crane operators have to always have their thinking caps on. A man who isn't extremely careful operating a crane can kill himself—or worse—an innocent worker or bystander.

My day started at six-in-the-morning. I greased and "prepped" my machine and filled the fuel tanks of the crane and the truck. Many evenings, I didn't get back to the yard until seven or eight p.m. This job made me so stressed and nervous, it had me drinking Maalox right out of the bottle. I was reminded of that old guy from the employment agency I worked for as a young man! The crane job was very demanding, both mentally and physically.

Imagine driving this huge rig in tight spots all day. I had to set it up, make all the hoists safely, and deal with disgruntled tradesmen and general superintendents. While doing all this, I had to maintain a courteous smile and display unfettered job interest and professionalism. It sucked! Half the days I worked, I wanted to strangle everybody who I came into contact with! People were always asking me to do impossible things with the crane. Thank God, I had some knowledge. I was a certified crane operator, with a lot of schooling from the apprenticeship school. Without knowledge, a crane operator can wreak havoc.

The drive home wasn't much of a break from my insane day. I had to hit the brakes on my thirty-ton truck crane whenever some moron in a compact car decided to cut me off in rush hour traffic near O'Hare field. I'm lucky I never killed anyone! God must have put a "special guardian angel" on my shoulder.

These pressures and responsibilities were eating a hole in my stomach. Thankfully, the company only worked us five-days-a-week. On the weekends, I was back at the Mockingbird—not as an employee but as a customer. I didn't return to my old bartending job. I was replaced by a good-looking female with size 38 double- D's and a good-looking "caboose" in a tight skirt to go along with them! Old O'Reilly really knew how to keep guys coming back to the bar! This old Irishman surely had some business acumen! He knew that sex sells!

One Friday evening, I'm on my favorite barstool sipping my scotch, enjoying the cleavage of the new bartender, and who walks into the bar but Katie "The Mystery Woman"! She sneaks up behind me, puts her hands over my eyes, and whispers in my ear, "Guess who?" I knew the smell of her perfume. I turned around and gazed into those beautiful blue eyes while putting my arms around her. I kissed her full on her smiling lips. This was a very impulsive move on my part, but she didn't pull back, and kissed me with equal fervor. My boat was floating now! Wow! Something was different about her. I couldn't quite put my finger on it, but she is definitely not the same girl she was a few months ago. She doesn't seem so sad and distant anymore. She has this air of happiness and self-esteem. I sense she isn't going to run away from me this time! We dance and converse until closing time. I'm falling in love with this girl! She holds on to me all night, as if we are meant for each other. This night, just as I sensed, she doesn't run away. She gives me her phone number. The real "acid test" will be tomorrow when I dial it, and either hear her voice or find out it's just a bogus number.

KATIE

I fell in love with her. The passion between us was dialed up very high. We couldn't get enough of each other. For a month or so, it was prom night every night. Then the shockwave hit.

She brought me to her apartment, and while I was making love to her, I glanced over to the corner of the bedroom. I saw a pair of size sixteen men's shoes! Needless to say, this really frightened me! I wanted to know who owned the damned things. Katie tearfully confessed to me that she was going through a terrible divorce. I found out that she had a five-year-old son with this man. The guy who owned these shoes was supposedly deer hunting up in Wisconsin! She told me not to worry; it was over between them. Yeah, sure!

Her admission did me no good at all! I visualized a six-foot, six-inch, three-hundred-pound football player-type guy wearing a flannel shirt and looking like Paul Bunyon, pulling the door off the hinges while I'm putting up my jockey shorts. The next thing I see in my mind's eye is the shotgun under my chin and the look of blood in his crazed eyes.

I said, "Why the hell didn't you tell me this before?" Katie tearfully explained, "I was afraid you wouldn't want me with all this baggage! I didn't think you'd want a Mother with a five-year-old son!" The light bulb came on in my head. Now I knew why she kept leaving the bar without giving me her phone number. She was out, cheating on her old man. She painted a grim picture of him. She told me he abused her and their son. Katie assured me that her relationship with her husband was over. He wasn't coming back. The big old size sixteen shoes filled my mind with doubt!

A LEAP OF FAITH

I loved Kate so much that I denied reality and also the uneasiness in my gut. An ominous feeling overwhelmed my senses. I might be getting myself in trouble again. The old adage, "Love is blind", rung loud and clear in my ears, but in matters of the heart, sometimes we are all fools!

I met her boy. He was a lovable little kid named Cliff. He was friendly and bright. We warmed up to each other right away. I felt wonderful being a part of this triad, and Katie never seemed happier. We did things together that young people with children do. We went to the zoo, kids' movies, and ate a lot of ice cream sundaes. I enjoyed every minute of it because these were all the things that my father never did with me when I was Cliff's age. I always wanted to have a child to love, and now I had the opportunity to be a father. Katie told me that her son "adored" me. I was glad, because I thought he was the best kid in the world. All was well in our world. We included my mom in our outings on the weekends. Mom enjoyed having us over to her house on Sundays, and cooked us her good German-Polish food! Mom felt a special feeling of family again.

Katie and I soon made plans to get a place of our own. We were looking out in the western suburbs. She was excited about renting a unit at an apartment complex out in Lisle, Illinois. This place was approximately, thirty-five miles west of Mom's house. The name of the complex was Four Lakes Village. The "Village" was a large campus of buildings in a rustic forested setting. The property had a ski hill, a nice pub and restaurant, bike paths and fishing lakes. We also had access to a convenience store, laundry facilities in our building, and organized athletics for young adults. We loved the place immediately! This was a happening place. It was a young people's community with all the amenities.

I spent all my money on new furniture. I purchased pots and pans, draperies, lights, end tables, a fancy new color TV, and stereo equipment. We also purchased a new bedroom set. We now slept in a brand new, huge king-sized bed. Cliff had his own room with a new bed, toys and new clothes. I went into some big debt to facilitate everyone's happiness. Money was no object to me. I loved this new little family of mine.

I packed a U-Haul trailer with our belongings and hitched it to my new Pontiac. Katie and Cliff followed me to our new home in her beat up Ford. The week was a hustle-and-bustle of shopping and receiving the new furniture. Katie "dragged" us endlessly here-and-there, accumulating more things for the apartment. She was on a mission buying all these things, which were so-called "necessities". We had to have these things! Oh well, "I'm in it for the long run now," I thought. Katie had everything a woman could want for a new life. As for me, I was broke and exhausted.

SOMETIMES FAITH LEADS TO DESPAIR

In the beginning, everything was beautiful for the three of us. Evenings were spent in front of the new television set. Katie sat next to me with her head on my shoulder, holding my hand. Little Cliff sat in my lap. We shared a lot of laughter and love. Katie made wonderful dinners for us and I enjoyed them immensely after a hard day's work running the crane. After family time with the boy, we put him to bed and then Katie and I made sweet love in our new king-sized bed. My darling always slept in my arms. I thought she was happy with me, and had what she wanted in her life. I was a dependable man who loved her and her son.

I didn't expect her to work. I was making enough money to support us both. I wanted her to enjoy the fitness center and take Cliff on walks through the woods. There were lakes for fishing and many things for a Mom and her little boy to enjoy throughout the day. I thought life for all of us was going to be beautiful.

I was seriously mistaken in my assumption. Inexplicably, after a few weeks, Katie started going out by herself at night. She told me she felt trapped. She yearned for some independence. She wanted more spending money. She was looking for a job as a cocktail waitress or bartender. I didn't like any of this at all. I told her I would give her more spending money if she stayed home, but she adamantly rejected my offer.

At first, dinners were made for the boy and me. Later, I ordered out for pizza. If I came home late because of an overtime job, Katie exploded at me with anger. She said I was purposely compromising her plans. This wasn't the woman I fell in love with a few months before. This wasn't the "Katie" I wanted.

The little boy was my only joy. I felt like he was my own son. Sometimes I took him fishing on one of the lakes before the sun went down. After dinner we might take walks in the woods, turning over rocks and deadfalls. We looked for worms, and other "secret" things that dads show their sons. I imagined that these were things that little boys like to do. I never had a father do these things for me. This activity with the boy eased the "fever" in my brain. I loved the little guy. We watched

TV together, and he asked me his little-boy questions. I knew how important it was in his development to have someone there who cared, someone to explain things to him. I made sure he ate well, and then while we watched television, he fell asleep in my lap. I wondered what would become of him? What type of man was he going to be? When he was sleeping in my arms, the tears ran down my cheeks. I made sure to wipe them off my face before I bathed him, put him in his pajamas, and watch him brush his teeth. I always read him a story and made sure he said his prayers before I tucked him in around nine-in-the-evening.

What really broke my heart was that he always hugged me and called me "Daddy". Sometimes, he asked me, "Where is Mommy?" I told him, "Mommy is looking for a job. Everything is alright Cliff." He knew all was safe-and-sound and that I would be there all night for him if he needed me.

When I was sure the boy was asleep, I went to the cabinet and pulled out the whiskey bottle. My game plan now was to drink and wait. I ran every dismal scenario through my mind. I knew she was cheating on me. I waited for her until past midnight most of the times, until I couldn't keep my eyes open anymore. Then I stumbled to my king-sized bed, drunk and alone. The alarm clock rang at four-thirty a.m. every morning. Sometimes she was in bed next to me. I didn't say anything to her anymore. Sometimes she woke me up after her carousing, looking sexy and feeling horny. She always had whiskey on her breath. I gave her what she wanted. I knew she must have been thinking of someone else while I made love to her. I gave it to her hard, just like a dirty whore would like it. I screwed her as if she had just stolen my wallet. It was bizarre using sex as a weapon. She was so sick in her mind that she liked it that way.

She tried to bullshit me with all kinds of lies. I was too numb to even dignify her remarks with a response. I was suffering a soul sickness that I had never experienced before. One day I worked up the nerve and blinding anger to tell her that if she wasn't gone with all her shit by that evening, there would be hell to pay. She looked in my eyes and knew I meant what I said. I must have looked like a madman.

I never shook with anger like this in my entire life. I thought I might lose all control and strangle her. Just looking at me, She must have known that she was in danger. I was shaking so badly, I felt as if I was going to have a convulsion! I knew I had to leave quickly, before I did something I might regret. I didn't want to go to jail. In my state of mind, jail wasn't nearly as bad as the life I had been living.

HOW LOW CAN I GO?

Life with her had been spiraling down for a very long time. She persuaded me to drive her beater car to my job while she drove around in my new Pontiac. I was a "fool for love". There's a song like that isn't there? She put a few bumps and dents in the car. The parking tickets she accumulated without telling me came after she was long gone. Receiving these little surprises in the mail was like pouring alcohol in an open wound. My experiences with her were like being informed by your physician that you have some type of incurable cancer. "The only way for you to survive, Mr. Cronborg, is for me to cut one of your legs off." Living with Katie caused my work to falter. It suffered because of my nightly drinking and the agonizing waits for her to come home. I was going into my job without enough sleep. I lacked the ability to concentrate on anything.

I lost my job finally, when I swung the boom of the crane too close to a 48,000-volt power line. The load came down, crushing the building we were erecting. Men were running everywhere. I thank God that no one was killed. I was rushed off by ambulance to Victory Memorial Hospital in Waukegan, Illinois. The paramedics put little rubber suction cups on my chest to make sure my heart wasn't going to go into fibrillation. I was released the same day after they kept their eyes on me for a while. I was lucky to be alive.

After she left, I was relieved to be alone. I embraced my bottle and solitude with a new enthusiasm. I sank into a deep depression and experienced extreme loneliness. I sat in my apartment alone with all the new furniture.

I was broke, drunk, and had no real friends to speak of. I thought, "What's the point of it all?" I crossed the line into alcoholic drinking that evening. I poured another drink because I just didn't care anymore.

LIFE AT FOUR LAKES VILLAGE

After Katie was gone I made a call to Gus Adams, a foreman at Plote Excavating. I had worked for him the year before and he liked me. I got my old job back on the dirt-moving crew. I needed this shot-in-the-arm. I felt just about as low as a man can go. Busy hands are happy hands. Besides, I had to pay for all the damned furniture and appliances that Katie so deftly acquired for us.

I loved pushing dirt around all day long, with my big Cat D-8 dozer. I was John Wayne up there in that seat. I listened to rock-and-roll or country music all day long. This was the only place where I felt happy. I was in my own little world with the wind and sun in my face. By now, I was damned good at what I did with all the dirt equipment. I didn't have to talk to anyone. I loved being alone. I just made hand signals to the truck drivers and scraper operators. They all had to do what I said, because I WAS GOD ON MY JOB! I told them all where to dump dirt or cut it. If they screwed up, I spit out my chewing tobacco and waved my arms at them. I'd have a conniption fit, just like one of those old "cowboys" who put the fear of God in me back in the old days. It's weird what happens to a guy when he gets whipped enough. You whip a dog all the time, and you get a pretty damned mean hound. No one fooled with me now. I had knowledge. I paid my dues in many ways. I could do the dirt-work job blindfolded. The job was a fairly simple process for me now. I had a good salary and less responsibility than being on a crane. I could get drunk as a lord at night and come to work and do the job with no complaints or complications. A lot of machine operators end up like this. It makes me sad to think of the guys I knew who died before they could change their lifestyles. I was one of the lucky ones. Most of them died with their smokes and whiskey after sitting in some dark old tavern all night long.

I discovered the pub at Four Lakes Village and all the "bar flies" who frequented this esoteric place. I quickly made personality evaluations of the patrons for future reference. I looked for the characters with interesting qualities to be my drinking companions. My discerning eye quickly dismissed the bullshit artists, cheapskates, egomaniacs, panhandlers, head cases, and assholes. I knew my way around a bar and the way the little social microcosm works!

The first rule of thumb is to always tip your bartenders well. This simple act of generosity immediately provides a person with respect. The bartender will always speak highly of you to all his customers. A man has to have a good reputation! When my bartender tells the people occupying the bar stools of my magnanimous nature, they immediately consider me as being a stand-up kind-of-guy. Bartenders break the ice for strangers, more quickly than you can imagine!

I always made sure that when I offered to buy a lady a drink, I also extended that courtesy to her girlfriends as well. Her girlfriends immediately become my faithful agents and make my pursuit of her favors much easier. My character appears flawless to them, because I bought them a free drink! It is money well spent! In the long run, this small investment saved me great amounts of money on preliminary dinner dates, flowers, and all other costly enticements.

I always showered, and dressed well when I made my appearance in a cocktail lounge. I never splashed on too much cologne!

Before I knew it, everybody knew my name, just like on that inane, old TV show! You remember this show! It's a comedy that lionizes alcoholic-types who display a broad spectrum of dysfunctional problems. I always enjoyed their quasi-intelligent quips while they wasted their time sitting in the bar. Cheers!

I made the pub my home at Four Lakes Village. When I wasn't running my bulldozer, I was in there looking for women. Just outside of the bar was a lovely swimming pool, which was readily seen right from my barstool. I enjoyed my weekends swilling scotch, poolside. A good-looking waitress ushered drinks to me outside as I lay on my lounge chair working on my tan. I fancied all the females in their bikinis who were also "out on the make". These young ladies were plentiful, and I enjoyed the conversational games I had to play to pick them up. I was usually successful in securing a social engagement for later on in the evening. I networked and multi-tasked to the max. This lingo wasn't invented at that time, but it serves me well here in this descriptive narrative. I did my laundry at the pub in the back room, met new girls, procured phone numbers, and bought drinks for all the "right people". I found out where all the good parties were going to be held at the complex. It was easy to meet women at the pub in 1979. Everyone out there was into sex, drugs, and alcohol. I certainly saw some bizarre things while I lived there.

One fellow got so drunk at an apartment party that he fell from a sixth-floor balcony into some "welcoming" shrubs down below on the front lawn. Believe it or not, he lived to tell about it. I saw him a few weeks later, sitting at the bar. He was puffy and bruised, encased in a weird-looking cast, which elevated his broken arm up in the air. It looked totally unorthodox and strange, seeing his arm up over his bloated head! I couldn't believe he hadn't learned his lesson.

His other arm wasn't afflicted in any way, so he held a double scotch on the rocks. He laughed his alcoholic laugh, his face turning red from high blood pressure. His cigarette smoke curled into his bloodshot eyes. With pride and grandiosity, he told us his tale of survival. I thought, "My God. I'd have to quit drinking if this happened to me!" It would be the A.A. tables for sure. A man has to know when to admit defeat!

Another guy I knew from the Four Lakes Pub fell asleep at the wheel of his sports car and lost his spleen as the result of the accident. He came back to the bar, contra his physician's instructions. He picked up right where he left off, drinking alcoholically. He was off to the races again, so-to-speak. This man was a top salesman with a major industrial corporation somewhere in Chicago. His was another classic case of "denial". Alcohol is the only thing that tells a man, everything is A-OK when his life is falling apart around him. It's sad, but true.

While I was living there, I dated an alcoholic high school teacher. She always had 5 or 6 empty bottles of House-of-Stuart scotch lying around her filth-encrusted apartment. Maybe she was going to make planters out of them for some high school project, but I suspected that garbage removal and housekeeping weren't her strong suit. She was content, as long as she had a full bottle on hand, ready to drink. We drank and laughed a lot together. She was a bright, young lady and her looks hadn't left her yet. The ravages the drinking would do to her body and to her mind were out there waiting for her on the horizon.

One strange thing about our relationship was that in the middle of having sex, she fell asleep. If she wasn't snoring, I shook her to make sure she wasn't dead. I'd get up and put my clothes on, leave her a nice note and go home. It all seems pretty funny if you can laugh through the tears. I didn't realize the shame and humiliation my past behavior would cause me, bringing this to mind now at this stage in my life.

One erudite drinking companion of mine always wore a cowboy hat, a big belt buckle, Levi jeans, and cowboy boots. He was going through the "urban cowboy" craze, which was popular back in 1979. Willie Nelson, Waylon Jennings, and all those millionaire rebel cowboys were all the rage. He decides to pull his jeans and underwear down one Friday night in the pub, and press his buttocks against the front window to welcome all the incoming patrons. We call this a "pressed ham" for all of you who are unfamiliar with alcoholic drinking anomalies. He pressed too hard and the glass gave way. There he was, stuck motionless, with his big white ass hanging out the window. I never laughed so hard in my life! Then I realized what a dangerous situation he was in. We rushed to his assistance, until the fire department could get there and extricate him from his predicament. One move and he would slice himself up pretty damned badly. His "hammy" was finally extricated from the jaws of the threatening shards of glass by the firemen.

The pub offered a birds-eye view of skiers whooshing down the big snow hill in the wintertime. The warming fire and the moose head mounted above the fireplace added to the bar's special ambiance. My claim-to-fame at the pub was known as the "moose head incident". One Friday evening, I drank shots of Ouzo and chased them with beers with some giant wrestler from Greece. He thought he was capable of drinking me under the table. He was an amiable sort-of-guy, but the war was on when he challenged me to a drinking contest! My friends at the bar were buying the drinks for us and setting them up. People were betting on their favorites.

I felt just like "Cool Hand Luke" in the egg-eating contest. Little did this oversized Greek know that I had the guts of a Billy goat and the tolerance for alcohol of a Charles Bukowski! I won hands down. I pocketed two twenties and a ten. My foreign friend was a good sport, and took it all in stride.

It was hot that night and for some reason the damned air conditioning wasn't working in the bar. The Greek and I were as drunk as a couple of sailors. He said in his broken English, "Let's take a swim my friend!" "Wow, that was a good idea", I thought! So here the two of us go out to the pool, knocking down bar stools, and anything in our wake to get to our goal: the cool, dark water, of the outside concrete pool! We stripped down to our jockey shorts and jumped in like a couple of whales. The whole house went crazy, laughing at our drunken antics. After about ten minutes, one of my bartender friends tells me that we had better get out of there! He thought, that maybe someone might call the police. Good logic!

I was so drunk I was in my own world and forget that I had an audience watching me. I proceed to pull my jockey shorts off and wring them out. The procedure seemed totally logical to me at the time. I wanted to put my nice khaki shorts back on, but I didn't want the wet underwear to ruin them! The crowd went wild with laughter! So I put on my khaki's, my tee shirt, and sandals and came back into the bar. People were clapping for me! I thought I had done something wonderful! I'm loving all the attention, and taking bows just like a performer. People were coming up to me and patting me on the back, offering to buy me a drink. I felt like I had just won a marathon! I slap my wet jockey shorts next to my drink on the bar and light up a couple of cigarettes for my new friend, the big Greek, and myself.

A bar maid inadvertently picks up my "whitey's" and starts wiping down the bar with them. You can imagine the laughter at her expense! She finally realizes what all the commotion is about and shrieks in terror. After all, what she had in her hand was cradling my crotch just a mere hour ago. She wings the jockeys all the way across the room and they hook themselves right up on the moose's antlers! Everybody cheers at her great toss! There they hung, in all their glory, for quite some time.

The famous jockey shorts held this place of honor in the Four Lakes Pub for weeks, maybe months, or maybe just a few days. Who knows? I was a drunk remember? It's all a blur to me now. This event established my legendary status in this bar. Now, everyone knew my name!

ON BEING THIRTY

I finally made it, the big "3-0". Where the hell had the time gone? What had I accomplished? How much money did I save? I didn't even want to think about it. I sure had a lot of fun along the way...also a lot of heartache. This was the result of my life up to this point. I now needed to get a roommate to defray the costs of living at Four Lakes Village. The rent was eating up my paychecks, and I had a huge bar bill! I advertised in the local papers and hung flyers in laundromats and grocery stores.

The interviewing process was painful for me at best. I couldn't believe the schmucks who were answering my ad! There are some really strange people out there in the world. I finally selected a guy named Steve. The fellow looked like he had just stepped out of an Armani ad in the Gentleman's Quarterly magazine. He had one of those Crest toothpaste, fraternity-boy smiles. I hated him right away, but figured he would pay the damn rent. This kid was squeaky clean! His fetish was driving out to Michael Butler's estate in Oakbrook, Illinois, to watch the Polo matches every Sunday. My God, I was ready to puke! I didn't know if I wanted him for a roommate until he pulled out a big bag of marijuana buds and rolled up a fat one. I fixed him up with a bottle of beer and told him, "Welcome to the apartment. You've got yourself a roommate, Steve!"

As clean as this guy looked, I had a gut feeling that he would at least respect my furniture. After all, he was into the Polo scene and all that phony, rich-guy stuff. He told me he drank Pimm's Chuckers! I thought, "You gotta' be kidding me! Shit, I'm a shot-and-beer man myself!"

All kidding aside, Steve ended up being a great roommate. We had a lot of fun together. He also dated some really good-looking girls. I sometimes ended up with their girlfriends. So Steve graced me with extra females! Steve always paid his share of the rent on time. The only crisis we ever had was when he got the "crabs". I banished him to his room. There was no way I was going to let him sit on my furniture! I sprayed Lysol all over the toilet and made a visual inspection of it with a magnifying glass before I sat down. I sure didn't want to pick up any of those nasty little "buggers".

It was a strange time in my life. I was in dating "Limbo". I gave up the idea of ever finding a suitable woman, who could be a compatible marriage partner. Most of the girls I met and had fun with were all barflies. These women came with all kinds of personal problems and extra baggage.

I hated women who had trouble reading through the funny papers. The absolute worst experience for an intelligent man is when a gorgeous girl asks him, "What's your sign?" My immediate reaction to this question is either to run away screaming (which is probably the best course of action), or to roll up the business section of my Chicago Tribune and "smack her upside the head" with it! I sat in the bar glumly many nights drink in hand.

Steve treated me on my 30th birthday and took me to the bars on Rush Street. We took the train downtown and bar hopped around via taxicab. Drunken driving accidents were fresh in my mind! I wasn't ready to spend my birthday in the hospital or jail. Luckily I had gained some maturity through my recent experiences of pain!

I had a wonderful evening. Harry Carry, the famous voice of the Chicago Cubs, was out with his wife, Dutchie, and actually bought me a drink! I should have had him sign the glass with a magic marker, but I was too wasted! Steve and I ended up at a twenty-four-hour restaurant in Lisle at about 5-in-the-morning for breakfast. It was a good end to a fun-filled evening. I went to sleep with a full belly as the sun was rising and the birdies were chirping. The cocktail hour would begin for me at the pub around three-in-the-afternoon. After I showered, shaved, and brushed my teeth, I would be there to occupy one of the stools.

I just knew I was going to be a lonely bachelor for the rest of my life! I had been burned enough, and felt that I was out of the game for good. Besides, I didn't have two red cents to rub together and was deep in debt. I needed to start saving some money! Little did I know that this troublesome little guy, Cupid, was pulling an arrow out of his quiver. The arrow would strike me, smack dab in the middle of my dark little heart!

DEBBIE

I had an attorney friend named Jim who lived out at Four Lakes Village. He was always trying to cultivate some class in me. He failed miserably most of the time. Jim was a clean-looking guy who was fastidious about everything. He reminded me of "Felix Unger", the character in the "Odd Couple". I must have reminded him of "Oscar Madison". We were quite a pair. We had two things in common: women and scotch. That was enough for a successful friendship!

One Friday evening, Jim suggested we go out to a nice place for a steak and "stalk" some young ladies. Sounds like a nice joint, eh? "Steak and Stalk!" He claimed if I wanted to meet nice women, I had to upgrade the caliber of the drinking establishments I frequented. We went to Houlihan's out in Oakbrook where all the rich people live. They had a nice menu, a big dance floor, and a show band playing the latest music. It was a nice place and it was crowded with a lot of well-dressed people in our age group.

If all goes "according to Hoyle", I could meet a nice church-going girl with a good job, large breasts, a nice ass, an insatiable sexual appetite, and great conversational skills. She would also have parents who owned a multi-national corporation, who had three country club memberships, and two winter homes—one in Cabo San Lucas and the other in Barbados. I always set the "bar" high for myself. This sounded like a good plan!

After Jim and I ate our dinner, he observed two females "eyeballing" us, way over on the other side of the restaurant. Jim had "laser-type" eyes. He said, "Hey, dummy. Don't you see that curly-headed blonde looking at you?" I said, "Huh?" I was either too myopic or too drunk to pick up on anything farther than three feet in front of my face. There were two of them. As Jim dragged me to their table, the girls came into view. They were cuties all right, and they were smiling at us! I knew immediately that the curly-headed doll wanted to meet me!

We found out that they were sisters and that the tall one—who was named Karen—had just arrived back home from Arizona. She was a tall, good-looking girl with suede fringe jacket and she sounded like a darned cowgirl! I liked her right away! The curly-headed sister was good looking as well, with a dynamite body, and a winning smile. Her name was Debbie. She was mine now! So we went out on the dance floor and the fun began! I thought that this gal, Debbie, was great fun! I think Jim was having trouble with his girl, Karen. Jim found a way of being anal-retentive sometimes.

I loved the way these girls were chugging the beer down! Most girls didn't drink regular-old draft beer. These sisters didn't drink those fancy "girlie drinks". I found out their Dad came from Wisconsin. This was definitely a point in their favor! I just love wild, beer-drinking farm girls with great boobs and butts! Their Mom hailed from Alabama. Yeeehaawww!

Debbie and Karen loved to dance. We all danced and laughed and talked until closing time. I hadn't had this much fun in a very long time. My girl Debbie exuded intelligence and good will. We liked each other right away.

We had a wonderful chemistry between us. This chance meeting was too good to be true! Just when I thought I was going to die a lonely bachelor in a single-room apartment with a cat for a companion, I met a girl with all the qualities I had been searching for!

I asked her for her phone number and if she would have dinner with me the next night, which was Saturday. She accepted and it was a date. I told her I was going to make dinner for her. I described to her a fancy meal with yummy food and a nice bottle of wine. I verbally built her a wonderful scenario of candles and soft music and described my beautiful apartment. I thought she would be putty in my hands! One thing I hadn't figured was how I was going to put in an eight-hour shift on the bulldozer the next day. Plus, I was going to have to clean up both the apartment and myself as well as make a fancy dinner all while having a hangover! I guessed I would have to cross that bridge when I came to it. I decided later on the next day that I would fix everything by taking her to a really nice restaurant for cocktails and dinner. I'd let her pick out her favorite place! Everything was going to work out just great! Finally, my luck was going to change!

THE FIRST DATE

I picked up Debbie at her lovely condominium in Lombard, Illinois. Her place was brand new and decorated tastefully. Her wonderfully appointed condominium displayed sculptures, art, and books. She had a variety of lovely plants and a cute little parakeet. I observed that everything she placed in her home was well thought out. She decorated with warmth and loving care. She dressed well. She had an artistic sense for style and color. This lady was refined, not the bar room floozy type I was used to seeing at the pub. Her makeup was done nicely. She was sexy, but she didn't flaunt her sexuality. Debbie, it appeared, did everything with flair and good taste. I liked her very much!

We went to a wonderful restaurant. I was extremely apologetic about my broken promise about preparing her dinner. Debbie was congenial, and took it all in stride. She was happy we were dining at "Arley's", which was one of her favorite restaurants. The restaurant served continental-style cuisine. The menu was filled with wonderful things to eat. The variety of appetizers and entrees was beyond compare! The wine list was more than adequate. The servers wore white gloves and the tables were adorned with genuine white tablecloths. The interior of the place was resplendent with beautiful art and comfortable furniture. I believe the cocktail lounge had a piano bar, but time has taken that from my memory. Debbie and I enjoyed a wonderful meal. We weren't rushed by our waiter, and luxuriated in every moment.

Debbie informed me that she had attended Madonna High School on the Northwest side of Chicago. Immediately following her graduation, she started training as a Ticket Agent for Eastern Airlines.

Eastern shipped her out for her training to Kansas City, Missouri. When her airline schooling was complete, she took a position in Eastern's Oakbrook, Illinois, office. Her job was well paying with excellent benefits. Debbie had traveled all over the world for free! These traveling opportunities were one of the "perks" of her job. Wow! I certainly was impressed! She had traveled to Africa, Europe, Japan, Ireland, Italy, Greece, The Caribbean, and South America. You name the place and there was a very good chance that she had been there.

My head was spinning. This woman was good looking, intelligent, and a world traveler. She had money and took good care of herself. She sure didn't need me! I wondered what she saw in me?

Debbie also owned a brand new Buick Regal, to go along with her condominium. The wheels were spinning so quickly in my head, I hoped she didn't see the smoke coming out of my ears! A relationship with this woman, I thought, was very desirable!

We went back to my apartment and listened to soft music on the stereo. We cuddled up and kissed right from the start. It all was so natural, as if it were meant to be. We both enjoyed the romance and the beauty of our togetherness. One thing that really impressed me about Debbie was her demand that on the way back to her place, I stop at a convenience store so she could purchase a Sunday-Chicago-Tribune! That whole evening, she never thought of asking me about my astrological sign! She had dimensionality to her! Never in my life had I met such a woman! She was that "special someone" for me. I just knew it!

A WHIRLWIND ROMANCE

I threw caution to the wind and called Debbie the next day. I was crestfallen when she told me she was busy. Her sister, Karen, who owned a black German Shepard named Morgan, was visiting her that Sunday afternoon. I said to her, "Bring your sister to my place with you and the black German Shepard as well."

Deb happily agreed to this and the three of them were on their way. I began hurriedly throwing beer cans and detritus away. I tried to hide my sloppy bachelor lifestyle. Exhausted by my efforts, I sat down on the sofa and lit up a cigarette. The three of them entered my apartment and I was amazed at the size of this evil-looking, jet-black, German Shepard! They reassured me that he was gentle as a lamb. Sure! In a few minutes, I was petting him, and he laid his head right in my lap. The girls were laughing at my unwarranted fears as we all settled in to eating popcorn and drinking beer. I poured a big bowl of water for the dog and he lapped it right up! He was a great hound from the very start!

We watched "The Omen"—starring Gregory Peck and Lee Remick—on my new Betamax. The girls were amazed by my recently-acquired piece of technology. The movie coincidentally featured a black German Shepard "devil dog". We all got a big kick out of this! During the film, the girls were laughing at my sidelong glances towards Morgan. I told them, "Anytime now, your dog is going to rip the carotid arteries right out of my neck!" All the while, I was petting him and scratching him behind the ears. He was a big baby. The girls stayed until about nine p.m. that evening. After I ordered a huge pizza, they were sent home with full bellies.

All of us had a good time. I kissed sweet Debbie goodbye, and went to bed that night with a smile on my face. I still couldn't believe my good fortune!

I went to work the next day, full of love. It was early October and the trees were showing their majesty with the colors of autumn. Everything looked and smelled beautiful! When I arrived home, I gambled and picked up the phone to call Debbie. She told me she was glad I called. I intuitively knew she wanted a relationship with me! From that day on, we spent every day together after work.

She filled my once-troubled life with joy. We spent the nights together, either at my place or at her condominium. Every evening, Deb made fabulous meals for me. I gained ten pounds by Christmas time. I brought her home to meet my mom. Mom absolutely fell in love with her! I told my mom, "This is the girl I'm going to marry, because she reminds me of you." Debbie thought my declaration to my mom was sweet! Now I had more confidence in the future of our relationship.

In December, after seven short weeks, I got down on my knees and proposed to Debbie at an Eastern Airlines Christmas Party. Debbie had tears of joy in her eyes as she said, "Yes!" Wow, Debbie was going to be my wife! I was so happy! The Christmas party turned into an engagement celebration as all our friends congratulated us. To top it all off, Debbie won two round-trip tickets to London, England! Life was really wonderful for both of us!

I met Mary, Debbie's mom, who was and still is the sweetest little lady. She had this lovely high-pitched voice and a cute southern drawl. She grew up "dirt poor" in Alabama, but you wouldn't know it listening to her good cheer and exuberance! Mary made the best-damned fried chicken that I ever tasted in my life!

She always made me feel at home and she had the gumption to tell me when I was wrong. Sometimes I made bad decisions in my life. I love her because she always defended me, even when I was at my lowest.

Mary is like a second mother to me now. I'm a fortunate man to have such a wonderful mother-in-law! Mary came up North when she was very young and met a young man named Al, who was Deb's father. He owned a heating and air-conditioning business on the North Side of Chicago.

Unfortunately, Al passed away from spine cancer at the very young age of forty. I always referred to him as "St. Albert", because according to Debbie and Karen, no man could ever measure up to their father. From what I was told about his life, Al and I would have been great friends. Al loved to watch sports and go fishing. He liked his beer and dancing at the Moose Lodge. He was originally from Green Bay, Wisconsin. I love all the "Cheese Heads" up there! They are my kind of people. He was a working man, and most guys who work with their hands are all right with me!

Debbie and I set our wedding date for May 3rd, 1980 at Christ the King Catholic Church in Lombard, Illinois. Debbie wanted a big church wedding with a lot of people. She bought a beautiful wedding gown and veil. We had a gala reception, at a brand new Holiday Inn in Glen Ellyn, Illinois. Debbie hired a wonderful band and forced me through the whole process of picking out invitations and doing things that men don't want to do! Men just want to get married and go on the honeymoon! All that other "girlie" stuff is not in our forte! I did everything Deb wanted anyway. I desired for my beautiful sweetheart to have everything just the way she wanted it! We had great food at the reception and a huge wedding cake.

Everyone in our families was there. All our old neighborhood friends and all our pals from Eastern Airlines attended our wedding reception. All the wonderful events transpired because of my wife's efforts. Deb was—and still is—a dynamo!

I'm so glad Deb and I decided on a big wedding, because every so often we pull out our beautiful wedding album and reminisce while looking at all the wonderful pictures. These memories remind me of what a wonderful life Debbie and I have had together and the good times we spent with family and friends.

We spent our honeymoon on the island of Oahu in Hawaii. We stayed in the brand new Hyatt Hotel on Waikiki Beach. We enjoyed cocktails, great meals, and the lovely sunsets. It was a romantic time for the both of us. When we returned home, I went back to work on the Deep Tunnel Project in Chicago. In the years to come, I spent a lot of my life underground.

DEEP TUNNEL

The Deep Tunnel project in Chicago was a huge undertaking. I worked this rock job (as we called it) on Addison and Rockwell Streets near Wrigley Field, home of the famous Chicago Cubs. This job was a federally-funded project. The Army Corp of Engineers was involved with it in a major way, as well as all the politicians that made Chicago "The City of Big Shoulders". We live in the City That Works, by God! The finished project was supposed to keep residential basements from flooding. Most Chicagoans were in favor of this project, for sure! Yet a few random voices claimed that the project was a boondoggle. The deep tunnel was supposed to clean up the Chicago River so that the effluent coming from the river wouldn't pollute Lake Michigan. Everywhere in the Chicagoland Metropolitan Area, drop shafts were being dug and dynamited. Huge construction companies were bidding for contracts. This vast project was going to last for decades!

I went to work for Ball-Healy-Horn Company, a joint-venture company. This was a top-notch tunnel outfit to work for. Our drop shaft was approximately 150 feet in diameter, and after massive amounts of drilling and shooting rock with dynamite, went way down to about 300 feet at the bottom. Our office trailers, change houses, and various types of equipment sat in a huge yard next to the Chicago River. The jobsite was located right where the famous Riverview Amusement Park once stood. I remember my mom taking me there on the Western Avenue bus when I was a little "shaver". Western Avenue came all the way from the South Side where we lived. We went on all the rides and ate cotton candy right there where I was wearing a hard hat now!

We "tunnel rats" stepped into a man-cage in the morning, lunch boxes in hand, wearing yellow rain suits and steel-shank rubber boots. We wore hard hats, rubber gloves, and carried air rescue masks on our tool belts. If we hit a seam of methane gas or there was a cave-in, the masks could save our lives.

We were lowered to the bottom of the shaft by a huge 100-ton Manitowoc crane, which was called a "friction rig". As we were lowered to the bottom of the shaft, we were greeted by the wet, dank, and gloomy conditions we worked in for the rest of our day. A huge 32-

foot-in-diameter mining machine awaited the "heading" crew. This is the crew that does the actual mining. We checked the 64 carbide steel cutting bits on the "monster" machine to see if any of them were worn out and needed changing. A bad cutter was wrenched or cut out with an oxygen-acetylene cutting torch. We had to get our backs into lifting the 350-lb. replacement cutters and get them into position so we could bolt them in. This is no treat for a man first thing in the morning! We were soaking wet with sweat after this "bull-work".

Once we greased the big bolts and wrenched them in so the new cutters were in place, we were ready to "rock-and-roll".

The mining machine operator began to turn the big wheel and when the huge cylinders stroked the wheel out to the rock face, the rumble from the contact was felt by all of us. The massive churning of the rock created vibrations through our bodies! The noise we experienced was akin to standing next to a huge 747 jet plane! I wore hearing protection— those little yellow "sponge" things. I rolled them between my thumb and forefinger and when they are compressed, I jammed them into my ear canals. I got proficient at this because I wanted to keep my hearing! Once the wheel was chewing up rock, it was thrown on a conveyor belt. My job was to control a "flop-gate" and load boxcars.

I ran an electric-hydraulic car-passing system, which separated cars and transferred them from the incoming set of rails to the outgoing set of rails. This process allowed us to mine continuously, all day long. I pushed the empty cars along with a big piece of steel called a "dog-ear". This facilitated the even loading of the boxcars and helped me to regulate the height of the rock in them. I had to be careful not to spill any rock because the resulting overspill would lead to derailing the boxcar. That would shut the entire job down! Not too much pressure for a man, eh?

The boxcars I loaded were pulled in and out by locomotives. The locomotives were big Deutsch diesel 30-ton machines. These old "whores" had scrubbers on them that were supposed to purify the exhaust, but they belched out black smoke all day long. I hacked up black mucous from out of my lungs for three years. In between the coughing, I lit up Marlboro cigarettes to calm my nerves and drank a couple of pots of coffee a day. With a flashlight, I signaled the locomotive operators who were backing the boxcars into the heading where I wanted to position them underneath the conveyor belt. When the last car was full, I'd signal the locomotive operator on the "loaded side" to pull on out. Out he went to the shaft to have the crane pull the loaded cars out for the dump on top. Up there was a huge mountain of rock, which was loaded into trucks and sent to crushers for road material that would be sold to highway contractors.

The mining machine was powered by twelve huge electric motors using 480 volts. The electricians on the job had to pull and hook up 100-foot sections of electric cable as thick as your arm. The cable was properly called "bologna cable". We had to shut down a few minutes in the dark for them to put the sections together.

The miners drilled holes in the side of the tunnel so short pieces of rebar steel could be put in the holes to support the heavy electric cable. As the machine ate up the rock and gained footage, the miners had to put up ventilation line, which allowed us to get fresh air pumped in from "top-side". Miners worked on a drill deck on top of the mining machine. Up there, they put up a chain-link mesh on the clay seams on top of the tunnel, so rock wouldn't come falling down on our heads. They drilled holes into which epoxy would be injected. Then the short pieces of rebar could be slid in and topped off with small circular plates to hold the mesh in place. The miners then tie-wired the mesh to the rebar.

On a good day, we mined about 30 feet of rock per shift. The company worked three shifts, 24-hours-a-day around the clock. This job never shut down except in the morning for maintenance or to change the bad cutters. Shut down time for maintenance only lasted two to three hours. I remember working on the tunnel job when it was 25-degrees-below-zero outside. We kept the diesels running so they wouldn't freeze up. Even though it was so cold up on top, down in the tunnel it was 45 to 50 degrees. I worked day shift, 9- to 10-hours-a-day, six-days-a-week. The tunnel ran for 5 miles on our leg of the job. I looked forward to a lot of work, a lot of rock, and a lot of money!

The men I called my friends—the miners who did the grunt work—came from the Southern United States. They were mostly young men with coal mining experience. They hailed from Kentucky, Tennessee, North Carolina, West Virginia, and Missouri. Some were from Southern Illinois. They were hardy lads who liked to drink and gamble. None of them ever missed a day's work or a day's pay. There were no "sallies" or crybabies on this job! Only real men worked here.

The crew nicknamed me "Dirty Dick", because I brought them Hustler, Playboy, Penthouse, and other "girlie" magazines. I purchased these "educative" reading materials at the local 7-11 in the morning where I bought my coffee. I loved my crew and the life in the tunnel. "Tunnel Rats" are a special breed of men. If your mind is right when you come down there, it won't be right by the time you leave. I guess I am living proof of that!

We had a lot of fun in spite of the bad conditions! My shift let out at about 4:30 p.m. There was no way in hell that I was going to fight the rush hour traffic on the Eisenhower or I-294. I went to the local tavern with the other "yokels" from the job and sat on a barstool, waiting for the traffic to thin out. We sat in Bill's Two-Way-Inn, a dive bar on Western Avenue. We listened to country music, drinking shots of blackberry brandy chased down by bottles of Old Style beer. At 6 or 7 p.m.—or sometimes if I was naughty, around midnight—I traveled back home to my sweet new bride. She worked all day at the airline and always managed to serve me a wonderful hot meal no matter what time I came home to her. Debbie put up with my carousing at first. She was a good girl. I loved her with all my heart! I used convoluted logic in an effort to legitimize my bad behavior. I complained to her about the rush hour traffic. I explained to her that sitting in the bar was better than sitting in my car for two hours. I saved time by sitting in the bar. This all made very good sense to me!

Debbie expressed all her doubts and fears to me concerning this bone of contention between us. I explained to her that I needed this "valuable" time to network with the higher-ups on the job. It was important to "unwind" with the boys. This was part of my subculture. The male bonding provided me with job security. Guys who didn't drink in the tavern were "suspect".

A man has to drink and tell lies with his buddies in the tavern. Men who didn't drink after work were dismissed from the job sooner or later. Tunnel workers were hard-living and hard-drinking men!

I always came home to a big hug and kiss! My wife gave me a very long leash! I loved Debbie for being so understanding. We both were making a lot of money in 1980. Times were good and we were both saving money and planning for our future. Our weekends were filled with parties and social events. We were both young and filled with the boundless energy of newlyweds. I made it to work easily with only 4- or 5-hours of sleep a night. The tunnel money would "fill our coffers" for at least three years, so Debbie and I decided that her condominium was too small for us. We planned on having a family some day, so we bought a brand new luxury town home in Wheaton, Illinois. We were busy picking out tile, cabinets, carpeting and all the things that were going to make our new love nest beautiful. These were wonderful times. They were the fulfillment of our "American Dream".

WHEATON ILLINOIS — CHRISTMAS SEASON — 1980

Debbie and I were trying to have a baby. Deb miscarried twice and was broken hearted because of it. The second time she miscarried, I was in the bar and she was in our garden apartment. This was the way-station apartment we rented before we moved into our new home. I should have been by her side, but I was with the boys as usual. My bad behavior started chipping away the pedestal Debbie once put me on. This was not to be the last time I took her for granted.

Mary, my mother-in-law, procured the garden apartment for us. She worked for the apartment complex and secured this little place for us to live in without a lease. Deb and I were living out of boxes, with the hopes that our new town home would be completed soon so we would be able to move right in.

Our new home was lovely. It had three bedrooms upstairs, three bathrooms, a huge living room and dining area, and also a comfy family room with a wood-burning fireplace. The kitchen was small, but adequate. We also had a full basement, which was dug deep. I was amazed at the amount of headroom down there. The only thing we regretted was the attached one-car garage. We should have looked for a home with a larger garage. We moved into our new town home the day after Thanksgiving 1980. Like most young homeowners, we were on the hunt for new furniture, draperies, towels, a washer and a dryer, lamps, et al. Deb and I were busy, but happy.

At the time, nothing surrounded our town home but cornfields. We were the first family to move into the complex. Now, in this year of 2008, I have to drive for 5 or 10 minutes to see any green-open expanse. Everything has been developed.

In the old days I enjoyed jogging along the shoulders of the empty highways. I loved looking at the snow in the cornfields and at the wild prairie flowers. These scenes in Wheaton reminded me of my winter runs in New Lenox, Illinois. There was hardly any car traffic to disturb me from meditating on my long distance runs. Debbie and I took long walks through the fields together. We held hands and kissed the way young lovers do.

Like most young husbands, I made a workbench in the basement and started purchasing power tools. I made a lot of furniture for our home in the early years. I loved working with wood. I learned a lot about woodworking from my brother, Jim. He was a master craftsman and made some beautiful furniture. I liked carving little low-relief designs in my finished projects. I learned staining and coating the finished furniture with sealing polymers. This process that I learned from my brother is an art in itself. I think most men need a private place in their homes where they can work at what they love.

Before our first Christmas in the new home, I took my sister-in-law with me downtown to assist in the purchase of a beautiful upright Kimball piano for Debbie. On Christmas Eve, we all gathered around the piano as Debbie played Christmas carols. My wife had a beautiful voice. The whole family sang along as we enjoyed this joyous holiday. We still have that old piano. It's against the same wall, although it hasn't been tuned or played very much for many years. It just stands there "stoically" as a reminder of happy days. It is a familial testament to what used to be in our lives. I bought a lot of liquor every Christmas for the guests who came to our house to celebrate. I'd purchase a bottle of expensive single-malt scotch for my personal enjoyment and a variety of tasty liqueurs for the houseguests. Invariably, I usually ended up drinking the liqueurs by myself, in January.

We also stocked up on plenty of beer and wines. Every year I over indulged. I thought I was the life of the party. The family always begged me to serenade them with my old accordion, late in the evening when we were all feeling good. I knew how to play all the old standards from the 30's and 40's. My mom and Mary sang along and just had the greatest of times for themselves! We younger people thought the whole event was hilarious! I smile now, thinking of the parties we shared in this home. Everyone was full of life back then. The grim specter of illness and death hadn't afflicted us yet. We felt the good times were never going to end.

After living with me for over a year, Debbie began to realize that the alcohol had a grip on me. I tried to manage my drinking and did my best to hide it from her. I failed time-after-time. A heavy drinker usually blames everyone but himself for his problems. Most of these problems arise from the overindulgence in alcohol. Alcohol systematically finds ways to undermine and wound relationships. As an active alcoholic, I lived in a state of denial for many years. I realized that things weren't right inside my head, but I couldn't live without my cocktails. My wife went up to bed on every Christmas Eve as I sat alone enjoying a few more drinks. I always gazed at the Christmas tree lights, waiting for something "magical" to click inside my head. Only then could I go to sleep like the "normal" people in my home.

BOB AND ME—TWO TUNNEL RATS

I met him while working on the Deep Tunnel Project. Bob was his name. He was a good-looking, young guy who reminded me of Burt Reynolds. He was a character who had a devilish grin and a sarcastic sense of humor. We liked each other immediately. His father was some type of executive with United Airlines. Bob grew up in an upper-middle-class home in Lake Forest, Illinois. Although he never attended college—which was a major disappointment for his father—he was one of the smartest guys I had ever met in my life. Bob was "dyslexic" and this affliction prevented him from pursuing the higher education route for his life's journey. Bob could do anything in regard to machine construction and fabrication. He also had a penchant for practical jokes and "storytelling". From day one, we were inseparable on and off the job. We loved each other's sense of humor and were constantly playing "head games" on our poor victims who worked the tunnel with us.

I'd laugh so hard watching Bob play his practical jokes that my sides would hurt at the end of the day. We were both crazy and fed off of each other's antics. This was a buddy-match made in heaven!

Bob could weld like no one I had ever seen. Since my old pipelining days, I never saw anyone lay a bead on steel like him! He fabricated with that old #7018 rod with great skill. He was an excellent mechanic-welder. He taught me fabrication shortcuts and pattern making. I watched him muse over various projects and always find a creative way to accomplish them with no fuss or muss. Working and partying with Bob was extremely educative for me!

Bob was muscular and lean. He loved football, women, gambling, drinking, fishing, and hunting. I thought, "What wasn't to like about this guy?!" When I discovered that we were neighbors in Wheaton, our fates were sealed forever! Right away, we started car-pooling together. He, his lovely wife, Joan, and their four kids lived a mere two blocks from Debbie and me! So now, Bob and I were driving to and from the job together every day. My new Pontiac had all kinds of dents and scratches on it. Both side view mirrors had been knocked from their brackets and were hanging on the sides of the car, swinging from the electrical wires. They looked like rusted Christmas tree ornaments. Bob laughed at my car. He got a big kick out of it. He said, "Dirty Dick, you're the only guy I know with a brand new car who has single-handedly destroyed it with his drinking escapades!" I gave him a dirty look and he laughed. We threw our empty beer cans and crumpled cigarette packages on my fancy suede back seat coming home from work every day. When it was his turn to drive, we did the same in his old Ford F-150 pickup truck.

Bob loved my selections of country western music. I "slammed" eight tracks into the tape player every day. He especially liked Marshall Tucker and Waylon Jennings, but his all-time favorite was David Allen Coe. Bob always asked me, "Dirty Dick, When are ya gonna clean all these beer cans and cig-packs outta your back seat?" I responded by telling him, "When they get almost to window level and the Illinois State Police can get a gander, then I'll get a coal shovel and do the job. Otherwise we are good to go!" This remark just made him crazy with laughter. As I said before, we always had a ball together.

Bob's wife, Joan, was a beautiful girl. She had long brown hair and beautiful dark brown eyes. Joan still had a beautiful figure, even though she had given birth to four kids. She was kind and generous and possessed a great sense of humor. She needed that, being married to a nut case like my pal, Bob! Joan was a devout Roman Catholic. She took herself and the kids to church every Sunday. Bob stayed home on Sundays nursing his hangover and watching NFL football pre-game shows. How the hell he ever got such a good woman to marry him, I'll never know! I should talk, eh? Lord only knows why Debbie ever married me!

On Friday nights, Bob and I always stopped at Bill's Two-Way-Inn Tavern. We drank shots and beers and waited for the traffic to subside. When we got home, we went into his rumpus room and poured ourselves some Jack Daniels and Coke. He had a pool table and we shot eight ball or straight pool until the wee hours of the morning. I was a helluva pool player, and would "whoop his ass" game after game. What made it even more humiliating for Bob was that these beatings happened on his own pool table. Joan loved this and enjoyed watching me beat him! She chortled with amusement and this infuriated Bob! He turned red, threw beer cans, broke pool cues, and screamed at me and swore. It was great fun for all! We ordered a huge pizza and all ended up sitting at the kitchen table, telling stories true and untrue. Bob had great kids. They sat in my lap and called me "Uncle Dick".

I always let my sweetie know that I was safe at Bob's house on these Friday evenings. Deb and Karen were usually at our house watching TV and eating pizza, just like Bob and I. Deb was probably content with the knowledge that I was safe at Bob's house, rather than on the expressway hitting guard rails.

Joan eventually put the kids and herself to bed. Bob and I drank more whiskey and ate pizza to soak up the booze. I'd usually leave somewhere around midnight and be back to pick him up for our Saturday shift at five-in-the-morning.

On Saturday's, Bob and I worked the maintenance shift together. We replaced cutters on the mining machine. We did other work, too, like inspecting and replacing damaged hydraulic hoses. We also did all the welding and greasing on the conveyor belt and mining machine. Before we went down in the "hole" we'd drink a lot of coffee and buy a dozen sweet rolls from "Dunkin Donuts". The sugar rush we got helped curtail the hangovers. Another mechanic nick-named "Nails" taught me how to suck pure oxygen from the tanks we used for our torches. This did a swell job to counter the effects of my hangover and always worked like a charm! Some of the miners always brought a bottle in and we all took pulls from it around two-in-the-afternoon when our work was done.

At the end of the day, Bob and I were all sweaty and greasy from lifting and pounding things with the sledgehammers. Actually, tunnel rats call sledgehammers "double jacks". We'd be cold and soaking wet from lying in water or hot from welding or cutting steel with our torches. It was a man's life. At the end of the Saturday shift, Bob would say, "Lets stop at Bills, just for one." I'd look at him with a devilish smile and my crazy eyes and say, "Yeah...one or twenty?!" After we changed in the hog house, we'd call Joan and Debbie to let them know we'd be home by six. Bob and I usually dragged our carcasses home by 8 p.m., too damned drunk and tired to take the "little women" out anywhere. Our poor wives ended up watching "Love Boat" and "Fantasy Island" with us. Bob and I always ended up snoring in our lazy boy chairs by ten o'clock, each of us in our respective domiciles.

We sure were lucky guys to have such tolerant women. They had all the right in the world to divorce us, or hit us in the head with a hammer. For some strange reason, God gives alcoholic men the best wives. This isn't true in all relationships, but for Bob and I the statement rang absolutely true! Bob and I couldn't have had stronger or more patient wives. I think they knew in their hearts how tough this job was on us mentally and physically. We brought the bacon home. I guess that's why they put up with all our foolishness. I think also, that Debbie and Joan knew how much Bob and I cared for each other. They saw that Bob and I had a special friendship. Now that I'm an old fart, I see how much damage we did to our wives. I inflicted more than a fair share of pain on Deb by not being home where I belonged. During these years, Debbie was a woman of great faith and resilience. She knew how much I loved her, but she came to realize that with alcohol, I didn't know how to help myself. It was sad for both of us.

THE WEEKEND FOOTBALL RITUAL

It's wintertime in Chicago. The "Hawk" is blowing and there is dirty snow and slush in the streets. While young mothers bring their children to church, their husbands pace the floors in anticipation of the Sunday newspaper. Men, who have beard stubble and cigarettes hanging from their lips, gulp their coffee down and curse that drunken, lazy newspaper deliveryman. Finally, the Chicago Sun-Times or Tribune hits the driveway. Actually, it usually ends up in the evergreens. The male homeowner curses to himself and retrieves the desired object.

All news about serial killers, crooked politicians, and the financial pages are discarded for the sports section. The Chicago Bears—the "Monsters of the Midway"—are playing football today!

The bets have been placed with the "bookies" and with the guys on the job. The refrigerator is filled with ice-cold beer. Liquor cabinets have been replenished and potato chips, peanuts, and pretzels have been purchased. It is law that wives are to shop on Saturdays, so the man of the house can dutifully prepare the "altar" of the pre-game feast. Male friends arrive promptly at 11:00 a.m. for the pre-game analysis. Good male friends always arrive bearing gifts of submarine sandwiches, beer, and whiskey. Guys who come with nothing aren't invited back to share in these "holiest of holy" male rituals.

On game day, I enjoyed putting a huge pot of spaghetti sauce on the range. My Italian buddies from Taylor Street in the old neighborhood used to tell me, "Its gravy, Asshole." Screw 'em. I called it sauce, 'cause Mom called it that!

I woke up early on Sunday morning to start browning and simmering the Italian sausage and meatballs that go into my special "gravy".

Real tasty gravy has to simmer on low heat for about four to six hours, so that all the delicious ingredients can meld together and produce the special flavor everyone loved. My Italian friends always knew if the saucepot was tended with loving care. Their moms treated them all as if they were "little princes", so my gravy had to be good!

A layer of vegetable oil is the first thing a chef has to put in the cooking pot. Then he has to build the sauce. The sauce consists of Contadina tomato paste. No other paste is allowable, other than Contadina.

Trust me! I use either fresh or whole canned tomatoes, fresh cloves of garlic, onions, green peppers, oregano, a bay leaf, and other secret ingredients. Also I added salt and pepper, according to taste. A good cook stirs and tastes as he adds these wonderful items. At commercial time, I stirred and tasted while I made myself another cocktail and threw cans of beer at the morons in my den. If I ever burnt the bottom of the pot with the mixture, it ruined everything! This is a heinous mortal sin! Sometimes it happened if I got too drunk! Otherwise, my only other recourse was to order pizzas from fine establishments such as Rosatti's or Giordano's Italian restaurants.

Also added to the gravy are authentic Italian sausage and meatballs purchased from the Italian delicatessen on the South Side of Chicago. These should be browned in a skillet with virgin olive oil and seasonings. Do not overcook! The sauce cooks the meat.

You add the meat once the sauce is bubbling and try and serve the feast at halftime. You have a lot of responsibility when you host the game. My advice is to try and stay sober until the second half! A good host also purchases a couple of fresh loaves of authentic Italian bread. I also bought freshly grated Parmesan cheese, mild and hot giardinera, and 5 lbs. of GENUINE Chicago Italian Beef and gravy for sandwiches! After all these preparations, what you end up with is a respectable Chicago football party! Eat your hearts out New York and Los Angeles! We are the center of the universe, not you!

The boys start drinking at 11:00 a.m., because most of them have hangovers. My friends are all tradesmen. These are the men who build America! I don't invite any "girlie" men to my house for football, only guys who have calloused hands and veins popping out of their forearms! My friends work in steel mills, factories, tunnels, dirt jobs, or swing hammers all day long building your homes. Most of us who didn't have to work on Saturdays, played football in the Lisle Park District league. Supposedly, these are "touch" football games, but everyone comes home bloody and dirty. We play for pride and a keg of beer. We even pay for referees, but we don't respect them too much! The games are really brutal. The ground is frozen or soaking wet. The grass is sparse. No pads or headgear are worn. In every game there is a lot of kicking, biting, and screaming.

Occasionally, "cheap shots" are taken and fistfights break out between the opposing teams. At the end of the game, we all shake hands and head for the local tavern to watch college football on TV. We share a common respect for one another; we all get along in the tavern. Most of the guys who play in these sandlot games had some high school or college football experience. A few of them I met played some semi-pro, or pro football. I played the game until I was forty-years-old. I played for the love of the game, but I had no business being out there at my old age.

I quit playing when one of the guys I knew dropped dead right on the field. He had a heart attack. He was a year younger than me! That's the day I decided to hang up my spikes for good. I left them on a hook in the garage and looked at them every year when the cold winds started blowing. Finally, I gave them away to a neighborhood kid. Anyway, the guys who came to my house for Sunday football were mostly the guys who played in the Saturday games.

We all wore jerseys sporting advertisements for local bars and pizza joints. These small businesses came up with the "trump" money to pay our park fees. If we won a championship, the sponsor got to display the trophy in his bar or behind his pizza counter. Sometimes they were given a picture of the team.

During the Bears game at my house, everyone gets to eat and drink his fill. No Green Bay Packers fans are allowed. I made one exception to this rule. My friend Bob, the tunnel rat, is a Packers fan. He is usually courteous and doesn't mention his freaking sick affiliation with that damned team! We all got drunk, yelled and screamed, and did the high-five thing. We held our heads in agony when the Bears blew it and lost the game. The day was always manic, male, and tribal. I loved it!

These games rotated from house to house, because any "sane" wife would never tolerate this locker room behavior, displayed by their loving husbands, two weeks in a row.

My habit was to space out my drinks so I could watch all the games from eleven-in-the-morning until the post games were over at ten-thirty-at-night. Sometimes, I became too inebriated and woke up in my chair with Debbie watching "Murder She Wrote". Horrors! I knew I blew it and would have to go upstairs to the bedroom to finish watching the Sunday night game! There was no more access to cocktails or junk food up there. Sometimes I sat with her, putting my arm around her little shoulders and toughed it through the "girlie" show. Deb used to say to me, "I'm amazed post-mortem lividity hasn't set in yet, for as long as your ass has been in that lazy boy chair!" Her well-informed quips always amused me on game day!

I always did pretty well with my "fantasy football" picks. I did just as well with the football cards and pools. Betting on the games always gave me an adrenaline rush and made the game action more exciting. If, on Monday morning you come to work to collect your winnings rather than paying out, the hangovers were always easier to bear! I loved the workday on Monday, with all the men recapping the games.

We always had a lot of fun prattling on about who was the best analyst or who made the most money betting on the games. This pro-football fun wasn't over yet, because the featured game-of-the-week is usually on Monday night! "Lordy," I thought, "Debbie isn't going to like this!"

Football is a "God-given right" for every red-blooded American man. This great tradition must be preserved and passed on from father to son. A true Bears fan supports the team through thick and thin, whether they win the Super Bowl or end up with a 3-13 record.

THE NEW BABY-1982

The tunnel job was winding down now. We finished the mining and fortunately, I had enough skills to continue working on concrete-finishing machines and hydraulic truck cranes. I operated a concrete forms carrier, ran locomotives, and served as a compressor operator and a welder on a drill rig. I ran a 30-ton crane next to the Chicago River on Diversey Avenue near the Cabrini-Green housing projects. One job I had on the Chicago River was across the street from a dog food factory. It was on midnight shift and was a horrible experience for me. The crane sat on the West side of the river, and with the wind blowing from the East, the smell of the dead horsemeat carcasses just about gagged me to death on hot summer nights. My throat was raw and sore when I went home every morning.

Debbie finally got pregnant and I was the happiest man in the world! We attended parenting classes and learned about the Sacrament of Baptism at St. James Catholic Church, our Parish in Glen Ellyn, Illinois. Deb and I also attended birthing classes at Good Samaritan Hospital in Downers Grove, Illinois, where our daughter Catherine was going to be born. I learned how to be Deb's coach in the birthing process. I learned how to help her with rhythmic breathing and "huffing". Doesn't sound like a job I would enjoy doing, does it? Don't be fooled! I loved every minute of it! I was a good husband and daddy. I was in the labor room feeding Debbie ice chips and holding her hand while she went through the delivery.

I give Deb credit for not calling me a million deplorable names for putting her in this "delicate" condition! A lot of men are the recipients of many profanities.

Some wives just don't have a sense of humor about giving birth to something larger than a football! My final job was to help the doctor cut the umbilical cord. This was an experience I shall never forget! I loved the beauty of this new, little human being, with all her perfect little fingers and toes! She was my beautiful little girl! I was very proud that I hadn't passed out and that my previous fears about doing something like this were unwarranted!

I handed this little pink baby over to the waiting arms of the anticipant mommy. Debbie was smiling from ear to ear. I was in awe of it all, being the proud father of a healthy little girl! There was no time for drinking with the boys in the tavern that night!

Before this glorious event every night when I came home from work, I rubbed Debbie's swollen feet. In the later stages of her pregnancy, I put my ear to her belly and listened to my little girl "thumping" around in there! Deb and I shared a lot of love and smiles enjoying this phenomenon!

Deb's stomach was really huge. She carried the baby way out in front of her. At first, the gynecologists thought we were going to have twins. They thought they heard two heartbeats. We now were expecting twins, but this wasn't the case. Towards the end of Deb's pregnancy, I actually could see impressions on the outside of her stomach from little arms and legs moving around inside of her! This sight is one of life's greatest miracles for a future father to behold!

I was pregnant at the same time as Debbie, because my weight ballooned from 190 to 235 lbs. I acquired a 44" waist! I didn't look like a marathon runner anymore.

I guess this happens to some dads who enjoy eating ice cream and candy with their expectant wives every night!

Deb and I still own a snapshot from those days where we are standing "belly to belly". It looked like a double pregnancy! These times are valued by me, especially now. I would love to have them back, to savor them once again. Finally, in early October of 1982, I was laid off from the tunnel job. The gravy train always comes to an end for a tradesman, if he buys a new home or car. A lay-off always comes if his wife has another child! This is guaranteed! If a guy has a job working construction, just like "Murphy's Law" a lay-off is sure to come every time, if he makes a major purchase or needs money for one thing or another.

I was happy anyway. I could be around the house to help with the new baby. On October 26, 1982, Debbie and I went fishing at a little farm pond not far from our house. The day was balmy, just like summertime. We caught a whole bunch of bluegill for lunch. It was a great fishing day, because of the warm fall weather. I cleaned 'em and Deb fried 'em up. We were both stuffed and tired after lunch, so we lay down in our bedroom upstairs and napped. As I remember it, Debbie seemed especially tired that day.

We went to bed early that evening, but Debbie couldn't sleep. It was time to take her to the hospital! At 11 p.m., I grabbed her suitcase, and in a frenzy, drove like a maniac to the hospital. Deb was laughing at me, and telling me to slow down. I was blowing red lights and disregarding every traffic law invented by man. I was a typical nervous young husband. I never thought I would react in this manner. At least I remembered to bring her along for the ride!

Poor Deb was in labor for 18 hours and delivered our beautiful daughter around 5 p.m. the next afternoon. We named her "Catherine" after my Grandmother. Later that evening, I called everyone in the world with my good news! I was a Daddy!

HOMECOMING

The baby didn't take to breast-feeding, so we ended up using formula. The only problem was that we didn't plan for this contingency and everyone in the house was running around, losing their minds! I sped to the Jewel grocery store to purchase the valuable nectar, which was to sustain our dear child.

The mothers-in-law were here trying to be helpful, but doing more harm than good. Our heads were spinning with information overload. I thought, "Why doesn't God issue parents a handbook along with the new baby?" She was more expensive than my new color Sony TV! I got a really nice handbook when I made that darned purchase! Anyway, after a couple of weeks, the Grandmas went home. Deb and I were both relieved. Now Debbie and I could rest.

Holding and nurturing a new infant is one of God's miracles! It really becomes your whole life. Men get over this "mystical" experience sooner than women, and pay the price by being called insensitive by their wives and all their "knowledgeable" friends. It was really cool, to have this little baby lying between us on the couch! I guess the most important thing for the psychological development of babies is that you hold them all the time. Deb and I always held our little girl.

I loved coming home from work, showering, and throwing on some hospital scrubs, because nothing else fit "fat daddy" at the time. I'd put my little baby girl on my chest while I was lying on the floor. She pulled out handfuls of my chest hair. Debbie winced with every handful as I smiled and let the baby have her way with me. Catherine was my entertainment now!

It caused me great pain, but anything for my little girl! It was great seeing the baby's little smile. Deb and I were having a lot of fun! It was my job to warm up the bottle for the 4 a.m. feeding. Catherine and I watched that old TV show, "Sea Hunt" every morning. If you're an old fart like me, you remember this show from when you were a kid! It starred Lloyd Bridges and was possibly the most boring show ever put on television. I fed my little girl and watched her suck on the bottle. Her eyes used to flutter as she was filling her little belly. I burped her periodically, per instructions from my wife. I loved how the baby looked into my eyes as I fed her. She put her little hand on mine as I held the bottle. When she was finished, I put her over my shoulder and rubbed her back, making sure all the gas was out of her. Babies sometimes burp up a mess on your shoulder, but you don't care because it's part of the program of being a daddy. Before I put her down in her crib, I checked her diaper for any "surprises". I then massaged her little back, while I sang her a lullaby. Always put a kid on her stomach after you feed her. This was another rule provided for me by my wife! These are the things that daddies remember. I loved doing all these things. A little girl grows up so fast! My daughter is 25-years-old now, but she will always be my little girl. This never changes for a loving father.

As Catherine grew older, Deb and I did all the things that good parents do for their children. Catherine was a well-behaved, smart little girl and never made a "fuss" in public. We brought her everywhere with us. We even brought her to Barbados with us to Heywood's Resort on a Caribbean vacation. She was only two-years-old. We bought her a million toys and games and we played with her on the floor in the den, teaching her how to put things like Legos together.

We read stories to her during the day and at nighttime when we put her to bed in her crib. Mommy and Daddy taught her how to say her prayers and we went to Mass every Sunday. I taught Catherine how to throw a ball and how to ride a bike without training wheels. We all played family games and did jig saw puzzles together. Every Friday night, Auntie Karen came over and we watched comedies on TV and ate pizza. Friday night was always pizza-and-TV comedy night at our house.

Catherine was a Girl Scout and she played baseball and volleyball. She participated in cross country running and basketball. She was a wonderful Ballerina. She took cello and piano lessons. She was with us on all our vacations and family get-togethers. The years went by too quickly as we all grew older together. It was like a "blur". One year just eased into the next.

I'm proud that I turned her into a pretty-darned good baseball player. To this day, Catherine can throw a baseball as well as any man! Debbie always used to say, "Thank God we didn't have a son, because you would have been much too rough on him." I suppose she is right. I always demand excellence. Sometimes I was too rough on my little girl, but I think today she appreciates my past demands for excellence in all her endeavors.

I also taught Catherine about automobile maintenance. She learned how to change oil, do tune-ups, and change tires, because she hung out with me in the garage on Saturday afternoons. Sometimes, when I did my woodworking projects in the basement, she watched me and learned.

"Cat" and I had a lot of fun pulling all sorts of practical jokes on her mom. I overdid it on this behavior. My wife used to tell me, "You need to be her father, not one of her friends!" Debbie was right. Some of the behavior I displayed was inappropriate. Debbie always said I was nothing more than a teenaged boy in a man's body! I guess Deb raised two children! I can't disclaim Debbie's notion in this regard. I'm still pretty much of a teenager at heart!

Catherine never developed the patience to become a fisherwoman like her mom. I'd clean all the fishing gear, the rods and reels, and the boat. I'd ice up the cooler with pop and beer. The boat, trolling motor, and bungee cords would be cleaned and inspected by me before every trip. I charged the battery for the trolling motor overnight and made sure we had life preservers. I mounted the swivel seats in the boat and always brought two paddles, just in case the motor went dead.

I thought my little girl and I would make a full day of it! I bought worms or minnows and hitched the boat to my truck, and then we would head out to the lake. I'd back the boat down the launch ramp and winched her down into the water. We'd motor out to a good fishing spot and "as sure as the sun sets in the west", my kid would be whining about going back to shore and getting a hot dog or an ice cream sandwich! Five minutes after that, she would be crying for me to take her home so she could play with her friends. I scratched my head, shrugged my shoulders, and started doing the bull-work to pack things up and head back home. Dads learn to do these things with character and aplomb if they are good fathers! It was OK. I could head out to the Gables Tavern in Wheaton and watch college football. When we came home early, Debbie interrogated Catherine. Hah! Deb wanted to get the lowdown on Dad!

Such is life! It was worth it! In my mind now—or what's left of it—I would trade anything in the world to have just one more day like this with my little girl.

When she was in grammar school, she was smart as a whip! Catherine was a little whirlwind of activity. I marveled at all the things she excelled at and was quite the proud papa! My kid had an iron will, just like her "old man". She accomplished anything she set her mind to do! Deb and I were really proud of her.

Then came high school. You know what I'm going to say if you've raised children! She turned into this horrible monster! My sweet little girl was wearing pink hair and black nail polish. The clothes she wore belonged on the back of a hooker! I was freaking out! What did I do to deserve this! Deb and I didn't think she'd survive to see her 21st birthday! I really mean this! Debbie spent a lot of sleepless nights. I hit the bottle. My biggest regret in life is that I wasn't available to my daughter when she needed me the most. I cut and ran on her. Being of strong character, she survived and ended up showing me the way!

I'm so very proud of you today, Catherine! You are my strength and my pride and joy! You, the reader will know why I speak of my daughter "showing me the way" later on in this book. I must proceed with other things first and foremost, so that you might understand later on!

ON BEING 40

It's called the big "4-0". It sounds scary doesn't it? Youngsters in their teens and early 20's call this prime time age "geezerdom". When a person turns "40", these kids picture the grim reaper "nipping at their heels". Well kiddies, I think you have addled logic. I'm gonna live a long time dammit! Forty is young! At forty years of age, I was in shape once again!

I did training runs between forty and sixty miles a week. I finally got my fat middle-aged body down to a respectable 170 lbs. I thought it was a hell of an accomplishment, since I was tipping the scales at 235 at the age of 32. My daughter, Catherine, was a happy and healthy seven-year-old. Debbie and I were getting along pretty well. Life was good. I felt and looked a lot younger than the dreaded forty!

At work I was running a brand new bulldozer for a new excavating company in the western suburbs. They had tons of work. All the work was close to my house, which was an added advantage for me in terms of traveling time. My foreman's name was Chuck, and we were on the same page all the time in regard to our concepts on moving dirt. Chuck and I worked together for two years and were friends on and off the job. We drank a few beers together after work every day. Sometimes we went out socially on double dates with our wives. Chuck took good care of me, giving me a lot of overtime. We worked 68 hours, six-days-a-week, weather permitting. I was making big money and doubling up on our mortgage payments. Deb and I decided to opt for a fifteen-year mortgage when we could re-finance for a better rate of interest. I never regretted this move.

I also made a lot of money working on the I-355 project in Illinois. I-355 is also known as "Veteran's Highway". They just finished the project this year, in November of 2007. I worked on it nineteen years ago, but it seems like yesterday. The project was a mere six miles from my front door. I remember working 12-hours-a-day, 7-days-a-week in the "drought year" of 1988. It never rained and we never had a day off. For ten months, we prayed for rain but it never came. I felt like a zombie. I lumbered along every day on "autopilot" just dying for a layoff.

My mind was turning into "burnt toast". I dreamt about pulling machine levers. I pictured myself on my Caterpillar end-loader, loading dump trucks in these surreal dreams. I asked Debbie if these dreams might be a manifestation of some deep-seated neurosis. Maybe something horrible was lying dormant in the corner of my brain, waiting to plunge me into madness! Debbie responded by saying, "No, Rich. You've been crazier than a "mad hatter" for years now. Plus you work too hard and drink too much!" I saw the plausibility of her explanation. Feeling relieved, I cheerfully went back to spreading mustard on my Pastrami sandwich. I planned to eat this delicacy on the "fly" between loading 18-wheelers today. I enjoyed the smell of the fresh coffee I had perking. Soon, I would be pouring it into my beat-up steel thermos for the day's work.

Debbie conspired to throw me a huge surprise party for my 40th birthday at the Arrowhead Country Club in Wheaton, Illinois. She set up a real killer of a ruse for me. To get my butt out of my lazy boy chair on a Sunday is no easy task! My wife had to use her tact, and a considerable amount of mental deliberation! Her lie precipitated my enthusiasm! She told me we were going to attend an Eastern Airlines keg party that day. All right baby! That's what I want to hear!

At the party there was going to be an open bar, plenty of food, a live rock band, and a lot of good-looking girls. "Do you want to go," asked Debbie? "Does a bear shit in the woods? Yeah, I want to go, for sure," said I! She knew she had me! It was a Machiavellian plan, executed perfectly by my sweet little wife. I never missed a chance to drink and dance at a weekend party. I wonder how many other times she might have fooled me over the past 27 years? Oh well, no need to dwell over that one. It will just make me crazier than I already am!

Wow! Was I surprised! Everyone from my immediate family was there. There were also neighbors, friends from the old neighborhood in Chicago, and all our Eastern Airlines friends. Also, there were guys there from the touch football league, and buddies I knew in the construction business and Local #150!

I felt like I was on that antiquated TV show called "This is Your Life", hosted by Ralph Edwards, way back in the 1950's! Tears welled up in my eyes. The party was marvelous! My family and friends purchased some really bizarre gifts for me! They knew me well! They sat me on some sort of "throne" in front of the audience, and I opened each and every gift. I got a big kick out of all the hoopla and the laughter surrounding every gift I received.

Debbie bought me a birthday cake in the shape of a coffin, and all sorts of ominous party favors to add to the flair of being "40". She really outdid herself this time! I was given a functional blow-up doll. You know, one of those sex toy things that perverts buy from adult-oriented shops, located in nefarious neighborhoods!

My 7-year-old daughter had a "ball" dancing with it all afternoon! People were laughing themselves silly, watching my innocent child and her new friend, rock-and- roll all around the dance floor! We still have pictures of Catherine with the doll. I received the traditional sex toys and erectile-dysfunction aids and manuals.

Of course, my "public" knew what I loved best! They blessed me with gifts of expensive bottles of single-malt scotch and liqueurs. I adored these gifts and put them to good use! A few cartons of Marlboro Reds were thrown in for good measure.

Forty was going to be a good year! I felt honored and privileged to have such a wonderful family and so many caring friends. My wife, Debbie, threw a wonderful party for me! I will never forget it. Some of the celebrants came back to our house and we continued drinking and laughing well into the night.

The next day was excruciating for me. I worked 12 hours in 95-degree heat, and high humidity. My tongue hung out like a leather strap all day long on that hot bulldozer! My old man used to say, "If you want to play, you have to pay the piper the next day!" Thanks a lot for the good advice, Dad. I paid the "piper" in spades that day!

When I finally got home that evening, I fell into my lazy boy in a lump and praised God for a functional air conditioner! I poured a couple of cocktails to "get well". I remember experiences in the past when I came home from work sweaty, hot and dirty. I'd be looking forward to a hot shower and a cold cocktail in air-conditioned comfort! Then it would happen! Debbie would say, "The air conditioner isn't working. Do you think you can fix it?"

Shit! I would get this sick feeling in the pit of my stomach. Then I would race to the basement for my toolbox of Craftsman tools and the halogen flashlight. I'd wrench on compressors and replace contactors or fuses in the dark. I did this so the family wouldn't have to sweat in bed all night long. This is what being "40" is all about, I guess. It's the life of a husband and a father. I muttered under my breath that in the 1950's at Mom's house in Chicago, we didn't need air conditioning! We slept with all the doors and windows open. We enjoyed the hot breeze mildly blowing on us! We had electric fans to cool us off back then and we had to breathe the "rancid air" that came from the Stockyards! Do you girls know that this air burnt your throat and nostrils? We were tough back in the "good old days"!

Somehow, I knew I couldn't use this logic on my wife and daughter. They would say in unison, "Just fix it, Dad, for cryin'out loud, or we're gonna rent a room at the Holiday Inn tonight!" I knew I was defeated. I worked and sweat until all was under control.

I ran my last marathon at the age of 40. I shouldn't have attempted another one. The drinking and smoking had taken its toll on me. Although I gave up the smokes in order to do my training, I used chewing tobacco as a replacement. I was drinking too much on the weekends. The race destroyed me. My time was an embarrassment, but I finished it. I'm proud that I managed to finish 5 marathons in my life! The first one was the sweetest for me. I think most marathon runners believe the first is the best! Finishing that first marathon is a lot like having sex for the first time!

In the winter of 1990, I was laid off from the bulldozer job. I hired on as a bartender at a "biker bar". This was going to be quite an adventure! Some forty- year-olds never grow up, because living on the edge is in their blood! Have you absorbed that concept yet, "kiddies"?

THE BIKER BAR

The place was a dump. It smelled of smoke and vomit, urine and sweet antiseptic cleaner that is used in such places to try and cover up the smells of nightly transgressions. The "parade" of fringe-type characters took their places on the bar stools as if they were in some type of bizarre drama. They were to provide me with endless hours of entertainment. Sometimes they produced alarm and fear in me. The experience of tending bar in this kind of place made me happy that I took a class in Aberrant Psychology! The fellow who hired me and who owned this biker-bar at one time was a well-connected politico.

❧

His political endeavors had fallen on hard times, due in part to his sleazy sexual activities captured on camera by a photographer with the local news media. I thought he was a pretty fair fellow in his dealings with me, and Lord knows, we all have skeletons in our closets. He just happened to get caught. His bar was an eyesore and the "squeaky clean types" in the local community wanted it shut down. To keep it going for this long, maybe the owner had greased a few palms. I didn't know and I didn't care. I just needed a job.

I got the job through Debbie's best friend, who was working for the bar owner in some sort of political campaign. Deb's friend knew I was laid off and that I needed work. Debbie's friend told the bar owner that I had plenty of experience on both sides of the bar. She also told him I wouldn't have any problem handling a rough clientele, because I was a pretty big boy and worked in the construction business. I had my doubts about this job, but interviewed with the gentleman and he hired me on the spot. Thus began my career in the "biker bar".

I showed up wearing a denim shirt, Levi jeans, a leather belt sporting a "Caterpillar" belt buckle, and well-worn cowboy boots. I also wore a leather jacket. I didn't want to look like Brian Wilson of the "Beach Boys" in this bar!

❧

I will never forget my first night. It was ten-cent beer night, on a Thursday evening. Two good-looking young girls familiarized me with the bar and its procedures. They looked tough, like they knew the score. Each of them was a no- nonsense-type of woman, wearing heavy eye makeup, tight jeans, and bras that forced their bosoms up out of their blouses, showing a lot of cleavage. They both wore high-heeled boots. These girls seemed like they were hip to any games that anyone could possibly play on them. They were nice enough to me, but seemed guarded in their mannerisms. My mind told me they were there for the money, just like me.

By 8 p.m., the bar was packed. People frantically waved dollar bills, hands held high, way up in the air. I served endless amounts of draft beer in plastic cups. The jukebox blared biker songs by southern rock bands. My clothes were soaked with sweat and beer and they smelled like smoke. In the back of the bar, it was tight, and the girls and I kept bumping into one another. This happened all night long. We all were laughing every time we careened off one another. I guess we needed a choreographer! It didn't help that we were drinking while we were serving!

The two female bartenders and I got along well. This made me relax. The girls worked the men sitting on the other side of the bar hard for the tips, using all of their feminine charms. The girl bartenders seemed to like me, probably because they felt somewhat safer in this atmosphere. I also proved to them that I knew what I was doing behind the bar. The bar had a small kitchen connected to it and served up some great-tasting burgers and seasoned "curly fries". Sometimes we had to cook up these delights while tending bar.

This "multi-tasking" added to the insanity. It was tough cooking and serving drinks at the same time. People were hollering and screaming for more beer and vodka! We told them to "shut up and chill"! Sooner or later, we threw a few bucks at some "homeless" guy who took over the cooking duties. He ended up being a pretty-darned good grill man, if and when he showed up for work.

❧

My back ached from carrying full kegs from the storeroom in back of the bar. I removed the empties first from underneath the taps, and connected the plastic lines to the new kegs. The girls thought I was amazingly strong, carrying the full kegs without the two-wheeled dolly. I guess all the lifting and carrying of oxygen and acetylene bottles on the deep tunnel project gave me an edge!

The bikers and their babes were throwing spare change at us behind the bar. I was really getting "pissed off"! Finally, I pulled the damned plug from the jukebox out of the wall and the music stopped. It got as quiet as a church in that bar. I said, "The next 'mutha-bleeper' to throw any change at me is going to get his ass thrown outside!"

Laura, the barmaid, grabbed me immediately and said, "Rich, you're screwing up. That's tip money they're throwing at us!" She continued, "That's their way of showing' affection!" With this new knowledge, I yelled, "I'm sorry, man. I'm new here!" As I plugged the jukebox back into the wall socket, everyone in the joint cheered and clapped! We all smiled and laughed. The evening rocked on with no more incidents. I found that these bikers and construction workers really tipped me well. They all took care of their bartender. I liked them all; they were mostly working people just like me.

At the end of the night, the other female bartender, Mary-Jo, looked me square in the eye as we were dividing our tips and said, "It's really nice to have a man here with us who knows how to tend bar. We're going to make a great team!"

The three of us closed the blinds to the bar and turned all the inside and outside lights off. In the dim light inside, we poured ourselves some drinks and toasted to our future success. We had to be careful because it was after hours and we didn't need a police citation. The girls and I were finally able to have a drink and a smoke and exhale with relief. We pulled our boots off and put our feet up for the first time in eight hours. I knew I was going to like this job!

A BARTENDER'S GUIDE FOR WORKING IN A BIKER BAR

1. Always let the customers know that YOU and only YOU are in control!

2. Legal Tender—money for drinks—must be presented to the bartender before any drink is poured. The owner must authorize all bar tabs. New bar tabs for any customers are not within the realm of my authority!

3. Bouncers are instructed by management to take all fights outside! Police and ambulances are never to be called, unless there is a chance that a "combatant" may lose his life or limb!

4. Never threaten me verbally or physically! If a customer reaches for me or touches me behind the bar, I am allowed to hit him on his head with my little hickory baseball bat!

5. I maintain the right to quit serving you at any time! I don't care whether you are sober or not, this is MY RIGHT as the bartender! If I over-serve you and you are stopped for a DUI or for some other malfeasance, I am going to jail! This is not going to happen in my bar for any reason!

6. Any patron caught snorting cocaine or any other substance off the top of the bar, or shooting heroin or any other substance in the bathroom, or having illicit sexual contact that is unlawful anywhere in "my house", will immediately be ejected from the premises! This law also applies to smoking controlled substances. All offenders are to be listed on the banned-from-bar plaque, which hangs behind me on the wall next to the cash register.

7. Bottles are to be weighed by the bar manager after each shift. Over-pouring always shows up after cash register tapes are cross-referenced with liquid weights that have been recorded prior to said shift. Bartenders who over-pour will be terminated after their 2nd offense. (The owner loved this little trick I had learned in Las Vegas!)

8. Bartenders and bar boys are responsible for stocking ice and bottled beer in the coolers under the bar. Re-stocking speed-racks and kegs, cleaning glasses, cutting fruit, and

general cleaning and maintenance is an ongoing process to be conducted continuously as needed, every day and night!

9. Ventilation fans are to be kept running until closing time. At the end of each shift, all lights are to be turned off, except burglar lights. Inspect the whole building inside and out before leaving and locking up the bar. The liquor room is to be inspected and padlocked before leaving the bar!

10. All garbage must be bagged and neatly placed into the parking lot dumpsters. All floors are to be swept and mopped. Bar stools are to be placed upside-down on the top of the bar at closing time. The bar must be wiped down with clean detergent and disinfectants. All ashtrays must be washed and dried. All glassware and cooking items are to be cleaned, sanitized, and stored properly!

11. Toilets and bathrooms are to be sanitized and cleaned every evening at closing time. Toilets in disrepair are to be fixed immediately! Any fecal matter, urine, or vomit in the bathrooms, is to be cleaned thoroughly by the bar boy.

12. The bar boy will assist the bartender in ALL jobs. A bar boy's refusal to do any job deemed necessary by the bartender will be fired immediately!

13. Any weapons confiscated by the bouncer or the bartender becomes their property, unless claimed by the local police department.

14. At the beginning of every shift, a "smart" bartender places a couple of large beer pitchers on either end of the bar for tips. A couple of dollar bills are placed in each pitcher. It is my experience that the bigger the receptacle, the more tip money the bartenders will make for themselves! Never use a dinky Tom-Collins glass for tips! (The girls fell in love with me, after I taught them this trick)!

15. SCAMS! Watch out for the $20-to-$10 switch. A bar patron sometimes keeps a $20 in front of him on the bar for a long time. He then tries to palm you a $10 when you are extremely busy! Always look at what you have in your hand and show it to the customer before you give him his change! This simple procedure keeps your bank from being short at the end of the night!

16. For all whiners, scam artists, and cheapskates, always float the whiskey you pour on top of their drinks. Don't mix it! They will think they are getting strong drinks, when in reality, they

are only getting a half of a shot! A bartender smart enough to get away with this is a good "houseman". He saves money for his bar and solidifies his position as an appreciated employee.

17. Finally, always watch your back! Remember to protect yourself at all times!

I kept this bartending job part time for a little more than a year. I began turning into the "type" of person I was serving. I didn't like who I was becoming. This type of job has a subtle way of numbing your mind and damaging your morals! The job cheapens you and involves you with dangerous individuals.

I slowly became extremely paranoid, and with good reason! I was smart enough to quit before my number was up! Life as a bartender is usually a losing proposition. The only way a bartender has a decent life is if he is lucky enough to procure a job in one of the fancy, upscale houses. These nice cocktail lounges and restaurants often pay well and include medical insurance benefits and profit sharing. You don't get anything GOOD from a dive! What you get from a dive is emphysema or lung cancer from second-hand smoke! Also, most bartenders working the "seedy joints" eventually succumb to alcoholism. Many bartenders in these places are attacked or sometimes even murdered. It's not a grand lifestyle!

Improvements are being made. It's state law in Illinois now that cigarette smoking isn't allowed in restaurants and bars. Second-hand smoke is a killer. I know one young woman who died because of her bartending job. She was diagnosed with untreatable lung cancer. After her diagnosis, she survived for only a year. She never smoked a cigarette in her life. She surely deserved a better fate!

Finally, it's easy to meet girls in these dives. But remember, most of these women are no good and come with a lot of "excess baggage"! A bartender should never think that he is superior to his customers. It's good for a bartender who works in a dive bar to realize that, "When you sleep with dogs, you wake up with fleas!"

JOBS 1990 — 1994

I was never happy just sitting around twiddling my thumbs. I hated the winter lay-offs. When I wasn't working construction, I worked in my brother's shop. I loved delivering flowers for good-old Kelly Flynn. The shop was located on 63rd Street and Fairfield Avenue, on the South Side of Chicago. I liked going back to the old neighborhood and sometimes rode past the old cold water flat on 65th and Francisco Avenue, which was my first home as a little boy. Kelly Flynn Flowers sat directly across the street from the beautiful St. Rita Basilica Roman Catholic Church.

Almost every Christmas I delivered flowers. I trudged through snow and slush and drove all over the city of Chicago. I knew all the streets as well as the back of my hand. I delivered flowers to the suburban areas as well. Starting with the firm as a youngster, I was a flower-runner at the age of 9. I sat on an old milk crate in the green Kelly Flynn van. Mr. McGill drove me to my stops. I got lost a lot and fell on the packages sometimes. He never was angry at my ineptitude, because he was an extremely tolerant man. He was an old-school Irishman who took his family to church every Sunday. He also had a penchant for Irish whiskey, which probably added to his humorous demeanor and acceptance of my youthful mistakes!

After I learned the business and my brother trusted my judgment, I drove the big green Kelly Flynn van. I worked on Mother's Day, Easter, Valentines Day, and all the holidays whenever I wasn't working at my construction job. My brother, Jim, always made sure that he had a job for me. Jim and I worked together for over 40 years until he sold the business. He bought the business from Jack Kelly, sometime back in the 1990's. Jack Kelly was like a father to us. He served as the father we never had.

From 1990 to 1994, I mainly worked excavating jobs for the Union. I had most of the winters off now. My body was starting to feel the wear-and-tear of the hard work I had been doing since the age of 22. After working some twenty-odd years riding dirt equipment like a cowboy a man starts to fall apart. One day, my ears started ringing. They haven't stopped since. I went to an ear specialist and was told I had a condition known as Tinnitus. I wore hearing protection all the years I worked, but the nerves in my ears were irreparably damaged. I lost the ability to hear high-pitched sounds. I had trouble understanding conversations in situations where there was a lot of background noise. Typical of the places where I had the most trouble were bars and restaurants. I'm sure that my love of listening to rock-and-roll all my life contributed to my otic degeneration as well.

The fat, Italian Otolaryngologist who diagnosed me, told me to stay way from coffee, cigarettes, and alcohol. Hah! I asked him if he was going to stay away from his mother's homemade Italian food so he could lose about a hundred pounds! I informed him that he was a "heart attack waiting to happen". He didn't have much of a sense of humor in regard to my observation and didn't crack a smile. I told him I'd rather have bells ringing in my ears for the rest of my life rather than give up my favorite things! I walked out of the office in a huff.

I now own a state-of-the-art set of hearing aids. They cost me around 4,000 bucks. They are really efficient and are adjusted by a computer for my personal hearing needs. I never wear them. They're a pain in the ass! Not wearing them helps me when I don't want to hear my wife's demands. I also feel that at my age and intellectual development, most people I meet don't have anything to say to me that I haven't heard already. I guess I'm turning into an old curmudgeon!

One of the jobs I had was in a landfill. You know what kind of place it is. It's a damned stinking garbage dump! I totally deplored this job. I hated pushing garbage around all day long with my bulldozer. There was no art or creativity to this mindless job. Also, the job was unhealthy. After a few days, the inside of my truck smelled like a maggoty garbage can. I started noticing, that even my mouth tasted like garbage. I knew this was not a good thing! Even after a shower, when I scrubbed the hell out of myself with all different kinds of soap, I still smelled like garbage! I couldn't believe that some guys worked in these conditions for 30 or 40 years! I quit after a week.

I hooked up with some crazy guys on a clay tunnel job. The outfit was a small one, just outside of Indianapolis, Indiana. The guys were a bunch of nutty hillbillies and ex-cons who loved to drink! They took me to the best "tittie-bars" that East Indianapolis had to offer! I took them to the same kind of bars in Lyons, Illinois. I quit this tunnel outfit because the equipment was antiquated and dangerous. We were asked by management to do some pretty risky things sometimes. Finally, I got sick from a broken sanitary sewer line. We were wallowing around in crap and used condoms in Maywood, Illinois. The crap was leaching into our tunnel. Even though I wore rubber gloves and a rain suit, I got sick with some type of airborne virus. I packed it in after that and never looked back. The next day I called the Union Hall for a new job.

✍

Working for another clay tunnel outfit, I found out that I had double pneumonia. I tried to treat it myself with scotch in the bar every night. Whiskey always worked for me to kill any bugs in my system! I switched to "light" cigarettes. Somehow, I wasn't getting any better. I felt like some German soldier in a World War II movie was jabbing me between my shoulder blades with his bayonet! Achtung!

The foreman on the job made me go to the hospital after observing my inability to climb out of the tunnel on my own power anymore. The steel ladder that I used to climb out of the 30-foot shaft might just as well have been a thousand feet to topside! I hung on to it, gagging and weasing, until my co-workers prompted me to go back to the bottom of the shaft and wait to ride the man-cage out. The hospital took all kinds of x-rays and CT scans and "imaged" a couple of masses in my lungs. I found out later that a microorganism created my lung masses. The little bugs came from the soil in Beaumont, Texas. It seems that the air ventilation lines we were using were never washed out properly and carried these little "critters" all the way to Chicago. They found a home in my nice warm lungs! The doctor told me that the masses probably would have to be surgically removed. He also told me there was a chance that my lungs might collapse during the procedure. I was getting pretty damned scared now!

I just knew I had lung cancer! It wasn't fun for me writing my will. For God's sake, I had a young daughter in grammar school! I was depressed for the two weeks before the procedure. It was tough for me to smile and pretend everything was all right. I had to hide all the morbid information from my kid.

My wife started researching all the lung diseases known to man and properly diagnosed what was wrong with me. I couldn't believe she was more erudite than the physicians that were diagnosing me, but that's my Debbie!

Miraculously, when the hospital CT scanned me before my procedure, the doctors informed me that the masses had dissolved. All I ended up with from the whole nightmare was some lung scarring due to the pneumonia and two weeks lost on the job. I was a healthy man once again! I vowed never to smoke or work in the tunnels ever again for the rest of my natural life! I lit up a Marlboro Red in a tavern a month after taking my vow!

The mind eventually forgets fear and pain. We all have the capability to deny our illnesses and ultimate mortality. I'm sorry folks, but no matter what you do, you're gonna die someday, Sucker! EEEEK!

THE DEMISE OF EASTERN AIRLINES

Eddie Rickenbaker was a tough-as-nails, World-War-I, ace fighter pilot. By sheer will and elbow grease, he single-handedly built a huge enterprise known to the modern world as Eastern Airlines. My wife, Debbie, worked there for more than 20 years. Eastern Airlines was a company with a heart. The employees enjoyed a fair salary and benefits. All who worked there, from top to bottom, loved this company!

The employees of this company were loyal and gave their best effort at work, everyday. The company reciprocated kindly, showing its loyalty to the employees.

On October 24th, 1978, President Jimmy Carter deregulated the airline industry. Eastern Airlines closed its doors on May 9th, 1988. The CEO of Texas Airlines, Mr. Frank Lorenzo, acquired Eastern, and didn't do too well with his new enterprise. Eddie Rickenbaker was "spinning in his grave" I am sure! As great a man as he was, if he were alive to see this travesty of justice and fair play, I think he might have strangled both Carter and Lorenzo! Eastern went under, and eventually so did Texas Air. Sometimes I wonder if Frank Lorenzo is living in a trailer park today? I doubt it! I have to let my anger and resentment go and forgive him, I suppose!

My wife lost her job on May 9th of 1988, along with many other hard-working people. Union busting was now in vogue. What happened to the steel industry was now happening to the airlines. People were out on the street who had marketable skills, yet the masses of them were told they were overqualified and subsequently, unemployable.

If you ever wonder why we are a nation of "burger flippers", look back to these days for the answers. Debbie, being an intelligent and resourceful young woman, landed firmly on her feet. She interviewed and was hired to do clerical work in the Records Office at the College of Dupage in Glen Ellyn, Illinois.

Her heart was heavy at first, but soon she adjusted to her new life. After a short time, she learned to enjoy her new job. Debbie loved that the distance to the college from our home in Wheaton was only a mile. Deb now would have more time for after-school activities with our daughter, Catherine. This change of occupations for Debbie strangely changed my life dramatically.

FEAR NO ART

In the winter of 1994, Debbie suggested to me that I should improve my mind. I thought my mind was working just fine! She informed me that classes at the College of Dupage were free for family members of employees who worked there. I could take a night or a day class. Deb reasoned with me that some type of scholarship on my part might keep me out of the tavern for a few days a week. Hmmm? I figured this might not be such a bad idea. My wife showed some "glimmers" of logic now and then. I decided to enroll in a drawing class.

When I was a kid, I enjoyed drawing "stuff" all the time. What I drew were scenes of army men engaged in war, with all kinds of blood all over them. Or I drew Cowboys and Indians murdering each other. I guess I showed signs of a dysfunctional personality at a very young age! Maybe television had something to do with my penchant for these violent scenes. At any rate, I loved to draw.

I loved receiving the Venus-Paradise pencil-type drawing kits. I also enjoyed those painting-by-the-numbers canvases. My aunties always gave me these at Christmas time. I never had the patience to stay inside the lines and experimented with colors. The paintings I ended up with always looked muddy or frightening. I was an "Outsider" artist at an early age and didn't even realize it! Usually my efforts at painting ended up in the garbage can. I'd rather put model airplanes together, or battleships, or cars with flames on the sides! That way I could sniff the glue!

I went to my first drawing class at the college with more than a little apprehension. I had a beat-up, 44-year-old body with a ruddy red face and a full beard. I weighed around 235 lbs. and wore a dirty Caterpillar bill cap, flannel shirt, Levis, and cowboy boots. I smelled of whiskey and cigarettes, because I usually spent the afternoon with "chums" at the Gables tavern in unincorporated Wheaton. The "Gables" was my favorite watering hole at the time. If I didn't have an art book or notebook under my arm, the kids in the room probably would have thought that I was a school janitor or some homeless guy.

They all eyed me suspiciously. I must have looked like one of those red-necked maniacs who throw crushed beer cans at college kids who jog on road shoulders! My mind gets funked-up with these unwarranted extrapolations at times, especially when I ponder what people think about my personal appearance! I looked at the kids and felt very awkward. I grinned sheepishly and sat down in an inconspicuous spot in the back of the classroom.

⌘

The students looked like generation X-, Y-, or Z-types that the news media guys are talking about all the time. Whatever the hell they are called, they looked pretty strange to me! Some of them had pink or purple hair. A few had nose rings or ears that were pierced with enough "bling" in the lobes that I was amazed that they could keep their heads upright. They all wore weird-looking clothes. I felt like I was "crashing" some bizarre Halloween party or interrupting some satanic ritual! Most of these kids were so skinny they looked anorexic! Some looked like anomie characters. They never suspected that I was more radical and anarchistic in my past college days than they could ever hope to be! I sat down, ready to draw. I burped and probably passed gas. Let's rock-and-roll!

⌘

Thankfully, the instructor was knowledgeable and urbane. I appeared bright and conversant and I knew he was pleasantly surprised, considering my hayseed appearance. Thank God for my Bachelor of Arts degree! I was enthralled with the class. I learned a lot about marketing art, the magazines to read about art, and contacts to make in the art world through my first instructor. I remember him saying on the very first day, "There are 80,000 artists in the state of Illinois. Only 3% of them make more than $20,000 a year from selling their art." Wow! He did me a great service by sharing this information! In regard to my own art career, I found his statement about artists' incomes to be very true! Yes, I became a professional artist! You can find my work and my "past-and-present glories" on my website:

⌘ Cronborgart.com ⌘

I loved the drawing class right away. We learned about gesture drawing, line, shape, and composition. I also learned about the concepts of negative and positive space. I never realized that art was such an involved process. There was a lot to comprehend. I listened to everything the teacher said about art. I felt young and alive again! My spirit was soaring because I found something that made me passionate once again. I realized that Debbie was right—I had allowed myself to become a worker-drone. I needed to stimulate my mind. Shame on me for waiting this long!

Once the kids in the class got to know me, they liked me. I liked them as well. I was learning about their subculture and how young people felt about things in this modern world of ours. They looked pretty freaky, but a lot of them had wonderful ideas and produced some fabulous-looking art. I told them about the hippie days at Southern Illinois University. They were in awe of my stories, and in their new age vernacular, said to me, "No way! Shut up! Tell us more, old dude!" I was digging the class and drawing some really "freaky-looking" stuff. The teacher told me I had a real talent for drawing. He thought I had an excellent feel for "value". He said that my work in black-and-white was "striking"! Debbie was right! This art class was almost as much fun as the tavern! Now I had two passions: art and drinking!

Artists "get away" with everything. They can be drug addicts, womanizers, wife-beaters, alcoholics, and head cases of all sorts. All the bad behavior is excused as long as the public believes the artist is a "great talent"! These artist types had a great con going on, and I wanted what they had! My whole life, I adored subversives and fringe-type characters. Now I had the chance to be one myself! This art thing is going to be a perfect fit for my personality.

I first started painting on heavy duty Arches 140-lb.cold-press watercolor paper. Then I graduated to using gallery wrap canvas. Now that I'm a "so-called" professional, I always use high-quality paint. I particularly enjoy using Golden Acrylics. I like the "immediacy" and quick drying time these acrylics provide for me. I paint quickly. I think that since the mind works on ideational processes at high speed, the effects an artist can produce for the appreciator are more honest if he works quickly. If the artist structures things and thinks too much about the results, the art usually isn't very good in terms of "quality". Art is not like science. When creating art, the artist always makes heuristic leaps in his mind. I let my "inner voice" rule my hand at all times when using the brush. If I don't like what the results are, I can paint over my mistakes.

Acrylics are plastics, and the worst-case scenario of a paint-over is a more textural production of art. Heavy impasto is not going to deter from the validity of the piece! Oils tend to be less forgiving and are more toxic. Artists have to be careful, because they die from the lead and fumes inhaled or absorbed by the skin in the painting process. Cadmium colors—like yellow and red—are dangerous, because of their lead toxicity.

I also learned printmaking. I learned how to carve reverse images on linoleum plates. My hand became raw and red from the carving, and I developed some awful blisters and carpal tunnel problems in my right wrist. I had to resort to leather gloves and wrist supports to continue to carve my linoleum plates.

I read all the important art magazines and joined the Chicago Artists Coalition. I also joined the DuPage Art League.

I constantly checked out art books from the Wheaton Public Library. I've done shows at both the Glen Ellyn and Wheaton Public Libraries. I studied all the mediums, the Old Masters, new artists, and the multi-varied processes that are utilized in the creation of art. I searched out images in magazines and old books. I have an astounding collection of old art books in my studio. At this time, I currently have over a thousand books related to art in my studio and scattered throughout our house. I have approximately 400 paintings in my house as well. I give studio viewings to patrons who are interested in collecting my work. Debbie says we're going to have to buy another house in order to store all the crap I have accumulated over the years!

I bought a variety of cameras to capture images. In essence, my belly has "the fire in it!" I am a man totally obsessed with his Mistress ART!

The psychology of planning and creating art led me inside of myself. Who was I? What did life mean to me? I was learning to see things in a special way.

When an artist is passionate and obsessive about his art, his life changes dramatically. His ability to sling "bullshit" at wealthy collectors dramatically increases as well!

OUR FIRST COMPUTER

My dear daughter, Catherine, was starting High School. Debbie told me it was absolutely necessary that we hurry to the "Best-Buy" store and purchase a computer, printer, and scanner. We also had to hook up with America Online so we could "surf" the World-Wide-Web. Huh? What was this foreign language? Had my wife finally gone "round the bend?"

"How much is this thing going to cost me," I asked. "I bet it's gonna cost me a fortune! Can't she use the computer at the public library," I thought? I presented my case well and had won this war! "NO," Debbie shrieked! I knew that look she was giving me. I was finished! "We're buying one right now and you're coming with us," she exclaimed! "We need you to load it in your pickup truck!"

Damn! It was a hot summer day and we drove down the road to the electronics store in my little S-10 Chevy. The three of us were squeezed together like sardines. We were sweating in the heat because my work truck didn't have air-conditioning. This was another one of my "good" ideas. I thought I would save money without the "air". It was not a good idea, because everyone was hot and angry when we finally reached the store. It was "total mayhem" inside of the place! The girls went through the process of trying to find a salesman and pick out the right computer and all the other "bells and whistles" that went along with the damned thing! I sat in an inconspicuous place somewhere in the store, in a little chair, wishing I were in the tavern. My hiding didn't work to well because Debbie and Catherine were onto me right away.

Catherine said to me, "You're not going to sit this one out, Daddy-O!" She was acquiring this new sense of female authority. I thought my wife had tutored her well! I was amused, proud, and pissed off—all at the same time! We finally got all these new-fangled devices into the shopping cart and stood in a line that seemed about a half-mile long. We waited for what seemed an eternity in this checkout line. What the hell were all these people doing here? I thought they were all crazy!

Of course, through the ordeal I was a total asshole. I wanted to be in my lazy boy chair, drinking scotch and watching the Chicago White Sox. Besides, this damned 'puter was going to cost me an arm-and-a-leg!

Shit! I could go on a junket to Las Vegas for the weekend, and party like a king with the kind of money we were spending today!

On the way home, we all calmed down. We were laughing and joking until the girls asked me to put the mess together for them. Women always have a way of putting you in good spirits before they drop another "bomb" on your head! Debbie said I wasn't allowed a cocktail until I got the computer up and running. Geez! I'd have to put my thinking cap on! Surprisingly, the instruction manuals were pretty damned-well written. What a small miracle! Praise the Lord and all the Saints! I put the components together, one by one, making sure to color code all the cables. I neatly harnessed the tangled mess of wires and hid them in back of the computer cabinet, which I also had to assemble. This thing came from China and the manual didn't make any sense at all! I cast all kinds of aspersions toward these little yellow men!

The wife and kid socked-in the AOL software disc into the slot of the 'puter and it was, "So Long, Dad"! They had a ball with the thing all night long. I returned to my chair to watch my beloved White Sox get their "asses handed to them" by the HATED New York Yankees!

Deb and Catherine kept screaming at me from the other room. "C'mon Dad! You gotta see this thing!" I said, "No way!" I wanted no part of the thing. About two weeks later, after listening to the girls laughing and having fun, I started wondering about the computer. Maybe there was something to this crazy thing after all. Finally, my curiosity got the best of me.

I sauntered over to the computer one day and received a tutorial on its finer points from my girls. They made a big mistake that day! From that day on, I was a computer junkie! I couldn't believe the information this "magic machine" could produce for me! Anything I wanted could be mine, as long as I typed the proper nomenclature into the keyword box. I was one "click" away from instant gratification!

Being a red-blooded American male, PORN was one of the first words I typed in the box. I was instantly rewarded with a veritable cornucopia of depravity! Some of this stuff was so "hard core" that it embarrassed the hell out of me! I had to make sure I did this thing ALONE! I also had to figure out how to delete all the nasty places I visited. I learned about all the parental control-type things. I consulted with all my "geek" buddies and figured out all the privacy tricks. After all this work, my "Catholic guilt" was too much for me to bear. I gave it all up! My 'puter was slowing down and I didn't want to "cook" my hard drive with any porn-related "viruses." One day, something amazing happened to me. I felt as if I were struck by a thunderbolt of knowledge!

I thought, "What if I used this computer to find art galleries in Chicago to sell my paintings?" This simple idea sent me on my way to a wild and crazy new life!

FAME IS ONLY A MOUSE-CLICK AWAY

In 1995, Wicker Park on Chicago's near-North Side was an eclectic and electric artist's community. The Flat Iron Building on Damen and North Avenue housed many artists and was the nerve center for "emerging" new art. An artist could rent "cheap" studio space at the Flat Iron. All my crazy artist associates were either living there or in other roach-infested crash pads in the area. We were all painting and raising hell at bars and in dance clubs around the neighborhood.

The area was really different back in the 70's, when I was driving a flower wagon for my brother, Jim. We delivered packages of flowers to the Chicago Metropolitan Flower Distribution Warehouse up near 1800 North Milwaukee Avenue.

Driving my van from Kelly Flynn flowers from the South side, I'd exit the Kennedy Expressway on North Avenue and head West from Ashland to Damen.

In the 70's, the Wicker Park area was infested with prostitutes and confidence men. Panhandlers, drunks, and gang-bangers roamed the streets. Gang symbols and graffiti were spray painted all over buildings and fences. Little by little, the area started gentrifying. After ten-years-time, the artists were moving in for the cheap rents and the large studio spaces. Reasonably-priced spaces were readily available to artists in the 80's. Little shops, record stores, and galleries began to proliferate in the area. Then larger enterprises started to move in. The "ultra hip" professional young people, started making the neighborhood their own. By 1995, the artists who beautified the community no longer could afford to live there. The last bastion for them was the Flat Iron Building. This studio complex remains affordable, even today. As the property values went up, many artists moved to Logan Square or other fringe neighborhoods to start the process once again.

It's a sad reality that we love the beauty that the artist creates, but we devalue the artist himself. The arts are usually disregarded by a lack grant monies and are deemed to be less important by our government agencies than the sciences in most schools. Our government always short-changes the Arts in America. Now in Wicker Park, the "yuppies" have claimed the neighborhood. The streets are thriving with Sushi

Bars, expensive restaurants, Starbucks Coffee, expensive boutiques, and upscale galleries that show inferior art at inflated prices.

Some of the Mom-and-Pop galleries still exist, but are few-and-far-between. A few dive bars and coffee shops still remain on the fringes. If you look hard enough, you can still find a good hot dog stand amidst all the glitter and glamour.

When I first arrived on the scene in 1995, I could purchase a double J & B on the rocks for about a buck-and-a-half at the Borderline Tap from my dear bartender, Amy. The Borderline tap is still there, but the clientele has changed dramatically from the working class or homeless "Nelson Algren-types" to the bland "yuppified" androids with the big bucks. In the old days, Amy poured heavy drinks for me because I always took care of her with a nice tip. This is the Wicker Park I knew and loved! It exists no more. Now, money is the bottom line. The same drink today would cost me between six to nine bucks! Thank God, that I'm a recovering alcoholic now! Even Starbucks gets deep into my pockets! I feel this is an affront to the artists who made the community! The famous Double-Door lounge is also located on Damen, North, and Milwaukee Avenues. Artists like the Rolling Stones and David Allen Coe sat in there and played gigs for free. Even though it has its "uppity side", Wicker Park is still a happening place. I love it, and it is still very good to me. Now, back to the old days once again...

The computer allowed me to make contacts with many of the galleries in Wicker Park and other areas in the city with galleries that featured artwork that looked similar to mine. I always wanted to show my work in Wicker Park. I "stomped" into Gallery 1633 on Damen with my ratty 22" x 30" watercolors on paper jammed under my arm. I wasn't too sophisticated back then! I showed them to gallery artist, David Moskow, and he liked them very much, so he led me to the gallery owner.

Her name was Montana Morrison, the radical, eccentric-looking, grand dame of the gallery scene. She knew a lot about the business and had shown her art all over the world. Hers was a co-operative gallery. Montana gave me a shot at my first shared show. Of course she was happy to get the $100 hanging fee, and the 25% commission on my sales. As I mentioned before, the art business is a gamble! I hung 8 paintings and got some good visual wall space, right next to the front door. People passing the gallery on the street saw my work. I also got lucky with the Northside Café next to the gallery. They hung 12 of my paintings in the bar. I got the restaurant show for free, with no hanging fees. I had two venues working for me, simultaneously on the same weekend. My work would hang in them each for a month.

I tried to sell art to people at the bar of the Northside Café while I slugged down scotch. I did pretty well at this, showing my portfolio at the bar. I was the inveterate salesman! The Northside even gave me fancy postcards and a small buffet on opening night to promote my show. The manager of the Northside was a nice guy. I made sure to always tip him well, if and when I sold a piece of art.

✍

The Northside owners figured that they would make out selling food and drinks to all my adoring art appreciators, and they were right! My crowd liked to drink and eat. I was always invited back there to show my art, because they made money!

They probably made a few-hundred bucks on me alone, swilling scotch, and eating hobo breakfasts in the morning to cure my hangovers! I made a lot of friends in Wicker Park. I bought drinks for everybody. I showed my artwork to the owner of the Eclectic Junction for Art across the street from the Northside Café and Gallery 1633. This gallery / boutique was more upscale, but I didn't get any "play" from the show. I figured, at the very least, I could add this gallery to my resume.

I was nervous and excited the night I first showed my work professionally. I called and sent emails and postcards to everyone I knew. Shameless self-promotion is the key to success for every artist. Artists who don't hustle always fail, unless they know someone with "clout". My first turnout was huge! That's always that way in the beginning. People came in off the streets to see what all the excitement was about. There were actually lines of people forming to get into the restaurant and the gallery to see my work. I was the new "Golden Boy" of Wicker Park! The magic was happening, and it was happening to me! The adrenaline rush I felt was unbelievable! I pocketed around $2,000 after drinking and smiling my phony smile, working art buyers to take the money out of their pockets. These were two days of drunken insanity and pressure for me, but I loved every minute of it! I sold 8 paintings. I thrived on the fast paced action of it all! I knew that quitting my day job would not be a good decision. Montana told me that I had beginners luck. I believed her, thank God! Times were going to get worse—they always do!

I felt like the new "Mayor" of Wicker Park. The neighborhood was "buzzing" with talk about the new artist who was selling a shit-load of work at the two venues. Other gallery owners were coming to see me with offers of solo shows. They knew I was "hot" and they wanted in for the ride on my gravy train.

I got gigs at The 13th Floor Gallery, The Flat Iron Building, The Dix Art Mix, Feitico, The Echo Gallery, The Gallery Café, and Excalibur on Dearborn Street. Over the years, I showed my art in a plethora of other galleries, coffee shops, beauty shops, and restaurants. In my early years, I was one of the hardest-working artists in Chicago. The hardest working artist I knew in the business is a gentleman and friend of mine named Walter Fydryck. The David Leonardis Gallery in Chicago represents him and had even featured a few of my paintings way back in the day. I bought a cheap digital camera and began e-mailing photos of my artwork to every gallery in Chicago. Of course, I researched the galleries to make sure they showed my style of art.

I maintained a hard-nosed tenacity in my efforts to contact newspapers, TV-show producers, radio personalities, and well-known Chicago artists. Doors were always slammed in my face, but rejections never impeded my desire for success. I knew that sooner or later, because of my hard work, good things were going to happen for me! Good things did happen for me, and they happened all at once!

My friends, Chas Kirstich and David Moskow-gallery artists at Gallery 1633—put together a web site for me and featured me on their Chicago cable access TV show, "Discover Art". Chas made copies of the videotape interview, which was shot at the Gold Star Bar on Divison Street, so I could use it as a marketing device. Most weekends, I hung out in the bars of Wicker Park with my briefcase of promotional materials and my portfolio of paintings. I drank at the Borderline Tap every weekend, showing my artwork to anyone who would bother to take a gander at it. I sold artwork out of the trunk of my car. I prided myself on the fact that I NEVER missed an opportunity for a sale! I was a flim-flam man, a regular Barnum-and-Bailey, Ringling-Brothers kinda guy!

I emailed the famous Chicago artist, Ed Paschke. Ed was the most famous of the Chicago Imagists at the time. He taught at Northwestern University and had paintings hanging all over the world. I showed him my web site via the computer. It blew my mind when Ed called my house to talk about my art. This guy had artwork in the Art Institute on Michigan Avenue, in the Louvre in Paris, and in River North at an upscale gallery directed by Maya Polsky. This man was successful. He WAS Chicago Art! I saw his face in the society pages of the Chicago Tribune all the time! My wife, Debbie, got so nervous one time when Ed called me, I thought she was going to have a heart attack! I told her, "Don't worry, Dear. He can wait a couple of minutes. He puts his pants on the same way that I do—one leg at a time." Ed heard what I said and was really amused. We talked about art for a while and became fast friends.

I went to all of Ed Paschke's lectures and ran into him, time and time again. He moderated a 9-11 show after the Twin Tower disaster in New York City. I had a piece of art in this show at the Jettset-Gallery run by Jett Walczak, another friend of Ed's. My friend Ed passed away suddenly in his sleep, over three years ago on Thanksgiving eve.

My mom had her stroke, the very next day. It was a tough time. Ed was my mentor. He represented to many others—and to me—what was "the best-and-finest" in Chicago art. I loved his style and learned much from him. He was always a regular guy. He made himself available to artists who had the "passion". He always referred to me as "Corndog"— my AOL moniker. We both laughed about this!

After Ed's death, Clyde Mlodoch asked me to participate in two Ed Paschke Memorial Shows. Clyde was a personal friend of Ed's and made latex skulls in a mold, which we all decorated in honor of our friend.

The shows were held at the Judy Saslow Gallery on Superior Street in the River North Art District in Chicago. I owe Clyde and Judy many thanks for the honor. I am thankful that Judy's gallery honors Ed with this Memorial Show every year.

Yes, I wanted success. Every artist does. I desperately wanted to make a name for myself in Chicago or New York. I chased rainbows, trying to grab that "brass ring." I was neglecting my family. I was "spinning out of control."

WHERE'S MY FATHER? WHY DID HE ABANDON US?

I thought my family was holding me back in the pursuit of my dreams. In fact, my family became a burden to me. Didn't they understand how hard I was working for them? I put myself under a lot of pressure in those days. I ran a bulldozer all day long. In the evenings, after having three or four "heavy" cocktails, I ate my dinner quickly. I got pretty hammered before dinner every night. Then I went to the computer screen to answer emails and pursue the dreams I had in regard to the art world. I left my wife Debbie to parent Catherine alone. I wanted nothing to do with them. I was too busy. I knew I had broken their hearts, but I didn't care. I failed miserably as a father and a husband. These teen years are the most important for a daughter to have a father involved in her life.

Catherine was in high school, and with all the negative peer pressure, needed me to be a good guide for her. A good father helps his daughter to make the right decisions. Catherine never came to me with her problems. I guess she knew what my reaction would be. I yelled or screamed at her too many times in the past, so I was not an option for her in the search for her solutions to her problems. After a while, I guess she gave up on me. I don't blame her! I emerged as an arrogant stranger to my wife and daughter. Day after day, I drove them further away with my alcoholic narcissism.

On rainy days and weekends, I went to the basement of the house and painted. I stood alone in my studio, listening to jazz or blues. I drank whiskey between brushstrokes. When Debbie and Catherine weren't home, I smoked marijuana.

Every weekend was the pilgrimage to the "artsy" districts, to see a new artist or to develop new business contacts. I brought Debbie with me to the galleries and bars for a while, but she saw through the phony veneer of the Chicago art scene. Right away, Debbie wanted no part of what I was doing. She'd rather be home for my teenage daughter. This is where I belonged as well! We needed to be a family again. Real wealth exists in the home! I threw all these gifts away, in a sick quest for some abstract dream.

I suppose I wanted to remain a teenager myself, forever. I used bad judgment in regard to my family. I never wanted to develop the maturity in myself to be a husband and a father. I thought in my alcoholic mind that I was smart enough to hide all my "dark secrets" from my family. I half-heartedly participated in every activity, which was worthwhile or meaningful to them. This is a heinous crime for any man who calls himself a husband or a father.

Today it's my responsibility to make amends for my past sins. Saying, "I'm Sorry," isn't enough. My family heard these words over and over again. If I lived an exemplary life, my example could become a "living amends". This decision is the only one that could carry me to the place where I needed to go. I wasn't ready to take these steps for a very long time. Some men remain children for a lifetime.

ART-WORLD ROCK STAR

In 1999, I was getting a name for myself in the Chicago art world. Lisa Black of the Chicago Tribune interviewed me for a front-page-spread, which was featured in the Metropolitan section of the newspaper. The story was biographical in nature and played heavily on the construction-worker, artist-dichotomy, in my life. The Tribune photographer came to my home to capture a picture of me, cigarette dangling from my mouth as I applied paint to one of my canvases. He posed me to capture the washer and dryer in my basement studio. I suppose he wanted to portray me as a struggling workingman with aspirations to be the next Jackson Pollack. This worked for me! My head was up in the clouds! It was a major victory for me to be the center of attention, as a "human interest story" in a major Chicago newspaper.

About the same time, CLTV News, a big-league Chicago Cable TV station, filmed me hard at work at my construction site. They filmed me on a steel drummed earth compacting machine on a hot summer day. I had my hard hat on my head and was grinning from ear to ear like some kind of moron!

Debbie, Catherine, and I got a big kick out of this one! My job superintendent was freaking out, because all the men stopped working to watch me, "the artist superstar". I was eating it up! I told the boss that he owed me for all the publicity the construction company was going to get on prime-time news that evening! My news story aired on the CLTV show, Chicagoland Journals. They also filmed me at the Dix-Art-Mix gallery in Buck town — an artsy neighborhood in Chicago — for the second half of the TV segment. I had 80 pieces of my art in this Gallery for my first solo show. I was on a roll and loved all the publicity. My dreams were becoming realities!

I was the "big cheese" now! Good-looking, young women wanted to be seen with me. They followed me from the galleries to the nightclubs and bars. I had an "entourage" of people now, who wanted to know all about me! People can "smell" money and success. I was on stage all the time. It's not what its cracked up to be! Lonely and drunk after my art shows, I drove back home to my house in Wheaton. I crawled into bed feeling tired and old, in the wee hours of the morning.

I contacted Harvey Moshman, producer of "Wild-Chicago," a popular TV show on channel 11, WTTW in Chicago. I hit it lucky; he was interested in my newspaper articles and videotapes. He contacted me to do a segment about my art and my life. The now non-existent Feitico art gallery was to be the centerpiece of the show. I wasn't going to be the main attraction. I missed out on having the whole feature story done on me, but was happy to help put together the deal. I got about 30 seconds of airtime. Hey! To this day, people still recognize me as being "that guy" on Wild Chicago! The Feitico gallery represented me and other "erotic" style artists on North Avenue and Wood Streets in Wicker Park. The gallery was one of the hottest in Chicago at that time!

The Feitico art gallery was really popular with the Chicago Fetish Community. Everyone showed up in "costume" for the shooting of Wild-Chicago. People had whips and chains and were wearing all kinds of leather. Feather boas, lingerie, and other things were worn by cross dressers, transgenders, dominatrix types, models, and regular artists. All kinds of weirdos showed up in other strange getups. I just wore a pair of slacks, a jaunty artist's cap and had my art portfolio in hand as usual, to sell my paintings. The whole scene had the feel of a circus! I was a media-darling once again! Millions of people got to see my "whiskey nose" on TV! It was no big freaking deal! Who cares? It means nothing to me now.

All of this groovy stuff went down, because I was one-hell-of-a-salesman and promoter. The time I spent as a clothing salesman wasn't wasted! I felt that this was going to be my year! My mottled face was all over the media. I was a hot commodity! I was on fire! People felt my enthusiasm! I WAS FULL OF CRAP!

The Wheaton Sun newspaper contacted me also in 1999. Jason Effman, a nice young man, interviewed me about my art and life experiences. He titled the article, "Renaissance Man". My phone rang off the hook.

Real big-time media exposure came after I emailed Mr. Harry Porterfield of Channel 7 television, here in Chicago. This was ABC! This was prime-time evening news! Harry was interested in my story and he interviewed me for his show, "Someone You Should Know".

Two million people watched this show every evening in Chicago and the surrounding suburbs! The ABC cameraman filmed me running a bulldozer and shoveling mud from its dirty tracks. The television crew came to my home and the camera guy shot me painting in my art studio. Mr. Porterfield also mentioned my art show at Excalibur, a huge nightclub on Dearborn Street on the near North-side of Chicago. This show at Excalibur was well promoted, and was mentioned in the prestigious New Art Examiner—the most prestigious art magazine to be mentioned in at the time!

My neighbors were craning their necks to see the Channel 7 van in my driveway. The phone was ringing once again! I owe Harry so much for taking an interest in me. He is an honorable man who, through hard work and interest in the "little guy", has won 11 Emmy Awards for his excellent humanitarian journalism.

Harry was always kind enough to answer my calls at Channel 7 News. He was also kind enough to do a story about the life of my dear friend, Bruce McMartin, a wonderful guy who creates fabulous "Outsider Art". I mailed one of my paintings to Mr. Porterfield for being such a nice guy. I hope he still has it and enjoys it very much! This was the least I could do for the wonderful stories he did about Bruce and me. Even now, I enjoy watching Harry Porterfield do his show on the TV.

With each new television show or newspaper article, I became more self-centered. People were sick of me talking about myself all the time. My poor wife, Debbie, had to endure my pomposity every single day. It had to be a nightmare for her and my daughter. I told them, "I'm someone you should know!" Yeah, they should have known me as a husband and father. I wouldn't let them know me. I didn't care about them. I just cared about myself. I had become "someone who should be disregarded". I had turned into an alcoholic ass and a fool. It wouldn't take long for my fall to come.

HITTING BOTTOM

I was worn-out by the age of 49. I woke up one sun-shiny Saturday morning with the red cardinals singing their beautiful songs in my ears... and I wanted to die. I went downstairs and the sun attacked me. I noticed that my hands were shaking as I poured that first cup of coffee. I was hung over to the point of desperation. The "pull" on the first Marlboro red of the day rattled my nerves even worse. I couldn't deal with the simple task of reading the newspaper. My mind and beat up body wouldn't allow me to relax long enough to comprehend the words.

Debbie had left for a "weekender" with the girls to visit an old friend from Eastern Airlines who lived up in Lake Geneva, Wisconsin. My daughter, Catherine, was gone for the weekend on some high school-related activity. I sat down in the living room and looked around. Everything I saw around me looked beautiful in the sunlight. All the furniture was elegant and expensive. The piano I had purchased for my sweetheart many years before, stood there in its same spot against the living room wall. That piano was an expression of my love, many years before. I thought, "Where are all those feelings now?" Something had gone terribly wrong.

In one-year's-time, we would own the title to our home. We had a nice savings and individual retirement accounts. Any man at the age of 49 would be happy to have these things. I put my head in my hands and started sobbing. I cried for what seemed an eternity. I cried until my damned eye sockets were dry.

I thought I was losing my mind, but I felt less nauseous from the hangover after letting all these emotions out of myself. I looked in the mirror at my ravaged face. I read somewhere that people get the face they "deserve" by the age of 50. I had the face of a drunk. I looked sick. I was obese and on high blood pressure medication. My face had that red-purplish alcoholic bloat. I owned a beautiful, veinous whiskey nose. I saw dark bags under my hooded eyes. I had deep lines in my face, which told me the story of my misspent life. I lived either in smoky barrooms or outside in the elements. The whiskey, wind, and sun had done their job on me. I looked at myself for a long time and was frightened by what I saw.

I took a long, hot shower, and then headed out to McDonald's to try and force two double-cheeseburgers down my gullet. My stomach was sour. With any luck at all, I wouldn't throw up after eating this poor-man's feast! I thought, "Thank God my stomach accepted the meal!" I was ten minutes away from the Gables, my favorite local tavern. I perched on my bar stool at 11:30 a.m. along with a few other "miscreants". I didn't want to be in that "tomb" of a house. It just reminded me of my failures. After two or three whiskeys, I felt on top of the world. I laughed and bet on football games with the other drunks. I went home for a nap at around 4:00 p.m. I set my alarm clock for 6:00. Two hours of sleep and I would feel like partying again.

When I woke up, I poured myself a scotch and called a buddy of mine. He was an alcoholic heavy equipment operator, just like me. I told him to come on over to my house and share a bottle with me. His wife and kids had left him because of his drinking. I felt sorry for him because he was broke and alone.

I knew I would have his undying affection and good fellowship for the evening, as long as I provided the whiskey! We both would laugh about the "good old days" together. We drank until about midnight and then decided to take my truck through a snowstorm to a local late-night restaurant. We ate well; I bought us a couple of rib-eye steaks with all the trimmings.

I slipped and fell getting out of my truck when we came back to my house. It was only by the grace of God that we made it back to my driveway in one piece. I did a couple of "donuts" on the way back home because of the icy road conditions. My buddy was laughing so hard as he fished me out of the snow that he almost fell down himself. As we both staggered into my house, I asked my pal if he wanted to "rack out" in the spare bedroom. He declined. He said he felt sober, but I knew he was drunk. I let him drive 20 miles back to his home in a snowstorm. After he left, I fixed myself a "nightcap" and passed out around 2:00 a.m.

I woke up Sunday morning feeling the same way I had the day before. What the hell was the matter with me? I never felt this lonely and sick before. I had another long crying jag. This day, I vowed to myself I wouldn't pick up that first drink. I had to pick up Debbie from her girlfriend's house at 4:00 in the afternoon.

I paced the floors of my house all day, sweating and "white-knuckling it" through my hangover. I cried and paced. I thought about what I had done to my family and myself. When I picked up Debbie, I was sober. I told her that my drinking had me "licked". On Monday, I was going to a twelve-step group for alcoholics. I felt humiliated and cried as I confessed this to her in the car. Debbie comforted me by saying, "It's time for that, Rich. I'm glad you're doing this for yourself".

THE NEXT SOBER DAY

I went to the alcoholics' meeting and my crying started all over again. I felt humiliated and ashamed. The other alcoholics told me that all of this was normal behavior. It was all a part of the initial healing process. You see, we alcoholics are in denial. Everyone around us sees that we have a problem. We steadfastly deny this reality! This is part of the insanity of our disease. When we finally realize that our drinking is ruining our lives, we are shocked. Alcoholism is the only disease that tells the person suffering from it that "everything is fine" when everything is falling apart!

All the drunks I met at the meeting were helpful to me. They put their arms around my shoulders and told me that everything was going to be just fine. Sure! They gave me meeting schedules and books to read. The stories they told me about their alcoholism sounded just like mine! They laughed a lot and smoked a lot of cigarettes with their coffee.

They told me I needed to go to 90 meetings in 90 days to insure my sobriety. They told me that if I did this, I had a good chance of staying sober. They informed me that every morning and night, I was to get on my knees and pray to a power "greater than myself". They called this thing, my Higher Power. My God could be anything I wanted "he-she-it" to be! I thought this was an interesting concept. They told me to start each one of my days with prayer and meditation. This would put me in a serene state of mind. I heard these alcoholics talk a lot about serenity, acceptance, taking it easy, letting go, and most importantly—"living one day at a time". I was told that this sober way of life was attainable by the "lowest of the low". Finally, they told me to come back. "Keep coming back," I heard at every meeting.

I had nothing to lose and everything to gain. The way I was living wasn't the answer for me anymore. My life wasn't working for me. I finally admitted to myself that I was a mess and needed some direction. I never thought I would end up like this! I never wanted to be the kind of man my father was, but lo-and-behold, I was just like my dad! I was ashamed by his behavior. I worked harder to be a better person than my dad.

I realized I ended up being a different kind of drunk, but I was still a drunk! You can dress up a pig in a tuxedo, put him in a Mercedes, or throw him in the mud in some slop pen. A pig is still a pig! This is the REALITY of the situation! I rationalized that since I was intelligent, hard working, and had enough money, I had carte blanche to do whatever I wanted to do. This is a pitfall in the thinking of the alcoholic. We alcoholics all have a screw loose in our heads! People in recovery come in all shapes and sizes. We come in all colors. We are rich and poor, educated and uneducated. Some of us wear high heels and make up, others wear bill caps and construction boots. We all have one thing in common—"We are alcoholic and we need one another to stay sober!"

My whole life I thought I could "control" my drinking. I thought all the car wrecks and tickets and just about everything negative that happened to me was caused by "bad luck". All the nights in jail, all the attorney's fees, and all the times cleaning up vomit were things that everyone had experienced! This is how my alcoholic mind works. An alcoholic mind doesn't think rationally. It only gets better when it is sober and even then it isn't normal! One old guy who was sober 45 years told me, "Rich, if I could take a drink and get away with it, I'd take that drink right now!" I thought he was out of his mind! Then he said, "The fact of the matter is, Son, that I can't get away with it anymore." This same old guy also told me that I had to get rid of all my anger and resentments. He said that they were poisoning my mind. He really was a smart man. Anger and resentment is the major cause of picking up that first drink!

When I first started coming around to meetings, I didn't have a clue about how to live the sober life. I just kept coming back like they told me to do.

cds

It was wintertime and I was laid off. I had a lot of spare time on my hands. Spare time is an "alkics" enemy. We alcoholics need structure in our lives, and plenty of it! I believe the well-worn old adage, "Idle hands are the devil's workshop." In the first few months of my sobriety, I read all the books recommended to me by the "drunks" who were staying sober. The first few days, I paced the floors, wringing my hands, counting the minutes. I went for long walks, meditating, praying, and asking my Higher Power to keep me sober, just for one day. I walked long and far to tire myself out and settle my nerves. I was fortunate to have my painting and interest in reading to keep me busy! Sometimes I needed two meetings a day. The drunks at the meetings told me to "pick up the 1000-lb. telephone" and call another sober alcoholic if I felt like picking up that "first drink!" I took their advice and did this a few times to save my life!

Initially, the worst times for me were the early afternoons. This was my favorite time to start pouring the whiskey in the glass. If I made it through the afternoon, I calmed down and felt relaxed in the evenings after I ate my dinner. I usually went to evening meetings. Debbie and Catherine were totally supportive. They saw the positive changes in my personality and physical health.

After a few months of sobriety, my face started to look healthier. I lost some weight. People noticed that there was a subtle difference in my looks and behavior. The "obsession" for alcohol was slowly loosening its grip on me. I enjoyed my flavored coffees, ice cream, and candy in the evenings now. Some say that we alcoholics need "sugary treats" to replace the sugars we get from our booze. On weekends, I took Debbie to dinners and movies. Deb was thrilled by it all. I never would take her anywhere before I quit drinking, unless I knew I had access to a full-service bar. In my alcoholic, irrational mind, I thought that everybody in the world drank all weekend long. My sober eyes were now seeing the real world. Fathers took their families out for ice cream at night or to amusement parks. They went to baseball games and all kinds of events. All of these enjoyments with their families were done without booze. Why hadn't I noticed this before? My mind was finally opened to a new reality. My mind was coming out of the alcoholic fog. My body didn't crave it anymore! Before I knew it, I had 5 months sobriety! I was getting well!

RELAPSE

I made it through the winter sober. I had almost 6 months without a drink. It was spring and a beautiful spring it was! The birds were chirping their songs and buds were starting to pop out of the willow trees. They were always the first to show the green. I enjoyed looking at the willow trees during my walk around Foxcroft Park Pond where I caught largemouth bass.

I was still attending my recovery meetings, but something was missing. I wasn't getting the same security and feelings of gratefulness anymore from the meetings. I started to think that maybe I wasn't an alcoholic. I felt I wasn't like these people anymore. I listened to their stories and began seeing differences between their drinking patterns and my own.

I never drank a half-gallon of cheap vodka every day. I never beat up my wife or served time in prison. Some of these people lived out of junk cars and ate food from garbage cans when they were out there drinking. I began to feel that a lot of them were "whiners" who liked to pose as victims of societal wrongs. I thought they were full of shit! Some of these people thought that staying sober was enough, and they didn't have to work for a living. These types just leached from the government. Sitting around all day, smoking cigarettes, and drinking coffee was their main aspiration in life.

Attending three meetings a day, when working was a viable alternative seemed somewhat irresponsible to me. I thought their behavior was pathetic. I don't mean to say that all the people in the group were like this. Many of them had important jobs, with many responsibilities and pressures.

I always made good money and took care of my family financially. I rarely missed a day's work because of my alcohol consumption. I usually drank a third- to a half-a-fifth of whisky a day. I thought I maintained myself pretty well. Of course, sometimes on the weekends I binge drank, where I could finish a fifth of whiskey or more in a night. I thought my main problem was binge drinking at art gallery shows and nightclubs. If I could get a handle on that, maybe I could drink again.

I drove my car after these episodes and luckily I was never issued a DUI. I'd been pulled over a few times, but always found a way to keep my head and beg my way out of it. I was feeling better now. I made the mistake that many of us alcoholics make—I thought I was "cured". My alcoholic mind started playing tricks on me. I started thinking, "Maybe I can enjoy a couple of cocktails after dinner, but only on the weekends. After all, I've earned it. Haven't I been dry for over 5 months now?" I knew I could control my drinking now! I didn't act on these ideas yet, but they continued to fester in my mind. The urge grew stronger every day. Instead of 5- to 7-meetings-a-week, I was down to only 2. One meeting I never missed was my Men's meeting on Wednesday evenings. I liked the guys there very much. They were honest, good, hard-working men, all with a lot of sobriety under their belts.

The Union Hall sent me back to work on a Federal job at a chemical plant. It was a good job that worked every day, rain or shine. I had to take a drug and alcohol test to qualify for the job. I passed with flying colors. No smoking was allowed on site because of the danger of explosions. Not many men in my union wanted this type of job. My machine was a brand new mobile crane, with a nice heater and air conditioning. It had a state-of-the-art, Load Moment Indicator System.

This device allows the crane operator to ask a computer a variety of questions, to determine if the hoists to be made by the crane are within safety parameters. I understood this new technology, because I had completed an LMI-class at the Local #150 training site. I was taught three of the most common LMI-systems and one of them operated this crane at the chemical plant.

The job was going well for me. I understood that safety was paramount since we were working in a dangerous place. One false move could precipitate fatalities caused by explosions or fire. I worked with a pipefitting crew. The men liked how smoothly I operated the crane. The job didn't keep me busy enough and my mind started wandering. I began thinking of the "good-old drinking days". When the obsession comes back to an alcoholic, he forgets the pain of the old days.

One morning, I had to move the crane. I was careful to assess the travel route and the area where I would be working. I used my 50-foot tape to check the radius that was required for me to swing the crane. I wanted to make sure there was plenty of room so the counterweight of the rig wouldn't hit anything or "pinch" any worker who inadvertently walked behind my machine while I was swinging the boom. I thought I had all my "ducks in a row" now, after I assessed the situation.

It was early in the morning as I started walking the crane to its new location.

The sun was in my eyes. I didn't see the overhead walkway ahead of me. I buckled a huge I-beam with the jib of my crane boom. The walkway was a crumpled mess. Fortunately, no one was on the platform at the time and no one was hurt! Everyone-and-his-brother was out there running around, calling on their radios and assessing the damages, reporting to the "higher ups".

You know how the rest of the morning went for me. It was an agonizing, never-ending, embarrassment. I had to fill out accident reports, affidavits, and speak with countless numbers of management personnel. They all asked me incredulously, "How could you do this?" I'm thinking in my mind, "Walk a mile in my shoes, Assholes! Shit happens!" I made an honest mistake. I was made to feel like a worthless piece of shit. Now I was a "social pariah" in this small work microcosm. I was to be dismissed...eliminated...let go. In other words, "Get the hell out of here, Asshole! You screwed up our job!"

Our Union Safety Director showed up out there. He was a nice guy. I knew him well because we had worked together on a job years ago. In fact, we car-pooled to the job together. He made my embarrassing pill easier to swallow. In regard to the accident, he informed me that I would have to write out an honest accident report. He was sure that I wouldn't be found legally culpable for the accident. This entire conversation was scaring me to death! My hands were shaking and I wanted to crawl into some hole and die. This is how I felt at the Waukegan Power Plant years before, when I almost electrocuted myself with a bigger crane.

Everyone looks at you when you screw up like this on a job. I don't blame them one bit. When life-and-limb is on the line, these men want a crane operator they can depend on. I didn't fit the bill that day.

I was so thankful to finally get the hell out of there that day. I jumped in my truck and tore out of there like a "bat out of hell"! Once I got past the gate, I started calming myself down. I thought, "I should get a recovery meeting, so I can talk about this."

It was a beautiful warm spring day. I had to call the union hall and put my name on the Out-Of-Work List for another job. I stopped at my old tavern to make the call. I sat at the bar and ordered a Coke. A bunch of my rowdy construction buddies were in there asking me where the hell I had been. They all thought I died or something. Before I knew it, I had a scotch in my hand. Three upside-down shot glasses sat in the "gutter" of the bar, signifying that the boys had bought me three more drinks. I was back out there again, drinking. I damned my luck and drank my pain away. I put a dollar in the jukebox to play Waylon Jennings and Travis Tritt. I thought, "What's the use, anyway!"

MORE ON MY FAMILY AND OTHER THINGS

That day when I came home from the tavern, Debbie smelled the whiskey on my breath. She observed the sheepish grin on my face and knew the merry-go-round ride was going to begin once again. She wasn't very thrilled to see the "old me" walk in the door. Just like all the other drunks who fall off the wagon, I started making oaths and pledges. I said, "This time around, alcohol isn't going to be a problem for me. I learned a lot about how to handle it. I'm just going to have a few on the weekends." Debbie sadly listened to these mindless soliloquies many times before.

My daughter was another story. I broke her heart. She cried and slammed her bedroom door in my face. She just dealt with my alcoholism by staying away from me at all times. Strange but true, this is exactly how I dealt with my father's alcoholism. My daughter, Catherine, was an intelligent child. She wasn't going to have any of my excuses. She knew the "ogre" was back in town.

I went back to work with A.A. Conte and Son, an excavating company in West Chicago, Illinois. Art Conte and his son ran the family business. They were always nice people to work for. They treated me well and I enjoyed working for them. I always gave them a fair-day's work for a fair-day's pay. At this time, I hit the big "5-0". There were no parties for me. Alcohol wasn't fun for my family anymore. I was tired from the work and was hobbling around like an old man. I liked working for Conte, because there wasn't a lot of overtime. We usually worked just five-days-a-week until the "big push" came on to finish the year's work. I had problems with arthritis in my shoulders and my ankles were always swollen with edema at the end of the day.

At this point in my working career, I had 28 years as a union member. The kids who were coming out of the Union Hall were young enough to be my sons. I enjoyed teaching them the finer points of the excavating business. I loved the dirt work and had a lot of knowledge to share with these young men. I always used to say, "Work smart, not hard!" I told the kids that old age has a way of teaching a man how to be inventive and accomplish the task at hand with a minimal amount of pain! I enjoyed my weekends off and the rain days to do my painting. My fervor "to be discovered someday" remained with me.

After my pledge to Debbie, my drinking was normal for around a month, but soon thereafter, I returned to drinking alcoholically once again. The effects of the alcohol were more pronounced and were more painful for me to endure, due to the aging process.

My brother, Jim, was finally selling his shop, and retiring at the age of 65. I was extremely happy for him! Jim worked 7-days-a-week at the flower shop for as long as I could remember. We both were kind of sad. We worked there over 40 years together. A lot of memories were shared in that shop. I learned responsibility, good manners, and respect from my brother, Jim. He was my mentor and my father when I needed one. My loving big brother taught me many things about life and work. He was a fine example of what a man should be for his family.

He sometimes lost his patience and made mistakes like any other man, but he was always working and staying sober. He had his problems with alcohol as well, but quit it by himself. He went cold-turkey at the age of 50. Jim was a real man! I always felt that he was a better man than me.

Mom was 88 years old now. Jim and I were concerned about her well-being. She was getting too old to take care of the big house in the old neighborhood. The Marquette Park area was changing. Buildings were falling apart. People who didn't care about the condition of their property were moving in. The police closed the park every night at 6 p.m. instead of 11 p.m. because of crime. The gang-bangers were spray painting symbols on buildings and mailboxes, claiming territories. Mom had been burglarized already and lost her diamond wedding band. She was lucky she wasn't home and didn't lose her life!

So, Jim and I sat with Mom and we made a decision to fix up her house and put it up for sale. We worked on Mom's house every weekend. Jim sold Mom's house and put her money into Certificates of Deposit for her retirement. Jim was a man good with figures, banking, and stock market decisions.

My brother also had Power-of-Attorney for Mom now. Mom moved in with Jim and his wife, Grace, in the big home he had built in Orland Park. The home was beautiful and spacious. Mom had her own bedroom and television set. My brother spent a lot of time in the basement with his woodworking projects. I would, too, with my mother and wife in the same house! He was a master craftsman who made absolutely beautiful furniture. I couldn't differentiate between his fine furniture and the type people buy in the classy "higher end" furniture stores. Jim was artistic and carved lovely plaques and canes. He made walking canes with heads of eagles, horses, clowns, and other bizarre things. I loved looking at his canes and he always tried to get me to trade my paintings for his canes. We bantered like a couple of old businessmen and laughed a hell of a lot about which items were worth more. I always lost the arguments! Hah! He was a "pistol," my big brother!

Jim and Grace raised four daughters. They are all grown up now and live all over the great continental USA. Jim and Grace took a lot of vacations that first year, visiting the girls and the grandchildren. Mom always came and stayed with Deb and me when they went on their vacations. My mom loved these mini-vacations with our family.

In Chicago, my art was in a variety of galleries. I reasoned that Wheaton, Glen Ellyn, and Naperville were untapped markets, which were right in my own backyard! I started pounding the pavement looking for venues there to sell my art. I hung paintings at the upscale Anamart Gallery in Naperville, Illinois. I developed a nice relationship with the girls who ran the gallery. It was a beautiful place. I found two nice restaurants with plenty of wall space in Glen Ellyn. I hung work in both and recycled the shows every month so these restaurants always had a different display of art. They liked me because I drank there and brought in customers. I met a lot of people and made sales without having to make the long trips to the galleries in Chicago. I was doing much better in my own neighborhood!

I hung paintings in a nice beauty shop named Shear Pandemonium in Glen Ellyn. I still do business with the owner, Andrea. I hung paintings at the Funky Java Coffee House in Villa Park, Illinois. This is a great place to get a cup of coffee and to enjoy conversations with a broad variety of interesting people. The owners, Joyce and her son Larry, have always been very kind to me.

My marketing of art and drinking got to be a lonely enterprise. I worked all day long in construction and sat in the bars more than a few nights a week to show my portfolio and make sales. I used to tell Debbie, "An artist has to drink with his upscale clientele to make any money in this damned business!" She didn't buy into this illogic I was trying to sell.

LIFE ISN'T FAIR

My company sent me to 179th and Lagrange Road in Orland Park to run a bulldozer. The job was a pretty good-sized one. Luckily, the job site was only 5 minutes from my brother's new house. I would leave my house early every morning to have coffee with Jim, Grace, and my mom, before I started my workday.

Jim drove over to my jobsite a few days every week to eat lunch with the crew and me. The guys liked him and used to kid me by saying, "How come your brother is so smart and good-looking, Rich? You must have been adopted!" I responded to these slings-and-arrows by saying, "I'm the smart one, but I look like hell because I always worked harder than any of you guys! Besides, I'm the bulldozer operator on this job and I'm your boss, so what does that make you?" We all laughed the way men do. Jim just loved the camaraderie going on between all of us.

One day, Jim told me he hadn't been feeling well for a long time. He told me he didn't have any energy, for some odd reason. His doctor was sending him for a blood test. I never will forget the evening I stopped by his house after work and Jim grimly took me in his basement to tell me he had a disease called Acute-Myeloid-Leukemia. Jim told me that if he didn't get a bone marrow transplant, he would have only 6 months to live.

· I never saw my big brother cry, but as I put my arms around him, we both were crying like a couple of scared little boys. Somehow, I sucked it up to let him know that he was going to make it! I told him, "Only God knows when you're going to die!" Jim told me he couldn't take care of Mom anymore and was depending on me to take care of her now. The next day, we got a room ready for Mom in our little town home.

I rented a small U-Haul truck and packed up her bedroom set, sewing machine and meager belongings. Mom was crying as I drove her to our home. I told her everything was going to be all right with Jim. Being elderly, she thought that my brother was abandoning her. This was not the case; Jim was gearing up for the fight of his life.

We had an extra bedroom now because Catherine had graduated from high school and moved out to get away from her alcoholic father. I put my arms around my mom when we arrived at my house and said, "Don't worry, Mom. I'm going to take care of you now!" I told her I would never abandon her and that I would take her to Confession and Sunday Mass at St. Daniel the Prophet Catholic church. This seemed to ease her mind and make her feel better.

Jim told me a few weeks later that I might be a candidate to contribute bone marrow. He asked me if I was willing to do that for him. I said, "Without a doubt, Jim! I love you! You're my big brother!" I went for the blood test on the appointed day. Sadly, we received the news that I wasn't going to be a good match for him. He was out of luck. I thought he was going to die. Between my drinking, family problems, and Jim's failing health, I felt my life falling apart. Sometimes I wondered what happened to my life. The sweetness of life left me like the air coming out of a balloon.

Being a resourceful and intelligent man, Jim did a lot of research on his disease. He looked at all the best hospitals in Chicago for the treatment of leukemia. He had an iron will and wasn't going to lie down and die without a fight! Jim found Washington Hospital in Seattle, and figured that was the best place for him to go for his treatment. They had done over 200 procedures before, just like the one he needed. With hope in their hearts, he and Grace boarded a plane. They lived in Seattle in a dormitory setting for 6 months.

ADJUSTMENTS

All of us in our family were praying for a donor. Deb and I were going through the adjustments of having Mom living with us in our home. Finally, after a lot of worry, Jim was lucky enough to get a donor. The bone marrow was airlifted to the hospital all the way from France. This was a blessed miracle for our family! Jim and Grace spent a lot of time with other leukemia patients in the dormitory and developed some wonderful friendships. Unfortunately, many of Jim's friends didn't make it. After 6 months of treatment, my brother was still here. He survived! Jim's body accepted the bone marrow.

His aspirations showed that a year after all of the pain and hard work, he was cancer free! He took large amounts of anti-rejection drugs and would have to take them for the rest of his life. The doctors were trying to wean him off the steroids, but the days without them were miserable for my brother. Jim was taking 40 or more pills a day. They were expensive. Having been a small business owner, my brother had been smart enough to prepare for his medical and pharmaceutical needs. My big brother was always prepared for any contingency! Jim paid a lot of money for his medical insurance. He paid a lion's share of taxes all his life as well. Until a person reaches the so-called "Golden Years", he doesn't realize what a nightmare the medical merry-go-round is for an elderly person. Sooner or later, we all get to take the ride! Things are confusing for elderly people these days, because the government bureaucracy is running everything now.

Insurance companies are getting rich and Americans are having trouble getting the medical care they need. It just doesn't seem right that our great country ranks low on the list for adequate health care. The most important thing for our family was that Jim's prognosis was good. The doctors told him that he was going to have a normal life. He was going to get well again!

My mom and Debbie got along really well. I was so proud of my wife! She was wonderful to my mother. She was nicer to my mom than I was. I was more interested in my selfish concerns.

It seems to me that if women like each other, they have a natural way of getting along. Men like me are just surly and lack patience! With

Catherine living on her own now, it was just the three of us—Mom, Debbie and me. Oh yeah, I forgot our two cats—Spooky and Fuzzy. They ruled the household! As time went on, having an elderly woman in our home wore us down. Having Mom in my house was an experience I liken to "Chinese water torture". I should have had more patience with her! Mom insisted on sitting in our small den with us every single night. Deb and I never had any privacy. Deb and I couldn't communicate well with each other, having Mom with us all the time. Because of my alcoholism, our relationship was strained to the maximum already! Mom wouldn't go to bed until 9:00 p.m. every night. This left Debbie and I with only one hour. Usually we discussed the problems of having an elderly person in the home, our daughter's needs, my alcoholism, or our money. There was no time for romance. Our marriage was pretty much dead! Sometimes my resentments toward my daughter really angered my wife.

✑

I always demanded a lot from Catherine. She was a lot like me. I felt that she was stubborn and opinionated. She never took my advice, but rather did things her own way and then suffered for it. Her cavalier attitude about work and school and her inability to prioritize things in her life drove me crazy! However, we were somewhat civil to each other. Sometimes the civility went by the wayside and we engaged each other in heated arguments. I was so troubled by my daughter; I couldn't rationally deal with her anymore. How can an alcoholic man be rational with his daughter? I don't know. I needed to clean up my act. I knew this in my "secret heart". Nevertheless, I blamed my daughter for my drinking. I am ashamed to say that one time I told her in my drunkenness that, "I wish you had never been born!" Writing this admission causes me a great deal of pain.

I dealt this brutal blow to my child, without any thought to what consequences the statement would have on her! Although I never physically abused my child, I single-handedly damaged her spirit. I mentally abused her with my negativity and my alcoholism.

I tore up my daughter's heart in the same fashion I tore up Debbie's heart. I hurt the people who loved me the most. I thought they both were in "cahoots" to undermine my authority as a father. This was the result of my insane alcoholic mind thinking that everyone was out to get me!

My life was certainly unraveling again. I worried about everyone and everything. Sometimes at work, my foreman saw me crying as I ran my bulldozer. One time he came up to me and asked, "What's wrong with you?" He wanted to know if I wanted to go home. He told me that I couldn't do my job crying, that I might hurt somebody.

I told him, "Mark, you can't send me home, because this job is all I have left that makes me happy in my life." He must have thought I was crazy! I remember him walking away from me, shaking his head in disbelief. Yes, all I had left in my life was this bulldozer, a bunch of crappy paintings, and a bottle. I was 53-years-old and I was tired. Life wasn't sweet for me anymore. I was bitter and angry. Things weren't supposed to end up this way. My life was supposed to be "like a song". It was supposed to be a wonderful success. My aberrant thinking came right from the bottle. My happiness came when I was in a bar or when I was alone in my studio with my bottle and my paintings. I kept the door locked and created a fantasy world for myself in my mind. The nicotine stained blinds were never opened to let the sunlight in. I smoked cigarettes, listened to jazz, and poured my troubles away.

THE LAST STRAW

No one understood my unique creative qualities. I didn't care one iota about what anyone thought about me anymore. Screw them! Debbie finally had enough of me and left in April of 2003. I was left with my elderly Mom and two feral cats. I never saw it coming; it made me numb. Debbie moved in with her sister Karen and her husband John. She told me she needed time to think. She needed time to herself. She had to get away. Deb also told me how sick she was of my drinking. I thought it was too late for me to go through all the promises once again. I had said, "I'm sorry" too many other times. I knew in my heart that this was the last straw for Debbie.

I looked forward to seeing Debbie a couple of times a week when she checked the mail. She would come over to visit with my mom and play with the cats. She wouldn't let me touch her. I couldn't put my arms around her anymore. I went through excruciating mental pain, not being able to hold and love my wife. I wanted one last chance. I needed for her to come back to me. Twenty-three years of marriage were going down the drain. It seemed like an amputation of an arm or a leg to me. I couldn't fathom losing her.

About a week after she left me, she came back on a Saturday to check the mail. I had a cocktail in my hand and we started arguing about my drinking. Because of the arguing and my nervous stomach, I staggered into the kitchen and threw up in the sink. I made another whiskey for myself and continued the argument. She had to have known that I had finally lost my mind. My life was a lonely agony now. I came home from work to feed my mother and the cats. Mom and I ate frozen dinners. Sometimes I ordered a pizza. I should have been cooking good wholesome meals for her. I knew Mom's heart ached for Deb and me. Mom knew I needed help with my alcoholism, but she was afraid to bring anything out in the open. After all, she allowed my dad to travel down the same path that I traveled on now. After dinner, I kissed my mom goodnight. I lied to her every night, telling her I was going to a 12-step meeting for alcoholics so I could stay sober. I don't think she believed me, but I didn't want to sit in the den with her and get hammered on scotch every night. Mom's heart had been broken too many times.

I went to a scummy bar not too far from the house. Some of the people I thought had drinking problems were telling ME that I was losing control! Some kind of "red flag" should have come up for me to notice, but I was too far-gone by now. I fell down the stairs most of the time I left the tavern. Sometimes I went out back to throw up in the parking lot, only to go back inside the bar and order another drink. No matter how sick I felt the next morning, I forced myself to show up for work on time. I punished myself by working really hard. I made sure that I "pulled my weight" on the job.

One rainy night, I donned my best attire to go out on the town. I knew I wouldn't have to work the next day because of the rain. I wore a nice suede jacket, dress slacks, an expensive shirt and shiny new boots. I ventured off to the upscale restaurants that had my artwork hanging on their walls. I wasn't going to let this separation get me down. I sat at the bar with all the "beautiful people" and ordered top-shelf scotch. I affected my grandiose demeanor, buying drinks for people and spinning my boring tales.

I soon had that warm glow, which shut down the terrible realities running through my head. They ran over and over again, like a perverse broken record. I kept telling myself that I would land on my feet once again, by hook or by crook!

There was always someone sitting at the bar whom I could corner and interest in my art. It gave me slight repose to forget about my troubles, and go into the fantasy world of my so-called "art career". I drank hard and fast. It was feeling like it was going to be one of my binge nights. I ended up down the street at another nightclub, enjoying my art glorifying its walls. I was really full of myself now! A good blues band was playing and the bar was packed! People knew me and were fawning all over me. I let my ego fly once again. I was pathetically drunk. My bartender should have shut me off or called me a cab at closing time. I stumbled outside in the pouring rain, looking for my truck. I forgot my expensive suede jacket on the barstool. I fumbled for my keys, losing my equilibrium every so often. I finally got in and figured out a plan for the drive home.

The rain came down in sheets and I could hardly see where I was going. I drove with one eye shut to negate my double vision. I fell asleep at the wheel periodically. The only thing that was waking me up was my truck, bouncing off the curbs. Thankfully, I took a deserted street without many cars. I was very lucky getting through the town of Glen Ellyn without side-swiping any cars. I was only a mile from home now and thought I had it made! Instead of my normal route down President

Street, I opted for Blanchard, a darker, less-driven road that would lead me home. I thought I had a better chance of avoiding the police. Soon, I saw the flashing lights behind me. I guessed wrong! My heart started racing while my stomach felt that feeling of impending doom!

I couldn't walk to perform the field sobriety test. I blew four times over the legal limit for the State of Illinois. I knew I was going to jail. The officers who arrested me were totally professional. They treated me with respect and they were gentlemen. I was full of alcoholic remorse. I felt ashamed and embarrassed. I tried to be polite in my drunkenness.

The cops gently handcuffed me and brought me to the station. I was fingerprinted and posed for my mug shots. I thought I was going to make the newspapers once again, but this wasn't the type of fame I deemed desirable. The policeman asked me if I had any distinguishing scars or tattoos on my body. My mind ran through past episodes of America's Most Wanted and the Cops TV Shows.

They handcuffed me to a ring with a chain bolted securely to a plate in the wall. I sat on a cold, steel bench for a couple of hours. Sitting next to me was some other unfortunate soul. He was a youngster, and was wailing like a banshee. He talked gibberish to me. I just sat there mum, like some kind of mental patient in a catatonic state. I knew this was the end of the line for me. This person I had become was a total stranger to me. I thought about my high school and college days and the innocence of grammar school. I was a clear-headed young man at one time in my life. I sat there and thought about a lot of things in my life for two or three hours.

An officer came to me and offered to drive me home so I could "sleep it off". I was shocked at his act of kindness! Apparently, they had checked my record. They found that I had no felony or misdemeanor arrests and was a homeowner in Wheaton at the same address for 22 years. The officers told me that they were driving me home because I was a "low risk" DUI arrestee. I thought this gesture was thoughtful, given the circumstances.

I was given all the salient information I needed in regard to my DUI, court dates, where my truck was impounded, and when I could pick it up.

The officer who took me home told me not to take it so hard. He said he felt sorry for me after I told him my story, but sternly reminded me that driving the way I had was dangerous behavior to myself and the people of the community. He gently helped me from the police car and opened my front door for me. He warned me to go to sleep and nowhere else that evening.

I set my alarm clock for 6:00 a.m. I would have an hour-and-a-half to sleep. My senses were assaulted by the unforgiving buzzing of the alarm clock. At first, I thought I dreamed this nightmare, but as I dressed I saw all the awful paperwork on my nightstand. I summoned up the courage to go downstairs into the kitchen and make a pot of coffee and lit up a smoke. I greeted my mother and daughter with the story of my night. I saw the disbelief in their eyes. My mom was expressing her elderly fears to me about who was going to take care of her. I was really angry! I said, "I need to take care of myself now, Mom!" It was at this particular moment I realized that I was fighting for my life. If I didn't save myself, I would be no good to anyone else. I hugged my mom goodbye and told her not to worry. There was plenty to eat and no one was coming any time soon to turn off the gas and electric! I needed to ask my daughter, Catherine, to drive me to work so I could pick up my paycheck, quit my job, and have her check me into Rehab at the Behavioral Center in Central Dupage Hospital. It was tough telling my mom and daughter what I had done the evening before. There were a lot of tears and sad faces that morning. I told my daughter to call her mother. Debbie had to take care of some business for me while I was away. She had to pick up my truck, and pay the towing and parking fees. She had to recover my jacket and take care of Grandma. I didn't know if Deb would do these things for me, but I was powerless now.

THE FIRST DAY IS THE TOUGHEST

As we were driving to the jobsite, I asked Catherine if she would pick me up a carton of smokes, and bring me a suitcase filled with some of my clothes and toiletry items like shaving cream and razor blades. She was kind to me and said, "No problem, Daddy-O!"

This was the first time I had smiled in a long time! I got my paycheck, as all the men on the construction site "ogled" my daughter. I told the foreman to call the Union Hall, because I was checking into rehab for alcoholism. He looked at me with wide eyes and said, "No way!" I said, "Yes, way!" On the way to the hospital, my sweet kid said, "Daddy, I love you! You're doing the right thing!" Her compassion made all the difference in the world to me! She gave me her support when I needed it the most.

When I checked into rehab, the nurse took a mug shot of me. "This is just like being in jail," I said. The nurse told me that they have to take the pictures so police and family can identify drug addicts and crazy alcoholics when we run off, in pursuit of our addictive substances. Sometimes we end up dead or get in trouble and the pictures help to either apprehend us or identify our dead bodies. That was supposed to be comforting?

The cute nurse asked me how I felt! GAWD! "I feel like shit," I said. "I'm still drunk, but I think I'm gonna have one 'hellatious' hangover!" My daughter was laughing now! She knew her dad! I filled out the paperwork—still drunk—laughing and having a good old time for myself. The blood-alcohol measuring device came out once again and I blew into it for the nurse. "Whew," she said, "You're still over the legal limit for driving in the State of Illinois!" "Wow Dad," Catherine chortled. "You must have been really messed up last night!" That was an understatement.

I kissed my little girl goodbye, thanking her from the bottom of my heart. She said, "Don't worry, Daddy. I'll take care of everything! I'll come with your suitcase this afternoon and visit you on Saturday." I was assigned a room—a humble institutional kind of cubicle—with two single beds. I was glad I didn't have a roommate. That would change in a couple of days! The mattress was horribly uncomfortable. I laid my body down and pulled the covers over my head. I was ready to sleep it off until sometime in the late afternoon.

Suddenly, this big guy comes barging into the room and says, "Let's go!" I say to him, "Get the hell outta my room. I wanna sleep! Who the hell are you, anyway! Are you crazy?" He tells me, "My name is Pat and I'm the Director of this Behavioral Center. You're not going to sleep! You have a lot of work to do today, so let's get going!" "My God. Welcome to the program," I thought.

This was not what I anticipated for my first day. I figured by checking myself in, it would look good to the judge when I went to court. I was a con-man alcoholic. I didn't want to give up drinking for good! The wheels were turning in my head. I figured I could phony-out everyone and get my driver's license back right away! I sure wasn't buying into this treatment-thing just yet! I was just a drunk, not a head case or alcoholic like these other assholes! I thought this was a "good faith" action on my part and it would be ancillary in getting Debbie's sympathy working for me. I would get her back! Deb was such a good and responsible woman that she came back home to take care of my mother. Debbie always had good character and moral fiber. This was something I sorely lacked all my life!

I didn't have to de-tox. The ravages of alcohol hadn't taken my body that far yet. The physical they gave me showed that my liver was still healthy. However, I had some numbers in my blood work, which suggested alcoholism. Mainly, my sickness was a "soul" sickness. I was depraved in my way of thinking. I got a good healthy fear of the disease, seeing people check into the hospital. The loved ones who checked them in were crying and carrying on. Some of the patients were shaking uncontrollably. Some pissed or crapped in their pants. It was horrible! Some were vomiting or drooling. A few of the people I saw had gone so deeply into their alcoholism that they had "wet brains". They were dead inside. The "lights were out" in them cognitively for good. My "dear friend" alcohol provided all these wonders for me to observe and enjoy! The "wet brains" stared at the walls. They looked like those people in the movies who had been lobotomized. The "surgical" destruction of the brain had been done not by a scalpel, but by a liquid—our Dear Mistress, Alcohol!

Some of the alcoholics who a few days previously were useless shaking messes, recovered after de-tox and looked like totally different people! They looked well-groomed and erect, laughing and walking briskly. A person would never suspect that they were a mess when they checked in. Drying out metamorphosed them into normal, healthy-looking people. It was strange and beautiful! Our "temples" are wonderfully recuperative!

I saw one beautiful 30-year-old girl in a wheelchair, who had the misfortune to suffer a stroke from her drinking. She tried to sneak a bottle of vodka in her room. She stuck it under a blanket on her lap. She waved goodbye to all of us, as a cigarette hung from her ruby-red lips. She was dismissed for breaking the rules. People who check themselves into rehab can expect to see just about everything!

Luckily, I had a "high bottom." I hadn't lost everything. I didn't have to go through withdrawal or delirium tremors.

Nowadays, the medical people control the shakes with Valium or other calming substances. In the old days, they lashed the drunk down to a gurney and hoped he didn't die from convulsions or a heart attack. Alcohol is patient. My "mistress" alcohol was hoping she could stay with me. "She" wanted to steal everything I had, than leave me for dead. I realized that "she" was evil because of what I learned in my 3-week-stay in rehab.

I gave this treatment program a chance to save my life. I went to all the A.A. meetings and did my best to be honest in group therapy. I cried rivers of tears, and learned a hell of lot about my disease. I also learned how to take an honest look at myself. I was given a brand new "toolbox" with a complete set of tools designed to keep me sober! I graduated from the program after 21 days. I made a few friends along the way. Out of the 23 in our group, just 3 of us are sober today. Four of us are dead. A few of us are in jail. I'm sober for 5 years now. I am one of the lucky ones.

HOMECOMING

I was afraid to go home. There were too many stresses, triggers, and reminders of "what was". I was safe in a cocoon at the hospital. I had support systems there 24-hours-a-day and no access to alcohol. My addictions counselor told me that "fear" is a common reaction of patients who are faced with the prospect of going home. She told me she would worry about me if I didn't have a healthy fear.

Debbie was at home now. She was distant to me, but amiable. Now we slept in separate bedrooms. I knew she wanted to see if I meant business about my sobriety this time. This was my third attempt and I knew in my heart that if I didn't succeed this time, I would be out the door! Three strikes and your out dude!

I remember the day Debbie forgave me. We were attending an outdoor concert in Lisle, Illinois. We were listening to John McKay and Steppenwolf. The concert was awesome! Deb and I were having a great time! Deb looked lovingly into my eyes. It was that look from "long ago". I gently kissed her, she smiled at me and ice was broken! We hugged and kissed all night like a couple of teenagers! I was glad to be back in the sober world. This is the real world! I was with the woman I loved, knowing that she also loved me! I wanted nothing more in the world than this. We listened to "Born to Be Wild". I was hearing it sober. I could really hear it! I didn't need a drink or a drug to have a good time anymore. I kid Debbie sometimes by telling her, "You were born to be mild!" I had two months sobriety the day of the concert. I never wanted to lose my wife or daughter or my mom ever again. I knew it all depended on me.

THE PRICE I HAD TO PAY

I lost my driving privileges for 3 months. I paid a fellow $150-a-week to cart my gnarly ass to work in the morning and back home at night. "Steve" was his name and he was never late. He never let me down. The reason for his dutiful commitment to me was because he worked a "good program". You see, he is one of "us". He is an alcoholic, just like me! Steve was on hiatus from his job as a garbage man. His back was all screwed up from having spinal surgery. He wore a brace and was in a great deal of pain. I met him at "the tables" in a meeting and told him I needed someone to drive me to and from my job. He was getting bored sitting at home and needed the money. We both thought that God had put us together that day for a reason! Steve was glad to get the extra money and I was happy to give it to him! When one drunk helps another it keeps them both sober! This is how it works! Steve has seventeen solid years of sobriety now. We get a meeting together once in a while, or go out to lunch. I KNOW he is my friend for life! I never had friends like him in the tavern. My "spirit guide" from up above sent Steve to me to help me stay sober. To-and-from work, Steve talked to me about "working" the Twelve Steps and how they helped him stay sober.

My attorney's fees and court costs amounted to around $8,000. Thankfully, my Union Health and Welfare Insurance Fund paid for my hospital stay. I lost about 3-weeks-pay while I was in rehabilitation. I know now that it was money well spent! At the time, I was just miserable thinking about all the costs. Now I think of these costs as a good investment! My life was saved by loss of money! What a strange concept, eh?

The State of Illinois required me to do six months of after care. One night a week, I sat with an addictions counselor. I sat in a room in a circle with a bunch of drunks and drug addicts who were just like me. My addictions counselor never had an alcohol or substance abuse problem. She wasn't one of us. I felt she lacked credibility. This is just my opinion. I think if you want to teach baseball to a bunch of young kids, you better have played the game yourself! The only counselors who ever helped me were the ones who had walked the same dark paths of alcoholism or drug addiction just as I had. As I sit here typing, I thank

God for my continuing sobriety. I am also thankful that I never killed anyone with my automobile while driving in a blackout. I feel this is God's special gift to me!

WORKING SOBER

When I went back to work I made up my mind to relax and put all my problems in the hands of God. I said the Serenity Prayer a-hundred times a day. It goes like this: "God, grant me the serenity to accept the things I cannot change, the courage to change the things I can, and the wisdom to know the difference." This little prayer has come to my aid countless numbers of times in my sober life! Think about what the prayer says! It is good, sound advice for anyone. Putting the prayer into practice in your every day life, takes a lot of patience and hard work. Practicing what the prayer says isn't an easy task!

I decided to quit yelling and screaming at truck drivers and operating engineers. This rude behavior did me no good, and was disrespectful to them. I calmed myself down and quit trying to immediately solve every problem that came to me throughout the day. I took the problems one at a time. I solved the important ones first. We alcoholics are perfectionists. We think we can control everything in the Universe. We have a difficult time understanding that in reality, we humans here on earth don't control anything at all!

The results of my new attitude were immediate and sometimes quite amusing! Most of the truck drivers in my company wanted to work with me. In my drunken life, they avoided my jobs like the "plague"! Now I did things slowly and methodically with a smile on my face. If something went wrong, I calmly tried to figure out a solution. Then, and only then, I took the correct action. If I couldn't fix what was wrong, I went to a higher authority on the job and asked for help. This is really a simple thing to do and it works every time! I decided to educate and instruct rather than to demean people. I also tried to educate myself, and admit to my mistakes when I was wrong. I purposely slowed myself down and got more production from my crew than I had in my old drinking days! They had more respect for me now because I praised their good efforts. I always tried to have a pat on the back, a smile, or a new joke for my men.

In my drinking days, I worked like a maniac to keep the trucks moving. I never wanted to see a line of trucks waiting to be loaded on "my" job. This "new me" worked at a normal pace on the job. I loaded trucks safely and efficiently with my new 973 Cat Endloader. If I had ten trucks waiting for me, so be it! I realized that I had no control over how many trucks management was going to send to me! I was just one human being who only could do so much! I wasn't God or Superman. I concentrated on doing quality work and on doing it safely.

The owner of the company came out to see me one day. Rumors were traveling around the company that I was "getting soft". I told the owner to look at my job. The job site looked beautiful and we were ahead of the completion date schedule. The general contractor was extremely happy with our work.

This old-school construction company owner looked at me and said, "I liked you better when you cracked the whip!" I replied, "If in any way you are dissatisfied with my work, then I suggest that you should call the Union Hall and get a replacement for me." It was as simple as that! I didn't pussyfoot around with people anymore because it impeded my quest for serenity! I always decided to be honest and "cut right to the chase"! I knew what my VALUE was to the company. I called the owner's bluff. He shrugged his shoulders and walked away. The problem was solved and I kept my job. I stayed on with the company for two more years and really enjoyed every day. I began to realize that I WAS MORE IMPORTANT THAN ANY JOB! This realization led me to great happiness!

LAST GASP ON THE JOB

My age was 55 in 2004. My life was wonderful because I was sober for two years. My relationship with my family was a loving one. Everything had changed for the good. I cultivated more good friendships than I ever had before in my life. I didn't have bar room buddies anymore, just good people who I could count on in the long run. If I needed their help, they were always there for me! Most of these friends I had were recovering alcoholics. The business of working in diesel fumes, dust, and dirt all day long started to negatively affect my health. I hacked and coughed all the time. I noticed the condition was getting worse and I was short of breath all the time. Finally, I threw away my "cherished" Marlboro cigarettes for nicotine gum. I hated the change. I chewed the gum nervously and didn't know where the hell to put my hands at first! I missed a cigarette dangling from my mouth, so I ate a lot of lollipops and chewed on their sticks during the days on the bulldozer. For some odd reason, my lungs continued to bother me. One night I came home from work and had a wheezing attack. This really frightened the hell out of me! Debbie sat with me for five hours rubbing my back and feeding me chicken soup and hot tea with honey. I finally calmed down enough to get some sleep. Each breath of air I drew into my lungs that night was a struggle for me. I called in sick in the morning and went to see my doctor.

The doctor sent me to Central DuPage Hospital for pulmonary tests. The nurse stuck me in a booth and asked me to blow into all kinds of tubes until I thought I was going to pass out from the exertion! Then they gave me some Albuterol—the stuff asthmatic people huff into their lungs—and they told me to do the tests again. The result of all these sadistic tests showed that I had a disease known as COPD.

It has a scary name: Chronic Obstructive Pulmonary Disease! EEEEEK! I was also diagnosed with mild Emphysema. This wasn't supposed to happen to me! This happens to old people! I wanted to work for seven more years until I was 62 and receive my full pension!

I went back to the doctor's office and said to him, "How come I have this, Doc? I quit smoking two weeks ago!" "Tsk, tsk, tsk," he told me. It should have occurred to me that previous to my quitting, I smoked steadily for 40 years. Also, I hung out in smoky bars all my life and had a job that damages the lungs. My doctor prescribed Advair 250/50, a bronchial dilator and muscle relaxer. This steroidal product was heaven sent! It sure did the trick for me! I took two "huffs" a day, morning and night. I could breathe again, but I noticed I couldn't breathe normally in any dusty or smoky places.

I tried to keep working on the machines, but my condition continued to worsen. I felt useless. I couldn't do my job anymore. Deb and I talked it over, and I decided to retire with about 87% of my pension. If I kept working, I probably would die in a couple of years anyway, so I took the money and ran! I felt a huge weight lifted from my shoulders after I put my pen to the retirement papers at the Union Hall. I worked in Local #150 for 33 years. I paid my dues and then some! Now I could paint my pretty pictures and join a gym to repair my damaged body. I was ready to put my game face on, once again!

THE GYM

I love the smell of a gym! A real gym is dank with sweat, and moldy kinda smells. My "ideal" stereotypical gym has an industrial feel to it! I come into this dark place lit with a few fluorescent lights and see miles and miles of heavy plates and squat racks. These devices of torture make me smile! My fantasy gym has free weights, Smith machines, and racks of "heavy-assed" dumbbells as far as the eye can see.

My fantasy gym doesn't play music by Brittney Spears or the Pussy Cat Dolls. It plays music by Hendrix or The Allman Brothers Band! I like to hear "angry" music sung by "angry" men when I pump iron. I like hulking, massive bodies pumping iron all around me. These are men on a mission to get bigger and bigger!

Ideally, the guys I work out with wear raggedy, stinking sweatshirts or muscle T's with holes in them. The shirts look like they had battery acid thrown on them! My ideal gym doesn't look like the upscale Northside Chicago gyms. We don't have pencil-neck executives working out in our gym with their "fancy-ass" Addidas or Nike warm-up suits! They would be afraid of us all anyway and wouldn't join our gym!

I like guys who put so much iron on the bar for their bench presses that the bar flexes and bends with each repetition! I love those big 45-lb. plates! I like men who scream like Ninja Warriors to get up a couple more reps! It means they are enduring pain to grow bigger muscle size! These men burp, fart, and scratch their crotches whenever they want.

Not many females in their right minds would want to work out at my fantasy bodybuilding club! The gals who work out at "my" club would have to be serious athletes or body builders. I would hate for my gym to be cluttered with those damn colored balls that are utilized for core work! They are an abomination! They get in my way and I want to kick them the hell away from my weights! I know how to work out my abs without those "girlie-looking" things all over the damned place!

I don't come to the gym to see a damned fashion show! I don't want to see scantily-clad, suburban "wifeys" fromping around with perfect hair-do's and manicures, distracting me from the work at hand! This place of mine has no place for cell phones! I hate damned cell phones! Leave the gall-darned things at home! My first reaction to a cell phone user is immediate "antipathy". In the gym, I feel like grabbing a cell phone and whacking the user right upside the head with it! Leave the damn thing at home and concentrate on working out! I hate all the damned clusters of television sets as well! My God, I feel like the gym has been turned into some Orwellian nightmare when I see all the damned things blaring at once. They distract me from my mission! I like pain! I don't need television to distract me from my joyous pain. Pain motivates me, not TV!

In my ideal gym, the guys I want to work out with are bikers, cops, ex-cons, second-rate boxers, construction workers, ex-professional athletes, recovering alcoholics-drug addicts, and lifetime gym rats! They know all the short cuts on how to pump up and form huge muscles. They know more about health than a lot of the doctors in the neighborhood!

I hate doctors who push pills to make you "healthy"! I'm not claiming all doctors are of this persuasion. Sometimes you need to take the pills the doctors prescribe for you! I'm just saying that you have to make "educated" decisions about your health! Some monetarily-oriented physicians are just interested in "perks" from pharmaceutical companies! Major-league bodybuilders know everything there is to know about nutrition and supplements! Don't fall into the trap of the human growth hormones! I don't recommend them to anyone. Stay away from the steroids! If a guy doesn't spend at least 2 to 4 hours in his gym every day, with only a day off a week, he isn't doing enough work. I like guys who spend maximum time in the gym. Fourteen-hours a week is the bare minimum, as far as I'm concerned. Most of us who are serious about working out, don't drink or smoke.

Serious bodybuilders all try and eat a gram of protein or more, for each pound of our body weight. Protein builds muscle, dude! We don't eat a lot of sugar and we radically limit our carbohydrate intake when we are "leaning out" for body building competitions! I gravitate to the biggest guys in the gym in order to soak up the knowledge they possess about "pumping up".

Some of the guys in my gym call me an amazing old man. I work really hard in the gym all the time! I have an endo-mesomorphic body type and worked hard all my life, so I get big, pretty fast. However, old age is a deterrent that keeps me from getting where I want to go. At my age it is really tough to add on more muscle mass. I'm stuck at a point right now in my training, where my body refuses to get bigger. It just wants to get fatter! I have to be happy with the fact that at 59 years of age, I'm one of the oldest and biggest guys up there, pumping some heavy iron. I like working out along side the "big dogs!"

By May of 2007, my body weight dropped from a "fat and sloppy" 235 lbs. to a svelte 183 lbs. It took me 3 years to get there, but I did it! My waist went from 44" down to 33". Last year, I actually could see my front abdominal wall of muscle, which we body builders lovingly refer to as our "six-pack". My biceps have grown from 13 to 16". I developed some huge calves and quadriceps muscles in my legs from climbing 35 degrees on an incline treadmill at 3.8 miles and hour. I did this for 90 minutes every day, besides my weight lifting. The climbing helped me develop ancillary lung tissue and developed my aerobic capacity. My doctors were amazed that I increased my lung capacity over three years, even though I have COPD!

My VO-2-Max, which is a number that measures aerobic capacity, was that of a thirty-year-old man last May! The most important thing for a person to do in the gym is to work their heart-lung machine!

If you don't know what you're doing, I highly recommend a personal trainer. These men and women at my gym are really helpful to this "old man"! A personal trainer can devise a good program for your specific needs! Some people think hiring one is too costly. The next time you think of the money involved, just think about all the money you threw away on booze, cigarettes, and fast food in your life! Compared to that, a personal trainer is cheap! It's money well spent! I threw my high blood pressure medicine away. My blood pressure now is 110/65. I have a cholesterol number at 165, which is pretty good as well! My triglycerides are looking like those of an athlete! I eat clean and live clean! My new credo is: Eat, Live, and Make Love just like a Viking Warrior! Don't rape and plunder. This is not good for you spiritually! Just live clean!

MOM

My mom's health was failing late in the winter of 2006. I told you about her mini-stroke on Thanksgiving morning of 2004. On Thanksgiving Day, I took her to the hospital for treatment. Her mouth was sagging on one side as she came down the stairs in the morning. We were all freaking out trying to figure out what the hell to do for her first! She was the calmest one of the bunch! She said, "For cryin'out loud, just drive me to the hospital!" That was the toughness of Mom! She was cool as a cucumber! Smiling and laughing later on that evening, she insisted on having a piece of pumpkin pie with Cool Whip on top of it and ice cream on the side! Her face had straightened out and she looked healthy as hell! We all scratched our heads in amazement! It must have been the Holy Spirit! Maybe Mom had a special guardian angel! She was 94 years old, for goodness sakes! Anyhow, it was cool to see her rebound like this!

Little by little, Mom started showing signs of her advanced age. She started falling down a lot in our home. We live in a home with a lot of stairs. We have a basement and bedrooms upstairs. We used to come home and find her with "knots" on her forehead and bruises on her arms and legs. Mom was afraid to tell us about her falling. She was afraid we were going to put her in a home. These are the normal fears of the elderly.

Mom was falling so much now, we were afraid she was going to kill herself. I had a "pow-wow" with Deb and Mom. I told Mom I was going to look at Villa St. Benedict in Lisle, Illinois—a Catholic Retirement Home. My mom reacted with tears. I gently told her not to condemn the place just yet!

I told my mom that I had a talk with a wonderful nun named Sister Joanne. She said that Mom could stay a week on a trial basis. If she didn't like her private apartment, she didn't have to stay. Mom acquiesced to the idea. She had her doubts, but I knew this place was a top-notch nursing home. Mom could still live independently and if she needed me, the residence was a mere ten-minute drive from our house.

Villa St. Benedict had a large cafeteria with delicious food. The menu was fantastic! They offered daily Mass and Holy Communion.

There was entertainment for the senior residents, games, and bus service. They enjoyed shopping trips, card games, and had all types of things to do! I told Debbie I might move in there and leave Mom at home with her! Mom got a big kick out of my declaration! Mom would get to meet people her own age and develop friendships, instead of sitting alone in the chair with the cats all day long. Also, she had nursing care around the clock if she needed it! Mom said that she'd give it a try. She loved it immediately!

I was glad I did the research on finding the right place for my mother. If I had been drinking, I never would have done the work for my mom. I was sober and available for her in her last days. I took Mom anywhere she wanted to go. I finally was being the son she deserved. We rented a truck, and family and friends helped me move Mom's furniture once again. Mom told me she felt like a gypsy these last years, moving from place to place. I brought Mom to all her doctor's appointments, delivered her pharmaceuticals to her, and took her to have her hair done once a week at Andrea's beauty shop in Glen Ellyn, where my artwork still hangs. Mom loved going to the beauty shop! Andrea always gave Mom a break on her hair. I got a kick out of Mom in this youth-oriented, upscale salon! Andrea and the girls just loved her!

On Sundays, Debbie fixed Mom's favorite meal for her: Barbequed ribs, candied carrots, and mashed potatoes. Mom loved these Sunday visits because she missed the cats. She loved playing with the cats! Sometimes we took Mom to a little family restaurant for cream of chicken soup. She loved this as well!

In March of 2006, Mom caught some type of virus. The nursing home called me at the gym and asked for my permission to send Mom by ambulance to the hospital. I told them to send her right away! I went flying out of the gym half dressed, to get to Central DuPage Hospital as soon as I received this phone call. The nursing staff at Villa St. Benedict had an epidemic on their hands. Old people were being taken to the hospital from their facility left and right! Mom was deathly ill when I arrived at the hospital. I didn't know if she was going to recover from this flu-like virus. She spent two days in the hospital and then was discharged. Debbie and I caught the same bug and it almost killed us! I'm amazed that my frail, little mother survived this damned thing! She sure was a strong woman!

The sad part of the story is that Mom was never the same after this flu. She lost 18 pounds in a few weeks. She lost her appetite and wasn't interested in eating anymore. I talked to the head nurse and dietician at the facility and they told me that there were plenty of things on the menu for Mom to eat. I think she made up her mind to die. I'll never know. We tried a protein drink for the elderly and all kinds of tricks to get her back on track. Everything failed. The next few months were filled with endless doctors appointments. I took her to heart doctors and pulmonary specialists. She just didn't rally from this illness. She didn't have any energy left in her. She quit her daily walks and had trouble walking with her walker.

I was told she had congestive heart failure after she complained to me that she was having problems breathing. My family doctor suggested that we put her on one of those portable oxygen tanks. She hated those damned things! She couldn't bear to re-arrange the tubing from the tanks in her apartment and I had to go over there every day to fix them so she could walk around from her living room to the bathroom. I bought all kinds of "gizmos" for her to get into the tub and to elevate the toilet seat. I was getting a lesson on caring for the elderly!

Mom's lungs were filling up with fluids more regularly now. I took her to the hospital every couple of weeks so the lung specialist could extract the fluids that were suffocating her. We had to take her off the blood thinners like Plavix for a couple of days, before they could put the needle in the lungs. The "docs" told me this was a necessary procedure because if they hit a vein, she might bleed into her lungs and suffocate. My mom was experiencing one horror after another. I felt powerless in regard to her decline. It saddened me to see her like this. My job now was just to be a good son and tend to her needs. It surely was a difficult time for her, but she accepted everything with dignity. She was a warrior goddess for sure!

Finally, she was so weak, all she did was sit in her chair or lay in her bed, gasping for air. She needed more and more oxygen. I hated seeing those tubes in her nose. It reminded me of my own pulmonary problems and what I might have to face in the future. My heart was breaking, seeing her like this. I thanked God to have the opportunity to be of service to her. I knew she didn't have much time left on this earth. Sometimes the strain got to me and I prayed to my "Higher Power" to take my mom to heaven. I prayed for God to take her peacefully in her sleep. Caring for an elderly parent for a long period of time wears out the caregiver, sooner or later. I doubted myself. I hoped all that I was doing for her was right. It's tough to make all the calls for your mom. We baby-boomers raise our children and then we have to take care of our parents. After they die, it's time for our medical problems to be addressed. So much for retirement and the Golden Years.

I have regrets about my lack of patience with my mom. If I had been a better man, I would have shouldered my responsibilities in regard to her more cheerfully and more lovingly. Our family doctor called me up one day and told me her latest blood test didn't look too good. He asked me if I wanted to make an appointment with an Oncologist. I couldn't see my mom suffering through cancer. This was just another horror to add to the mix, along with all her other medical problems. Without hesitation I replied, "No, Doctor. I want to see my mom die peacefully. I don't want her to suffer anymore." My doctor reassured me by saying, "I'm glad you said that, because I agree with you." Maybe I was just sick of caring for her. I felt a lot of guilt. I was worn out, but maybe I was being selfish. At other times, I thought I was doing the right thing. I guess we all try and do what's right when the time comes for our parents to leave this life.

Some people want to keep their parents alive forever and fight the good fight until the end. This is their right. I can't cast any aspersions their way. I think it's too much torture for a patient who is going to die anyway. It's tough on the rest of the family as well. It was devastating for me telling a doctor that I wanted my mom to die. I felt like the judge, jury, and executioner for my poor mom. To "pull the plug" is an awfully tough decision for any caregiver.

I was advised by Sister Joanne to take advantage of St. Thomas Hospice out of Oak Brook, Illinois for Mom's final days. They were wonderful caring people and they made the death process much easier to deal with for Mom and our whole family. Mom was taken off all her drugs now, except for her morphine, antidepressants, and oxygen. I was with her every day until the end. My dear cousin, Kathy Bannon, was an angel for me. She was right by my side for days before the end, to provide me a shoulder to cry on and offer me her wonderful support in every way. My daughter Catherine, my wife Debbie, and my sweet niece Irene, who loved my Mother so very much, were all there all there for me as well. Dear Irene, my niece, was named after my mom.

I held my mom in my arms and asked her to forgive me for my anger, drunkenness, and impatience with her in the past. My mom smiled at me and wiped away my tears. She did this so lovingly; just the same way she did it when I was a little boy. I still was her little boy! She made it all easy on me. She said, "I asked my mom to forgive me for those same things when she was on her death bed." Then my mom told me that I was a good son. I was her angel. She said, "You took care of me all the way to the end. Only good men do this for their Mothers." Then she said, "I always knew I was right to have another baby! God knew I would need you at the end of my life." She said to me, "This is why God finally got you sober, Dickie. Your job now is to stay sober and continue to take care of yourself and your family. Don't ever forget to pray. Promise me you will always remember God." I made that promise to my mother.

My mother's life was a sweet song. She endured things with patience and dignity. She was an inspiration to me. She lasted for 9 days after we decided to eliminate her medication and put her fate in the hands of God and St. Thomas Hospice. She died in my arms at 5 p.m. on August 21st, 2006. She lived to the ripe old age of 95. She wanted to make it to 100 so she could appear on the Smucker's Jam Label and on the morning TV news. My Dear Mother, she was a special lady!

AMEN

LIVING WITH ADVERSITY

This year I decided that my new heroes were all those blue-haired, little old ladies I see in shopping malls. They shuffle along pushing walkers with those "funky-assed" green day-glow tennis balls on the legs.

Once you reach a certain age, getting up in the morning becomes an Olympic event! If you are lucky enough to survive and "claim" your senior citizen status, it becomes probable that you will face more pain and adversity than an NFL quarterback! You won't care, because the mission now is to wake up "vertically" in the morning; rather than to be found by your hysterical wife in the "horizontal" position with your tongue hanging out of your mouth like that deer you shot in Vienna, Illinois, while hunting with your drunken buddies!

Much of your day consists of reading the obituaries, watching the weather channel, and making countless numbers of phone calls to other "geezers" to discuss various diseases, hospitals, and locations of funeral homes. Older people visit endless numbers of departed friends and enemies in the funeral homes. We get fat because we eat a lot of pastries and sandwiches there! You finish your day by watching The Wheel of Fortune while eating a large bowl of premium brand ice cream. The ice cream advances the clogging of your arteries! The closest you get to pornography is Vanna White! You fall asleep in your chair before 9:00 p.m. watching some rerun of Murder She Wrote on The Hallmark Channel. (You've given up control of the TV clicker to your wife by now, and will never see Rambo movies again!) These are the "Golden Years" dudes! I think they suck!

I've made a short list for you of all the physical maladies I've faced since my body started going "south" on me at the tender age of 53. I'm amazed I made it to age 58! God willing, I'm going to make it to 59! A man has to hope for the best!

THE LIST OF TERROR

1. 2003—COPD: Chronic Obstructive Pulmonary Disease with "mild" Emphysema. What the hell is "mild"? Is this diagnosis supposed to reassure me? It didn't! To me, emphysema means you're gonna die, Sucker!

2. 2004—Pre-cancerous esophagus and colon: The esophageal symptoms are heartburn and a whiskey voice. The colonic problems are signaled by blood in the stool. This is a freaking nightmare! My brain immediately tells me I have cancer! I suggest a colonoscopy every three years! I knew I shouldn't have eaten all that damned Mexican food, peanuts, and strawberries all my life! All the scotch I drank didn't help matters much either!

3. 2005—Erectile Dysfunction: This malady is the real heartbreaker! I never thought I would be anything other than a prized stud horse until I reached 90-years-of-age. Thank God for the Pfizer Pharmaceutical Company! My battle cry now is: "Viva Viagra!" For me, 50 milligrams does the trick. If I really want to get "down and dirty", 100 milligrams turns me into a sex star! I'll risk the damned heart attack! I get to romp like a 20-year-old and the purple haze I see from the drug is really cool! The headache afterward is a major bummer, so take care! OUCH! Maybe I ought to go and see that gal Alice!

4. 2005—Non-Specific Colitis: The non-specific part means that the "Poop Doc" doesn't know what the hell is the matter with my colon! He puts me through yet another colonoscopy. After perusing his bill, I figure he must have needed a new set of titanium golf clubs. I don't get angry. I like keeping the AMA strong! After all, I am a good union man. The doctor sends me off with a prescription for Sulfasalazine, which makes me sick to my stomach! I throw them down the toilet after enduring two weeks of senseless nausea. I solve my problem by eating whole grains, fruits, and vegetables. I vow not to see this guy ever again. This "poop doctor" is now on my "shit list!"

5. 2005—Diverticulitis: Next time you eat popcorn at the show or sesame sticks while you're watching television, think about the agony you might have to endure when your colon develops

little pockets and sores because of your advancing old age. Husks or little seeds stab your insides "like little knives!"

6. 2005—Yeast Infection on the Vocal Cords: For all you folks using the Advair inhaler, make sure to rinse your mouth out and gargle after each "huff"! Not rinsing causes a yeast infection, which is impossible to rid yourself of, even though you take massive doses of antibiotics and other exotic prescriptions. The guys in the gym sadistically "razz me", saying my affliction is caused by my affection for indulging in oral sex. I hope I live to see them reach my age! I'm going to get even! Payback is well, you know!

7. 2005— Surgery on the Vocal Cords: My Otolarygologist wants to scrape the mucosa off my cords because I'm starting to sound like Marlon Brando in the "Godfather". My doc says, "We do this just to make sure 'Mr. Cancer' isn't lurking under there!" How reassuring! My doc says that if he is, we will "zap" him outta your life with a laser! Wow! I have visions of Flash Gordon. This is a day surgery. I thought it was a "piece of cake"! This surgery only kept me out of the gym for one day! I begged the Anesthesiologist to let me return the next day and he acquiesced because he looked like Hulk Hogan! I was sure he was one of our brethren! I pumped more iron painlessly the next day because I was still anesthetized!

8. 2005-Mass on the Adreanl Gland: My family doctor says every year that he will "keep his eye" on this one! Huh? Yeah sure! Scare me some more, dude! How do you keep your eye on an adrenal gland?

9. 2007— Scoliosis: This is curvature of the spine. My spine looks just like old Lake Shore Drive in downtown Chicago! Way cool! I still remember that old rock song about LSD.

10. 2007— Degenerative Spine Disease: This one really scared the shit out of me! Just the name freaked me out beyond belief! I was wondering how the hell I shrunk from 5' 10" down to 5'8"! Now I knew! The diseased discs kind of compress together! I still can bench press 260 lbs. and do standing curls with 45-lb. dumbbells in each gnarly hand, so I don't worry too much about this disease! Maybe someday I will just crumble like an old building and the janitor in the gym will get a dustpan to sweep up my remains!

11. 2003— Arthritis in my knees and shoulders: I should have had a desk job! I just knew it! Pulling levers all my life on the

machines and looking over my shoulder when backing them up put me in this predicament. Stomping on accelerator pedals and brakes didn't help my knees too much I guess!

12. 2006—High Glucose Levels: I responded to this by giving up Alcohol and sugar. No more Krispy Cremes, ice cream, scotch, and I still don't put the gun in my mouth! Amazing!

13. 2006—Exercise-induced Anemia: Heavy duty Aerobic training burns up magnesium, potassium, and iron reserves in your body. Beware! I drink a lot of water and sports drinks now! I take iron and magnesium supplements and eat more bananas than a gorilla!

14. 2007—Aneurisms in the popliteal arteries of both legs: This requires immediate attention! These big boys can kill you! After surgery, I was flat on my ass in my Lazy Boy enjoying lots of Vicodin and grade "B" movies. I suffered and made myself walk every day. He did the right leg first. This was the "bad one."

The aneurysm in my right leg was the size of a tennis ball. It was too big for a stent. The surgeon showed me all the diagrams of what he was going to do to me. I was freaking out! It was a horror movie! The surgeon tied the big thing off and used a gortex prosthetic to bypass it! The graft ties the big artery together into a single "entity" once again! I have two 7-inch incision scars above and below my knees on the insides of my legs! These are my badges of courage. I feel I went through some dark primitive ritual and came out a brave warrior! I am "the man"! I had a grand total of around 60 metal staples holding my wounds together! The doctor pulled them out about 3 weeks after each surgery. The second surgery—the left leg—was easier for me. We still had to use the bypass procedure. I'm the bionic man now! I imagine how big my quadriceps muscles are going to be a year from now when I can get back to the squat rack! I have superman arteries in my legs! I enjoyed frightening children this past Halloween when showing them my Frankenstein legs! The Vicodin I was taking, coupled with Clonazepam for anxiety attacks, made it so much more enjoyable!

After each of my leg surgeries, I crawled back to the gym after 3 weeks. The day the staples came out of each leg, I forced myself back to the gym the next day! I worked my upper body in a non-weight-bearing position. My surgeon and his partner were amazed when I walked into his office for my staple removal, without a damn cane!

I'm not "out of the woods" yet. I have what they called a "deep vein thrombosis". This is a blood clot in laymen's terms. The damned thing can kill me! The doctors put me on a blood thinner called Coumadin. They keep upping my dosage and I'm still clotting inside. I guess I have Jell-O in my arteries now. The drug is making me bleed internally. So now I have to inject a steroid called Proctafoam up my rectum. I get my steroids in my lungs and up my pooper! Maybe they will help me build more hard muscle! I don't let myself get depressed. I go to the gym every day and walk over 2 miles a day on the treadmill in about forty minutes.

I'm going to get healthy again. I'm pumping iron and getting big! I look like the picture of health! At the end of the day, my legs are swollen from sitting at this typewriter. I elevate them all night. I'm still in a lot of pain, but kicked the Vicodin. Remember, I'm an alcoholic! Today is February 6th, 2008. By summertime this "Viking Warrior" will have "gutted out" the pain and look and feel good once again! I hope the Coumadin does its job to pulverize my "evil" blood clot! My job is to stay focused! I need to keep my eyes on the prize!

I miss all my green leafy vegetables. I can't eat spinach, salads, broccoli, and all the things that help me stay fit! They contain vitamin K, and the doc says they are a no-no for me. I guess I just put all of this stuff in the hands of my "Higher Power" and do the best I can do! Sometimes I get depressed and wonder, "What's next?" Hey! Don't be sad for me! I have dreams and plans and a sense of humor! I have a year-and-a-half to work out so I can win the Illinois State Master's amateur bodybuilding competition. I've got my professional bodybuilding friends in the gym ready to train me! I plan to compete in the 60+ age division. I kid with the guys in the gym and say, "The only way any other guys in my age group are going to beat me is if I die before this competition!"

There's always a silver lining in each dark cloud! All you have to do is look for it! If I didn't have these leg aneurysms, my book never would have been written! I don't know if it's a very good book. You will have to be the judge of that! But it's mine! I'm proud to say that I used my time "fortuitously!" I value every second in my life now. If God throws me a "ringer" I have to go to "Plan B". Adversity makes me want me to press on! As soon as this book is published, I plan to start painting again. I might write a book of stories about each and every one of my paintings!

I plan to sell this book out of the trunk of my car, at the gym, at Twelve-Step meetings, and on street corners! I will sell this book at all my art shows.

You see, I'm a Ringling Brother's, Barnum and Bailey kinda guy! I've been called the Renaissance Man!

MY DAUGHTER, CATHERINE

My 25-year-old daughter, Catherine, is my pride and joy! Not only is she "strikingly beautiful", but also she possesses an intellect that amazes me! Catherine is entering her senior year at DePaul University in Chicago. Catherine majors in Anthropology, but also has a strong background in science and mathematics. She did her required student observations at the Latin Elementary School and plans to do her student teaching there as well. The Latin School is the top elementary school in the city of Chicago. My kid just finished the first phase of teaching certification. Catherine works at a variety of jobs to finance her education. She works full time, yet manages to carry a full class load as well! I believe my daughter, Catherine, is a member of the Phi-Beta-Kappa Society, but I'm not sure. One thing I know for sure is that she doesn't settle for less than an "A" in her schoolwork. I tell her that sometimes a "gentleman's 'C'" is alright, but she expects more from herself.

Catherine's boyfriend is a terrific guy! His name is Peter. He is a fine young man who comes from a loving family and Deb and I think the world of him! Peter has his degree in Construction Management from Purdue University. I don't hold that against him even though I bleed blue-and-gold for Notre Dame! Peter works in his father's electrical contracting business. We enjoy having dinner with his family on occasion. Debbie and I consider ourselves fortunate that we developed a nice relationship with Peter's family.

↭

Time and maturity have healed the wounds between my daughter and I. We both grew up. I never gave up on her and she never gave up on me! To know my daughter, read this wonderful letter I received from her in a card last Father's Day.

I will treasure it until the day I die!

Dear Daddy:

Thank you so much for everything you have given me! I feel like it was just yesterday when you were teaching me how to ride my bike without training wheels. You gave me courage and faith in myself.

I can remember playing catch with you on sunny afternoons. You always were encouraging me to do better than my best! You have been such a warm, caring person. You taught me qualities like respect, commitment, bravery, pride, persistence, affection, love, and integrity.

You are these qualities, Dad. I hope to measure up to become "half" of the person you are. I know you have struggled in your life, but I always knew you did your very level best! Besides your being such a great provider, I adore how much you love and respect my mother. I am so proud of you for overcoming obstacles in your life! It is truly a joy for me, to watch you grow in sobriety.

I love you so very much!

Your daughter, Catherine

These words really touched my heart. I will always keep this Father's Day card. I will read it when I need strength or a re-affirmation in my life. These beautiful words are special to me. They are what every father wants to hear from his little girl!

Catherine gave me another card when she visited me in the hospital after my 2nd leg surgery in October of 2007:

Dear Dad:

It takes so much courage to walk through a difficult surgery with the amount of grace and dignity you display. You are such a great example of strength and fearless perseverance to me! Keep up the good work, Dad. God is looking out for you!

I love you! Catherine.

I'm certainly no hero, but I'm proud of my little girl! She continues to get upset with me when I meddle in her affairs. I go overboard sometimes in trying to give her "fatherly advice." I always tell her, "That's my job as a father. Don't ever forget, I'm still your dad!" I wouldn't have it any other way! AMEN!

MY BROTHER JIM

It is December 2007 and the weather is still reasonably cool. I call my brother Jim every morning before I go to the gym. We joke about our surgeries and talk about what we read in the morning's Tribune. I like to get him on a "rampage" about all the news in the paper because he is a conservative Republican. He realizes what I am doing to him and calls me a sadistic "sumnabitch," which I am! I tell him I learned it all from him, which I did! We usually talk about our surgeries and the old days at the flower shop. We laugh at our situations now and relive the old days. We are amazed at how much energy we had in those days. We worked really hard together. I told my brother about how I always felt immortal. He laughed, then he told me, "You're not a kid any more Dick; you're coming into my world now." I had to agree with him. I certainly wasn't a young man anymore, and these leg surgeries had me in a lot of pain. I hobble around now, like a wounded sparrow!

Jim and I had gotten so much closer together over the last seven years. I think the catalyst for our closeness was threefold: Jim's leukemia, Mom's death, and my sobriety. As I aged and matured, I cared more about people. Jim told me that my sobriety had a lot to do with my maturity. Jim loved having a sober brother. He told me my mind was so much sharper since I gave up the "sauce"! He always gave me strength!

Jim wasn't doing too well these days. He enjoyed having me read him chapters from this book every day. I read them to him over the telephone. I got a big kick out of his chuckling in the background. He was really enthused about this book project. He thought I had something good to offer and urged me to have this memoir published. I couldn't refuse him this request. If I ever forgot to read a story to him during our daily phone calls, he reminded me by saying, "Hey brother, you forgot my story!" I think my reading to him provided him with a little bit of pleasure in his life. He was so ill that it hurt me inside.

I didn't know what to do for him anymore, except to call him every day. I had to remind myself that my brother should have died 6 or 7 years ago. He beat the odds. My brother never took to being a whiner or a victim. Jim survived every illness that fate threw his way! He beat acute myeloid leukemia, prostate cancer, mitral valve surgery on the heart, perforated colon, bladder infections, and adjusting to a colostomy after having his colon re-sectioned. He was my hero, this "iron man" brother of mine! They gave him beta-blockers for his "ticker" and all kinds of drugs to keep him alive. Some days it all just overcame his spirits. The next day he would be his "chipper self", talking about his plans for the future. He told me that he had a lot of traveling to do when he regained his health. He spoke of visiting his children and grandchildren when he healed from the upcoming surgery on his colon.

A normal man would fall to depression and give up. Not my brother. Once my brother started regaining his strength, he and Grace went shopping at the deli. Jim loved shopping for food. He cooked up different delicacies for me. He loved making his homemade split-pea-and-ham soup. All his life, he was svelte and trim and I was the "fatty"! Now he looked like the Pillsbury Dough Boy! I tortured him about his "roly-poly," appearance and told him about payback! He laughed and always reminded me that he was smarter than me! This truth was hard for me to deny! I loved his teasing so much! Jim loved to tease me. I guess that's how big brothers relate and bond to their little brothers.

As ill as he was, he worked in his woodworkers shop and made a table for Gracie's sewing room. I talked him into buying a new computer! He was much like I had been in the past, denying the need for the "newfangled" thing!

I nagged him for 3 years. Finally he purchased a nice Apple-Mac 'puter. He really enjoyed it more and more every day. Jim got a kick out of being able to eat all the spicy food he wanted. He said, "I have a colostomy now and can eat all the hot Mexican food that I love so much!" What a trooper he was! I really laughed when he made fun of the colostomy and how he gained from having it! That was my amazing "iron man" brother!

Jim went into Northwestern Memorial Hospital in downtown Chicago to have his colon put back together after Thanksgiving. He was looking forward to getting rid of the colostomy and getting well again. The surgery wasn't a success. The doctors told him that when he was strong enough, they were going to have to reverse the procedure and give him the colostomy again. I think this is when Jim gave up.

My heart ached for him. He started telling me he didn't think he was going to make it. He told me that he wanted to die. I tried to say all the right things, but felt inadequate in finding the words. I didn't want to see him suffer anymore. I felt the same way about Jim, as I had felt about Mom. I told him to hang on, in spite of what I really felt. Jim was told by the hospital that Medicare wasn't going to pay for his hospital room anymore. He was angry. I don't blame him. He told me that they were going to warehouse him in a nursing home somewhere in Hinsdale, Illinois. That was the last time I talked to him.

Jim's children and his wife Grace were with him every day. I am grateful that they were at his side in the hospital. Jim wouldn't talk to me on the phone during the last couple of weeks of his life. I think he was trying to protect me. I think he wanted me to remember him as the "Iron Man". I cry sometimes because I miss him so much. Jim died on December 16, 2007.

I didn't feel he had much more time on this earth, and I was right. The doctors did their best, but they couldn't do anything for him anymore. It didn't seem fair to me that my brother, who led such an exemplary life, had to be cursed with endless medical problems. He endured agonizing pain with the guts of a soldier.

I have to remind myself that my brother, Jim, was granted a "miracle". He had some quality life and times those last 6 years. I expected him to have one more ace stuck up his sleeve. He didn't. Sooner or later, we all fold up our cards and have to go home.

WHAT I HAVE LEARNED

With a little effort every day, a person can sure accomplish a lot! I never intended to write a book. I started journaling on October 3rd, 2007. This was the day I was released from the hospital after my second leg surgery. If you find any mistakes in this book, don't blame them one me! Blame them on the Vicodin...or Eric Heinz, my Editor! I figure I put in over 600 hours in doing this project. A book is a major task for a heavy equipment operator. I am abysmally deficient in my skills at punctuating and spelling. Being an artist didn't help me too much either. I like painting "outside" of the lines, so please excuse my mistakes. I do think my honesty and what I want to say comes through to you, the reader, loud and clear!

This whole project has been very therapeutic for me. I figured out during the process, that I was merely "painting" with words. I also found out I have so much to be thankful for in my life. I am a survivor. I "choose" to be happy! I am very grateful to God and to my surgeons that I can walk! I know I will never run another marathon, but that's OK! I have five marathon finishes in my memories. No one can ever take my memories away from me. They are sealed in my heart forever! We have to seize each day.

No one is ever going to read what I write and accuse me of having any talent. I'm just a "ham and egger" when it comes to laying down the written word! I try to stay humble, and have no delusions about the level of my talents. I just hope my memories will make someone smile or cry or feel some emotion that makes them more human! Maybe some of what I write can aid a reader to avoid the mistakes I made on my life's journey. I would love it if my words inspire a reader to go on to greatness in some endeavor! We are all—each and every one of us— living miracles!

I want to inspire passion in the people I meet on my journey. I want them to share their passions with me! I love feeling and hearing exuberance in people! We all need each other on this "Spaceship Earth". The most important time in our lives is right now! You see, there isn't anything else! Your past is over and done now. The way you remember your past is delusional at best. Your mind cannot perfectly replicate the past. The way it "really happened" is lost forever to your mind. I try and learn from my mistakes, but I don't dwell on them. I let them go, because they serve me no purpose.

The "future" is nothing but the mind's construct of "possibilities." Of course an individual must plan for the future, but he has no control over the outcomes! The "fickle finger of fate" always has its way with you! Heee! It's a cruel joke isn't it? I love that old bumper sticker, "Shit Happens"! Well, it does, doesn't it? The simple statement, "Shit Happens", is direct and to the point! Believe it and carry on with your life!

I like to start out my day with some "quiet time". I ask God to help me! I pray, "Dear Lord, please help me not to be a big asshole today!" I ask my "he-she-it deity" to help me do the will of the good universe, not mine. It is good for me to start out each day with humility. I pray for my friends and enemies. I forgive everyone who has hurt me. I don't need to carry around the poison of anger and resentment. I learn discipline and humility from the simple act of making my bed every morning!

I then go into the kitchen and pour a cup of coffee and start some meaningless argument with Debbie! My old man "crotchetiness," which usually involves some ridiculous thing of no importance, usually precipitates the argument! I realize my prayer and meditation have gone down the drain! I apologize to Deb immediately and start my day over again, promising God and all the Saints that I will do better! We always fail! We are HUMAN! Individuals who are "winners" keep on trying! People who always try to be better, make great progress and eventually end up doing great things!

I remember one day remarking to my wife, "I'm 2 years sober now and really proud of myself!" Debbie rolled her eyes and said, "Yeah, you're two years sober and still yell and scream and make the same stupid remarks." She was right! I wasn't anywhere near where I needed to be! I wasn't the "Holy Man" I claimed to be! I watched too many "Kung-Fu" television shows as a youth, I guess. None of us are really unique, but we can be unique in special ways through our good works. We all have a lot of work to do each-and-every day to become better people!

When I go out the door in the morning, I try and smile and be nice to everyone I meet during my day. Be friendly! Try to listen to people. People I meet have interesting stories. I talk about myself too much. I need to LISTEN more!

A lot of people think I'm "crazy friendly", but I don't care! I'm having great fun by being friendly, and it makes me feel good inside. Rewards keep rolling in when I practice "crazy friendliness"! I am constantly amazed by how many interesting people there are in this world. I get to meet them everywhere!

Somehow, I always seem to fail in my attempts to be a "holy man". I brag about my accomplishments, give the finger to old ladies who are driving too slow, and bitch and complain if things aren't going my way. I complain about the government, religious leaders, and the way things are going in the good old USA! I need to take a "chill pill" a hundred times a day! When the light bulb finally comes on in my head, I calm down and start my day over again. I realize that I poison myself with anger. Nobody does it to me! I allow it to happen to myself! I'm only serene, if I'm not insane.

Remember, life is beautiful! Always do what you love. Make your work a marvelous joy! Whatever you do in life, make the world a better place. Don't ever choose a job for your life's work that you hate. Hate is poison for your soul. If you hate your job, quit it and do what you love! Don't worry too much about money. When you're dying and look at your Lexus in the driveway of your mansion, you will realize that these things are meaningless. I never met an elderly person who said, "I wish I would have spent more time at work in my life!"

Make your "Higher Power" and your family number one in your life. Spend a lot of time with your children. Be moderate in all your habits. Stay healthy and eat good food. Laugh as much as you can! Always tip your bartenders, waitresses, and the people who don't have as much as you! It all comes back to you tenfold! My old man used to say, "Make sure you make friends on the way up the "ladder of success. You might meet the same people on the way back down"! This statement from my father makes me realize he wasn't such a failure after all! Dad was just a human being, comprised of good and bad qualities.

Get outside and fill your lungs with fresh air. Exercise, walk, and look at flowers. Look at clouds, sunrises, and sunsets. Play with children and pet as many dogs and cats as you can, as long as they're not "the biting kind"!

Don't get obsessive about fiddling around with I-pods, computers, digital cameras, GPS systems, video games, and cell phones. This crap will take over your life and you become a slave to things that really don't make you happy! I put a lot of this stuff away. I don't miss them because

I pretend I don't own them anymore. If you happen to want all the crap items again, they're always going to be there for you! All you have to do is dust them off!

᪻

I love books. I like libraries and old bookstores. I like the smell of books. I like licking my fingers to turn the pages and writing things in them. I like underlining things that are important or life altering in my precious books. Owning a book collection is wonderful, even if they are never read again. I have so many books, my wife, Debbie, gets mad at me when I bring them home! I have to hide them and sneak them in the basement, where I work. It's like the old days when I tried to sneak in an extra fifth of scotch! We need another house to store all my books and my 400 paintings! All these things give me joy, so it's all right! I see my books and paintings as my "children"!

᪻

I love to make art. Make art, not war! Actually, God creates my art. I decided that I was only His "middleman". I'm nothing but a minion. I'm God's "idiot savant" in the creation of His art. I've always loved making things with my hands. There is something primal and universal about making things. It connects us with our past and with our neighbors throughout the world. I think a lot of us have lost our sense of history. I've heard somewhere that they don't teach Geography in American schools anymore! I hope this isn't true! I recently read in the Chicago Tribune that 40% of the U.S. population can't find America on the world map. If this is true, it makes me very sad. What's happening to us? Are we losing our minds?

I was a lucky child! I grew up poor. I got to go garbage picking in the alleys of Chicago. I got to make my toys or find treasures in garbage cans! I made soapbox racers and slingshots. I carved all kinds of things with my cheap little "pen knife". I found those old fashioned 78-rpm records and launched them higher and farther than a Frisbee! God help me if they went through one of the neighbor's windows!

I planted vegetables from little seed packages in Mom's backyard. I grew strawberry's back there as well. I got up early in the morning to pick them before the birds could eat them. I put 'em on my cornflakes. I camped out in the back yard when I was a Boy Scout with my old buddy Mike. We listened to Dick Biondi on WLS radio.

We ate all kinds of candy and junk food and when we woke up in the morning, the transistor radio would still be playing rock-and-roll.

Then we went and played baseball all day long, after we did our chores, of course! I had a beat up red Radio Flyer wagon and picked up bottles from the alley to cash in at the local "mom-and-pop" grocery store. Geez! Did I write that already? I hope not. I don't need Alzheimer's disease to add to my list of terrors!

We "poor kids" had to use our bodies and our minds to be resourceful. We had to learn how to entertain ourselves! In grammar school I learned how to read and write. I had to learn how to do long division and fractions. I had to learn my multiplication tables and learn the Constitution of the United States of America. I could make change without a calculator! I "ciphered" with my brain, y'all! Isn't that amazing!

Today, with the new math, the new spelling, and all the other "new fangled" educational philosophies we have, our children are entering high school and they can't read or write! They can't figure out simple mathematics without a calculator or some other "gizmo". The schools keep on graduating them. The kids are "processed" out and believe me when I say, "They are D-U-M "dumb"!!!

I meet "so-called" college graduates every day who are dreadfully lacking in a good liberal arts education. A good old-fashioned liberal arts and science education has gone by the wayside in favor of "specificity". We are training culturally inept automatons, ready and willing to serve corporate America for minimal pay and benefits. This country needs children who can do a variety of useful things. We need inventors and scientists. We need to start manufacturing things again. We don't need more rock stars and burger flippers! Thank God, we have an influx of intelligent children from other countries still serious about the American Dream! These bright children aren't afraid of hard work and long hours. They are willing to do what it takes for success! They will have their success because they are willing to figure out a way! The strong will find a road to success, even if it is against all odds! They are going to keep America strong! I condemn laziness in American educators, American families, and American students. We just don't get the job done anymore! It's time to wake up and smell the coffee!

I think it is our responsibility as parents to take an active interest in our children's educations. Don't sit in your country club, sipping martinis, thinking your $80,000-a-year suburban educators are going to magically transform little "Lance" or "Muffy" into paragons of intellect! It isn't going to happen without your help!

Continue to search for truth. Don't settle for less from your television stations, newspapers, and politicians. Don't accept bias, lies, and yellow journalism. I am a child of the 60's, therefore I never felt much affection for politicians. I always felt they were people who made too much money and had a penchant for lining their pockets with our money. Their interests usually weren't in the interests of the hard-working American middle class. My general definition of a politician is "a person who spends your money while demonstrating no meaningful skills of his own." This definition certainly doesn't apply to some of our politicians. We have some honest and hard-working people who have served with dignity and honor. We need people of honor, knowledge, and integrity in office. Get out and vote for these people while you still have that right! You're only going to miss one episode of your favorite television show!

I hate it when our television media scares us every night with nonsensical studies. I guess fear sells advertising. Fear runs rampant on the evening news. Just tune in tonight and think about it! I don't watch the evening news anymore. I get most of my distorted media bias from my Chicago Tribune or Sun Times. Some of it is truth and some is not. My job is to extract the truth from the "gobbledygook"!

To sum up, I guess this "beat-up old man" is threatened by my gut feeling that the inmates are now running the insane asylum! I wonder what ever happened to the middle class in society? I don't see the America that I knew as a kid. My beautiful America is melting away. No one knows what the "truth" is anymore. I sure don't. I feel more and more confused by what I see. What I do see is a polarization taking place in this country. I see two "classes" taking shape—the rich and the poor. I don't think the government serves the people who do most of the work! Is this right? I must be getting paranoid!

In my thoughts, I see government being run by a cabal of evil men in a worldwide collaboration to keep the rich very rich, and the poor very poor! All I can do is vote for the candidate I feel is worthy of my trust. I will continue to vote until my "right" is taken away from me!

I promise to respect all living things. God sees everything I do. I promise to understand that all work is to be respected. No matter how menial the work seems, I will reward the people who do it with tips and praise. I won't waste gas or travel unnecessarily. I will recycle and put out my garbage nicely so my garbage man won't have to work so hard! I will try and remember what Sister Elizabeth taught me in grammar school. She said, "Your personal freedom ends at the tip of your nose!" In other words, don't mess with the freedom of other people.

☙

I will never see myself as a victim. I won't be a whiner. I will continue to work in whatever capacity God has allowed me to possess. Work defines me and allows me to soar with the eagles!

I promise to visit the sick and the elderly. I promise to continue to go to the jails and the drug and alcohol treatment facilities in order to share what I have learned. These simple tasks keep me "grateful" and give me direction in my life.

I believe if we all share with one another, there is plenty on our planet to go around. We need to get all the greedy people on our planet to share. This simple action will make their lives more worthwhile. I believe in miracles! I'm a silly heart!

Greed is ruining our world. It always has. The world is going to survive in spite of us. I think my job is just to take care of my own backyard. Things are going to get better! I'm going to continue to live "One day at a time"!

☙

Today, it is snowing in Chicago. I'm sad the "hated" Green Bay Packers weren't in the Super Bowl this year. I wanted them to win the Super Bowl! I could tell Green Bay fans their Super Bowl Champions were beat "handily" two times this year by my "revered" Chicago Bears! Hah!

I am still grieving for my brother and Mom. I am the last one now. It is gray and snowy outside. Debbie is at the gym. My mother-in-law, Mary, had a mild heart attack last weekend. I go to the Coumadin nurse today to have my blood levels checked. I need to go and get new ink cartridges for my printer. I have to get more medicine for myself from Walgreen's. I look forward to putting on my jeans, cowboy boots, and knit stocking cap. I will fly through the snow in my truck, singing along to the songs along of Travis Tritt and the Allman Brothers! I woke up "vertically" this morning! I thank God for another day!

AMEN!

Made in the USA